Josiah Oldfield

This book is dedicated to two men named John:

John C. Q. Roberts, who began the quest for Josiah, and
my husband John, who has been involved in the search
willynilly for the last ten years.

ISBN 978-0-9553903-4-0
09553903-4-6

Published by Rainmore Books
Rainham, Kent ME8 0HA

2008

Printed by Minuteman Press, Rochester

Front Cover Illustration:
Josiah Oldfield, about 1933

Josiah Oldfield
Eminent Fruitarian

by

Rosemary Dellar

'To be a good biographer requires a generosity of
spirit, the willingness to enter into the heart and
mind of another person, to try to divine what moves
and motivates them. Above all it needs more than
puritanical censoriousness and an unwillingness
ever to give the subject the benefit of any doubt.'

Lucia van der Post

'Eccentricity has always abounded when and
where strength of character has abounded'.

J.S.Mill - 'On Liberty'

Contents

List of Illustrations

Introduction

Chapter   Page

1 Early Life and Oxford   1

2 Vegetarians in London 1885-95: Josiah, Mohandas Gandhi and Arnold Hills   12

3 Medical Student at St Bartholomew's Hospital   22

4 Animal Welfare and 'Animal Rights': Josiah's Views   30

5 St John's Hospital for Diseases of the Skin   38

6 Growth and Activities of the Vegetarian Movement in London   46

7 Josiah and the Legal Profession   55

8 The London Vegetarian Association   61

9 The Oriolet Hospital, Loughton   65

10 Relaxations in Essex   79

11 The Order of the Golden Age   87

12 The Humanitarian Hospital of St Francis   93

13 Josiah's Companies   108

14 Marriage   112

15 The Fight for the Abolition of Capital Punishment   115

16 Visit to India, 1901   120

17 The Lady Margaret Hospital, Bromley   129

18 Domestic Crisis ?   139

19 A Flourishing Establishment: Bromley 1905-18   144

20 The 'Fruitarian Colony' at Doddington   159

21 The Fruitarian Philosophy   167

22 Josiah's Military Career   175

23 Margaret Hall, Tulse Hill and Lawn House, Broadstairs   191

24 Doddington in the Aftermath of the First World War   197

25 Publicist and Pundit   208

26 *Truth*'s Vendetta   221

27 Events and Eccentricities at Doddington   226

28 Josiah's Travels   240

29 The Red Lion Square Project   248

30 The Declining Appeal of Doddington in the Later 1930s   253

31 Josiah's Contribution to the War Effort 1940-1945   261

32 The Post-War Years   267

33 An 'Arbitrarily Eclectic Brand of Theology'   276

34 Celebrated Author   280

35 The Final Years   288

36 Josiah's Contentious Views   295

37 Postscript   305

    List of Josiah's Publications   309

    Acknowledgments   311

    Sources   313

    Index   315

**Josiah with staff at the entrance to his hospital
at Doddington in 1932**

List of Illustrations

Interior of the Church of St Andrew and St Mary, Condover   1
Cottages at Ryton   2
The Interior of Newport Grammar School   4
The Examination Schools at Oxford   7
William Axon   13
Arnold F.Hills, President of the Vegetarian Federal Union   17
Josiah and Gandhi at a meeting of Vegetarians in London, 1890   19
(CopyrightGandhiserve.org)
The Courtyard of St Bartholomew's Hospital   23
St Bartholomew's Hospital   24
A Ward at St Bartholomew's   26
Title page of *The Evils of Butchery*   32
Leicester Square about 1900   39
Josiah the keen Committee Member   43
Brochure advertising the 'At Home' Company   47
Illustration from Report of the Educational Food Fund   49
The Relaunched *Vegetarian Messenger*   51
Mr and Mrs Henry Salt in costume for a performance of *Hamlet*   53
The Congregational Memorial Hall, Farringdon Street   54
Mitre Court   55
Josiah   60
Loughton Village   65
Map of Loughton, on the edge of Epping Forest, in 1890   66
Professor John Mayor   68
Loughton from Earl's Path   71
The Outdoor Ward at Oriolet   73
St Ethelburga's Home, formerly the Oriolet Hospital   75
Althorne, still rural in 1937   79
St Andrew's Church, Althorne   80
A Little Wooden Hut...   81
Vestry House, Walthamstow   85
Sidney Beard   88
Objects of the Order of the Golden Age   91
Plan and Elevation of a Fourth-Rate House   98
Front Extensions to Fourth-Rate Houses in City Road   103
Map of Newington, South London, in 1894   108
Josiah's Answer to Punctures   109
Prisoners at Work at Bhownagur Jail   117

Romilly Society Writing Paper   119
William Oldfield   120
Map of India in 1901   122
London Lane, Bromley   129
Tea in the Garden   132
Free Letter admitting a Patient to the Lady Margaret Hospital   135
Josiah surrounded by some of the Staff at Bromley   145
The 'School of Embroidery'   152
The Refectory   154
Once the Lady Margaret Hospital, now the United Services Club 156
The bricked-up Chapel Window   157
Josiah's Evening Hymn   158
The Main Street at Doddington   159
The Lavender Harvest at Doddington   160
The Oasthouse, later known as 'Ellen's Oast'   163
Preparing a Salad   165
Appeal from the Fruitarian Society   168
Henry Cocking   170
An RAMC Field Ambulance   176
Josiah with Vegetarian Soldiers at Burleigh Castle   184
A Field Hospital in England   186
1st Eastern General Hospital   187
Ward at 1st Eastern General Hospital   189
The Operating Theatre at Fort Pitt Hospital   190
Brochure for the Margaret Hall Nursing Home   192
Dickens Corner, Broadstairs   195
Doddington, with Windmill on the Horizon   198
'Some Sick Babies being Mothered'   199
Pamphlet available to Pregnant Women   201
The Chapel at Margaret Manor (exterior)   205
The Chapel Window   206
Carved Head at the Entrance to the Chapel   207
Some of Josiah's Bestsellers in the 1920s   214
Request for a Royalties Statement   215
First Reference to a new Venture in Bloomsbury   216
Map showing Location of Lady Margaret Manor   225
Josiah's sister Ellen   226
Announcement of a Lunch for Gandhi, 1931   227
Josiah, daughter Josie, and Gandhi at the Lunch   227
Ellen's home, 'Newlyn', at Doddington   228
Josiah inside his Cottage, Little Greetynge   231

Little Greetynge	232
The Monks Hut	233
Oxford University Robes, Doctor of Civil Law	236
Tea for the Children in 1932	237
Josiah with Josie	238
A Fyffe's Banana Boat	244
Red Lion Passage	248
Red Lion Square in 1946	251
Elderly Workmen Resting	255
Josiah and some of his 'Refugees' at Work	256
Philip Yarnitz	257
Josiah aged about 80	260
The Buildings at Margaret Manor seen from the Chapel Roof	261
Roy Ashby and Jim Babbington	264
The Interior of the Chapel	267
'Spindly White Legs'	268
Ken Parfitt	270
Title Page of *The Penalty of Death*	272
Aerial View of Lady Margaret manor	275
Josiah at a Lunch in 1951	280
Ellen's Oast, converted to a Youth Hostel	282
Interior of the Youth Hostel	283
Entrance to the former Hospital in 2002	287
Doddington Church in 1900	290
Josiah's Grave	293
The Chapel and adjoining Pumphouse after Josiah's Death	294
Dr Robert Bell	296
The Remains of the Chapel, now forming part of a House	305
Construction of a Chimney in the 1930s	306
Remains of the Pumphouse	306
The Monks Hut Today	307
Josiah's Entrance to the Monks Hut	308

Introduction

Attempting to write a comprehensive account of Josiah Oldfield's life is a biographer's nightmare as far as chronological arrangement is concerned. Some years ago there existed a series of books for children called 'Choose Your Own Adventure', in which, at the end of page 1, the reader could turn either to page 2 or to page 27 to pursue different threads of a tale. Further choices could then be made at the end of these. Because of his multifarious activities the story of Josiah Oldfield seems to demand a similar treatment.

He studied theology and law before turning to medicine; he was the inspiration behind three hospitals and was closely associated with at least one other; he founded a society devoted to the abolition of capital punishment and companies concerned with the production of items as diverse as oils, jams and rubber for puncture repair; he was a prolific author and a passionate advocate of Fruitarianism; his career in the Territorial Army was important to him... At any one date at least three of these topics are relevant: in 1895, for example, while still a student at St Bartholomew's Hospital, he was on the Board of Management and two sub-committees at St John's Hospital for Skin Diseases, he was speaking and writing about the evils of butchery, and promoting vegetarianism through lectures and articles in the magazines he edited. He was composing the thesis which would lead to the award of the Doctorate of Civil

Law, and, although his name did not appear on the Circuit List in that year, he acquired a legal address at Mitre Court Chambers in the Temple. Presumably it was as relaxation that he was at the same time cultivating a plot of land in Essex and taking part in exercises with the Volunteers. Had any diaries survived it would have been instructive to find out just how much he could pack into a single week.

What was he really like? He was an outspoken idealist when young, condemning cruelty to animals, the existing penal code and many then current medical practices. He was not afraid to stand up for his principles even if this led to the scorn of his fellows, and he wholeheartedly believed that one day a more civilised world might be achieved through Fruitarianism and the existence of societies such as the Order of the Golden Age. In midlife, as he achieved fame and prosperity, he would modify some of his views on medical matters, but continued in his unorthodox treatment of certain conditions.

He was unconventional in his attitude towards sex and marriage, and ambivalent in his vision of womanhood - the practice of his ideas giving rise to headlines such as that appearing more than thirty years after his death: 'TINY COTTAGE WAS ROMEO DOCTOR'S SECRET LOVE NEST' prior to the sale of his former home at Doddington.

This attempt to paint a fair picture of a larger-than-life character, now almost forgotten, still has tantalising gaps, but I hope that readers will enjoy learning about Josiah as much as I have.

Chapter 1

Childhood, Youth and Oxford

Josiah Oldfield was born in Condover, about six miles south of Shrewsbury in Shropshire, in 1863, one of seven children of whom six survived infancy. His father, David, was the village organist, and also, although he had been blinded by smallpox at the age of three, a grocer. Theirs was not a wealthy family, but William, the eldest son, held an Exhibition (and later held a Scholarship) at Christ Church College, Oxford, and by 1881 the youngest boy, Frederick Henry, was at a small private school. There were three sisters, Sarah, Julia and Mary Ellen, all older than Josiah: Sarah's twin, Amelia, had died just before her third birthday. Their mother was called Margaret, a name which was to figure largely in Josiah's later life.

**Interior of the Church of St Andrew
and St Mary, Condover**

Josiah's book, *The Penalty of Death* (1901), is dedicated to his 'Mother, from whom I learnt most that I know of the beauties of humaneness and of the power of love to conquer all evil passions'. In 1881 the family lived at Little Moor Cottage, Ryton, half an hour's walk from the Parish Church.

Josiah seems to have had a happy childhood, recalling in later life how as children he and his brothers and sisters made daylong excursions to pick bilberries on the hills five miles away at Church Stretton, returning with blue-stained tongues and equally stained jackets, frocks and white pinafores. In winter they were sent to pick watercress from nearby brooks, which their mother served in winter and spring as a 'blood purifier'. No doubt it was for such excursions that Josiah was 'packed in flannels', yet he still caught frequent colds. His father eventually cured Josiah of adenoidal troubles (Josiah's brothers teased him, calling him a 'grampus' when he snuffled) by teaching him to avoid all hot foods and drinks, and to persevere with breathing always through the nose. Father recommended treacle and figs to prevent constipation.

Cottages at Ryton

Sometimes the family went further afield, for one of Josiah's boyhood memories is of a bout of food poisoning after dining on mussels while visiting the seaside. He was taken to see the first exhibition (of electric light) at the Belle Vue Gardens,

Manchester, and watched the installation of the spluttering carbon candles in the roof of Paddington Station. When at home Josiah enjoyed reading, a love that he maintained throughout his life. As a boy he preferred tales of adventure, particularly stories by Fenimore Cooper involving Red Indians. One book which made a particular impact was *Captain Cook's Voyages Round the World*, where Josiah first met the description of scurvy - of sailors covered with sores and with gangrenous fingers and toes, whose teeth dropped out, who died despite anything the ship's surgeon could do, but who made a seemingly miraculous recovery if the ship made landfall where fresh herbs and fruit were available to supplement their diet.

His relationship with his father is remembered affectionately. In 1924 he recalled his father telling him 'If you're not well enough to get up, you're not well enough to eat' - a principle that Josiah put into practice. Another of his father's habits that made a lasting impression was his response to the question 'Would you like another cup of tea?' The answer depended not on whether Father was still thirsty, but on whether he had already drunk two cups. Josiah was to quote this when recommending his 'dry diet cure' fifty years later.

Things were not always peaceful, however. 'I remember when I was a tiny boy my sister and I used to pray for my father when he was in a bad temper. We almost hoped, even though we hardly dared to raise our voices above a whisper, that he would hear us and be converted to what we thought was proper in a father, though not applicable to ourselves when we got enraged. We should perhaps have done more good by advising our father to try a short fast when he felt his temper rising than by waiting till he had exploded, and then sanctimoniously praying for him! I am not sure whether the immediate effect might not have been more personally painful, but I think that if patiently persisted in the final result might have been very effective.'

This was written with the benefit of hindsight in 1929. At the same period Josiah wrote that his father was introspective and very sensitive to pain, and that the fear of the pain of dying was constantly on his mind. Even when his sons were still boys their father would argue that since birth was painful, death would be also: although he did not fear death, he shrank from the pain of leaving this world. In the event David Oldfield lived to be over eighty, and died peacefully one evening in his customary armchair.

Josiah's grandmother too played a part in shaping his eventual career. He records that she would gather plants with which to prepare herb-teas for her poor neighbours to combat the usual outbreaks of anaemias and skin eruptions in the spring. The village doctor derided her efforts, equating the efficacy of her remedies with that of brick-dust. But although she was unaware of the existence of vitamin C it was Grandmother who was right. Later Josiah would recommend the young shoots of stinging nettles as a useful spring blood tonic.

The Interior of Newport Grammar School

Like his elder brother, Josiah attended Newport Grammar School, and there he determined that he would do everything possible to do so well that his parents and his school would be

4

proud of him. He worked late at home after school hours, and when the lists came out his name appeared in Class I with a distinction in Greek and Mathematics. But he also joined his classmates in what were then considered normal boys' amusements, for in *The Mystery of Birth* he would relate how, when he was a boy at school, he was keenly interested in keeping ferrets, and going ratting, and delighted in the excitement and joy of fishing. He described graphically the setting of several ferrets on a rat in an empty classroom, with the added comment 'How we boys enjoyed the sport'. Josiah also learned to ride, and to hunt the 'gentle stag'.

After leaving school he was employed for a short time as a master at Chipping Campden Grammar School. This was in the charge of Rev. Joseph Foster, who was Curate of Wotton-sub-Edge. As well as day-boys there were fifteen boarders, whose ages ranged from eight to sixteen. The period spent there apparently made a deep impression on Josiah, for a letter which he wrote to *The Times* in 1922 on the subject of diet in public schools begins 'Having had years of experience as a housemaster, long before I became a doctor...' and goes on to point out the necessity for variety as well as sufficiency in boarding school food. Those 'years of experience' cannot have been more than three, assuming that he began teaching at the age of sixteen.

This may not have been his only way of earning enough to pay for a university education, for in later life he spoke of doing manual work to provide fees. According to his obituary in the *East Kent Gazette*, he earned his keep while studying at Oxford by working as a road-mender at 6d an hour for two hours every day before breakfast, work which he continued during vacations. (A press report in 1935 had the remuneration at only 4d, and the hours as 5.30-8.30) A resident of Doddington, where Josiah spent his later life, remembers him saying that he had also blacked boots to earn money.

In 1882, aged 19, he went up to Oxford, although like many poorer students he was not attached to a particular college, but lived in lodgings in the town, thus halving the necessary cost. Alan Bullock, in his chapter on the 'Toshers' (unattached students) in the *History of the University of Oxford*, gives an idea of the sums required. 'In October 1874 the Delegates reported that, following a study of 46 student budgets, a man could study at Oxford for three eight-week terms at an annual cost of £50.14s.0d. Board and lodgings could be obtained for 28/6d per week, and dues and fees amounted to no more than £16.10s.0d.' This, however, did not cover clothes, travel, books etc. In practice poorer students could find lodgings outside the city centre at rents of 8/- to 12/- weekly. Perhaps it was in lodgings such as these that Josiah lived for some years in a house where the husband and wife had occasional storms, and where there was a constant undercurrent of distrust and dislike, almost of hatred. There were numerous occasions when Josiah thought that their quarrels would end in murder. Once he heard the woman threaten to brain her husband with the hatchet, shouting that she would swing for him.

The Delegacy responsible for admitting and regulating unattached students, of whom there were approximately ninety each year in the 1880s, had been set up in 1868, and was ultimately to become St Catherine's College. Most of its students were the sons of clergy or other professional men, and many were later to be ordained or to teach. Josiah was to comment in later life that as an undergraduate he found himself very much alone. The Delegacy had its own small library, although this had seats for only four readers, and a room attached to the University Church was made available for use as a chapel. There was then little provision for formal tuition.

But 1882 was the year in which Jowett, the Master of Balliol, became Vice-Chancellor and began the implementation of better facilities for the unattached students. They were assigned lecture rooms in the newly-built Examination Schools, and a reading room in the adjacent building in the High Street. In about 1883 tutors were introduced for those students reading for Honours. Two guineas per term for tuition was the standard charge.

Josiah read Theology, achieving second-class Honours in 1885. The Oxford Theology School, founded only in 1870, was considered inferior to long-established subjects like classics or mathematics. 'The average man who takes up Theology aims at a third, and usually gets it with a very moderate amount of work - perhaps an average of 3-4 hours per week.' But Josiah's aims were higher. To obtain his second class degree he would have had to learn Hebrew in addition to the Greek with which he was already familiar. Detailed knowledge of the New Testament and four Old Testament books was required, plus some study of liturgy, textual criticism and dogmatics (Christian doctrine). He commented later 'Many a University Double First has a tired brain for the rest of his life'.

The Examination Schools at Oxford

As a theology student at Oxford Josiah appears to have held orthodox Christian views, tending to the High Church. He observed the Lenten fast, talked of his Catholic faith and appreciated ritual and ceremony. There is no record of his regular place of worship, but he does mention visiting the Cowley Fathers on at least one occasion. Perhaps this was when he encountered a 'young Father of the Church who had inherited more muscle than wisdom from his ancestors, telling me that he no more consulted his stomach than his portmanteau as to what he should put in it'. By the date of this meeting Josiah had

7

evidently been converted to vegetarianism, and was zealous in his desire that others should follow suit. Josiah was not impressed by some priests whom he saw as social workers rather than spiritual leaders, but he had a sneaking regard for the Jesuits, admiring their 'power of prayer', if not always agreeing with their objectives.

Having obtained his Theology degree Josiah did not, as might have been expected, proceed to ordination. By this time his brother William, who had been ordained in 1880, had served his curacy at St George's Everton, become the incumbent of St Mary, Belize, and since 1883 had been Commissary (representative) to the Bishop of Jamaica, and Chairman of the Standing Committee of the Diocese of British Honduras.

Instead Josiah went on, after a further two years of study, to gain another second class honours degree, this time in Civil Law. This was at a time when up to 70% of college students might be reading only for a Pass degree. Law was another 'new' subject, having been separated from Modern History in 1872. By the time Josiah was studying he would have been able to benefit from the publication of textbooks on different aspects of the course - an innovation at that time. He was also one of the first students who had to produce a 'dissertation or book' in order to gain his Doctorate, for until 1887 a DCL had followed a BCL after due lapse of time with no further requirement of work on the candidate's part. In future years Josiah was particularly proud of his success in attaining the DCL.

It was while studying the lives and works of spiritual leaders of other religions that Josiah realised that many of them, particularly those 'aspiring to reach the higher walks of spiritual attainment' abstained from meat. Following his own first Lenten fast he had decided that such a vegetarian diet must have much to commend it. He was also influenced by attending a lecture given by the physiologist W.B.Carpenter, probably on temperance. In 1884 there was a discussion at Keble College on the merits of Vegetarianism, at which 'the advocates of the pure diet were in the majority'. It was hoped that Keble would 'lead the way back to a simplicity of life and diet which has unhappily been lost sight of during recent years in the University of Oxford'.

Josiah's religious faith was firmly grounded on the Bible, and his dietary beliefs had the same foundation. Particularly relevant was verse 29 in the first chapter of Genesis: 'And God said "Behold, I have given you every herb bearing seed, which is upon the face of the earth, and every tree, in the which is the fruit of a tree yielding seed; to you it shall be for meat"'. Moses was a hero to Josiah, who regularly cited the Mosaic Law when he advised the avoidance of blood, dead flesh or decaying material. In *The Crown of Grapes* he would explain how he had been overwhelmed with wonder at the stupendous task that Moses undertook and at the enormous difficulties he overcame. 'To convert a posse of degraded offal-eating slaves into a courageous conquering army of stalwart Fruitarians, and to enthuse them with a hope and to encircle them with sanitary laws which have remained with them for thousands of years, was a superhuman undertaking'. But Moses had difficulty in keeping the people true to the vegetarian diet. '"While the meat was yet in their mouths" says the Chronicler (Numbers 11 v 33), "the wrath of God came upon the children of Israel". And why? Because they would not be content to be Fruitarians, like the angels in Heaven, but, chained by the belly to Egypt, must needs despise the manna of the heavenly inhabitants and long for the old gross carnalities of the quivering flesh and the dripping gore to satisfy their appetites withal. It is the same today...'

The Bible, to my knowledge, does not describe the diet of angels, and Josiah was selective in what he chose to quote. Had his meat-eating acquaintances been equally familiar with the Pentateuch they might well have retorted with verses from Deuteronomy - 'Ye shall buy meat of them for money that ye may eat' (Ch.2 v.6) or 'I will send grass in thy fields for thy cattle, that thou mayest eat and be full' (Ch.11 v.15).

It was while he was an undergraduate that Josiah changed his views on the 'sports' he had previouly enjoyed, realising the cruelty involved. The passage on ferreting quoted earlier, which

9

was published in 1949, continues 'Today I would not join in such a fray. I have learned to be a victim, to go down into hell, and to be one with the damned'. There is no clue as to what this statement refers, although it may relate to his experiences during the First World War. The cruelty involved in the slaughter of animals for food was another factor urging Josiah to give up meat. This particular aspect was stressed by a small group known as Fruitarians, an association of which Josiah was to become perhaps the most fervent apostle. He decided to adopt a Fruitarian diet, a regime which he maintained until the end of his life.

A letter published in the *Dietetic Reformer and Vegetarian News* in 1884 from a lady in Leicester gives a glimpse of early Fruitarianism:-

'We have been Fruitarians more than eight years and can safely recommend the system. I always tell people that we are FRUIT-arians, not VEGET-arians. We take fruit in place of flesh. We do not eat as many vegetables as when we took the less pure food. We cannot understand how it is that 'Fruitarian' does not commend itself to most members, for I find that many folk rather like the idea. That term does not bring to their imagination a dinner of turnips or cabbages, as 'Vegetarian' does to many. Whatever the name, our cause is gaining in favour day by day'.

During his time at Oxford, presumably in search of vegetables to extend what was normally available in early spring, it occurred to Josiah that the nettles he was idly knocking aside as he sat on a stile might be used. This happened to be just after he had seen some cases of utter destitution in a village just outside the city. He came back the next day with a basket to harvest the tender tops, which he then washed and boiled. He does not say whether he then recommended them to the poor families he had met, but later he would recommend serving the boiled nettle tops with cream. Young fresh dandelions could be treated in the same way and served on toast.

He was far from alone in regarding nettles as wholesome, and the magazine *Fun* printed some verses on the subject mocking the Vegetarian Movement in 1892. That the movement's members were not, as some thought, lacking in a sense of humour is demonstrated by the fact that the whole poem was reproduced in the *Vegetarian Messenger*.

The second and third verses read as follows:-

That burning question 'How, alas!
Must people of the humblest class
Exist when they are short of brass?
We now at length can settle:
For as the breezes freely blow -
As village streamlets freely flow -
So freely through the land doth grow
The healthy stinging nettle!

Then rise, poor folks, at break of day,
And out into the country stray,
Yet linger not o'er bird on spray
Or flower with dewy petal:
But there, with well-rewarded toil,
Luxuriant nettle-beds despoil,
And carry to your homes and boil,
And eat, the stinging nettle!

Chapter 2

Vegetarians in London 1885-1900: Josiah, Arnold Hills and Gandhi

After graduating from Oxford Josiah moved to London to continue his law studies. The Admission Register of Lincoln's Inn records that he was admitted on May 13th 1887, and he was called to the bar on 29th June 1892. One of his fellow students at this time was Mohandas Gandhi, who was a member of the Inner Temple. It is believed that the two may have shared rooms in Bayswater (52 St Stephen's Gardens) for a short period. Gandhi's autobiography does not comment on this, although there is considerable detail concerning his meagre diet. Gandhi was by upbringing a vegetarian, but on coming to England had at first rebelled against this regime, thinking that perhaps meat-eating contributed to the apparent superiority of the British. This phase was brief, and once he had discovered the vegetarian restaurant in Farringdon Street, and had read some of the literature he found there, he became vegetarian by conviction.

Gandhi spent less than three years in England, where his associates were largely 'a group of aged, crusading vegetarians who talked of nothing but food and disease'. Josiah, at least, was of a similar age, and the two had many discussions about diet - could one live on fruit and bread alone; would a diet omitting starchy foods be sufficient; should milk and eggs be permitted since their consumption did not harm animals? Gandhi thought that even these were luxuries to be avoided, and declared that the real seat of taste was not the tongue but the mind. He taught himself to prepare and enjoy such dishes as plain boiled spinach, and perhaps invited Josiah to share his meals. Josiah's views on the consumption of foods such as milk and honey were later set out forcefully in a pamphlet entitled *Honey for Health*. 'There is a certain childish mentality amongst some undeveloped human minds which says "milk is produced by the cow for her calf only. Honey is produced by bees for their queen and larvae only. Therefore will I neither rob a cow of her milk or a bee of its honey, but will abstain entirely from the use of both."! Higher intelligence has grasped the fact that Nature's plans are interwoven in the principle of Cooperation which replaces Antagonism'.

William Axon

Josiah too had been influenced by the Vegetarian Society's literature, and in particular by the efforts of Mr Bailey Walker. The Society had been founded in 1847, its main aim being 'not to found a sect but to influence a nation'. William Axon, in his history of the movement published in 1897, cited many reasons for its existence, including economy, the alleviation or removal of physical ills, and abstinence from flesh meat in abhorrence of the cruelty involved. To the rich it offered, as **a contribution to social reform** [my emphasis], a way in which 'friendship and social intercourse can be made easy between all classes'. It was most in harmony with the divine will and formed a means of attaining fuller physical and mental development.

Membership had fluctuated considerably since the Society's foundation, but by 1875 there were 91 full members and 187 associates (sympathisers who did not pledge themselves to complete abstinence from meat). By 1896 these figures had fallen to sixty and fourteen respectively, but other vegetarians belonged to separate organisations with similar aims, especially in London. The *Vegetarian Messenger* was the Society's main organ from 1849 to 1861; it continued publication with the title *The Dietetic Reformer* until 1886, and then resumed its original

13

name from 1887 onwards. These changes were in part due to conflicting opinions amongst vegetarians based in different parts of the country.

The Vegetarian Society had close links with the Bible Christians of Salford, and Manchester was the centre of its activities. The semi-religious fervour of some of its members is vividly described by Reginald Payne in his autobiography *The Watershed* published in 1961. He tells how, as a child, he was hurried past butchers' shops by his Vegetarian parents with eyes averted, since dead things were synonymous with contamination and sin, guilt and taboo: all who partook of flesh were unclean. Vegetarians were the Elect, whose difficulty was 'not so much in maintaining their principles as in maintaining their spiritual humility'.

London in 1875 had seen the birth of the Dietetic Reform Society, whose members abstained from meat and also from tobacco and alcohol. This society was housed in the newly-built Memorial Hall in Farringdon Street, and it was in this same thoroughfare that London's first vegetarian restaurant had opened. Two years later the London Food Reform Society came into being, among its early members being T.R.Allinson, remembered today because of the wholemeal bread bearing his name, and Professor J.E.B.Mayor, of Cambridge University. By now Vegetarianism was beginning to be recognised as 'respectable', with some eminent practitioners, many of them from the middle classes. Henry Salt (1851-1939) was a Master at Eton, a socialist and a Fabian, a friend of Shaw and William Morris. F.W.Newman, who was brother to Cardinal Newman, had become the Vegetarian Society's President in 1873: he had become committed to its ideals after learning, while a student at Oxford, of the cruelty inherent in vivisection.

Josiah himself attempted to change the general perception of vegetarianism as 'crankiness and faddism... associated with back alley meetings and the great unwashed', as he put it. Instead he favoured the term 'Aristophagy', (from the Greek 'aristos' - best, and 'phagein'- to eat) referring to consumption of the **best** foods. 'What is Aristophagy?' was to be the title of a lecture he would deliver in Hampstead in November 1900. Earlier he had discussed his reasons for adopting both the name and the practice, writing that in childhood he had been taught that in order to develop his musical taste he should select only the **best** music to listen to, persevering if at first he found it difficult to understand or appreciate. Enjoyment of art and literature were to be developed similarly. Only by gradual but persistent application, therefore, would the healthier diet come to be fully prized.

In order to get the new name adopted Josiah arranged for no fewer than 10,000 copies of his original article to be printed, making them available at 1/- per hundred. Despite his efforts the word (which does not appear in current dictionaries) did not gain popular support, any more than the verb 'to vegetare' which Josiah also used (from Latin 'vegetare' - to animate or vitalise). In 1897 his *Why I Vegetare* was 'in the press', but whether it actually appeared is not clear. The London Vegetarian Society would ultimately settle on the words 'Vegetus - Vital, Healthful, Wholesome' to head its stationery.

The London groups were attracting younger recruits, Josiah being one, and gradually the links with Manchester became weaker. When the Food Reform Society adopted the title 'National' rather than 'London' there was initially some antagonism from Manchester, but by 1885 this had been largely overcome and the new group became the London branch of the Vegetarian Society. The merger, however, was not to last, and in 1888 the London Vegetarian Society was founded as a separate entity. Its President was Arnold Frank Hills, at 31 just a few years older than Josiah, who became Vice-Chairman of its committee. The minimum subscription was set at 1/-; 10/- entitled a member to free tickets for four monthly receptions, four debates and four conversaziones, refreshment tickets, and, post-free, all literature published by the society priced at 1/- or less. This gives some idea of the activities of the LVS, whose main aim was to promulgate the knowledge of the advantages of a Vegetarian diet. Associate members, who need not necessarily be strict vegetarians, were also accepted.

At the first Annual General Meeting of the London Vegetarian Society in 1889, chaired by Arnold Hills, the year's activities were reviewed. There had been debates at Oxford and Cambridge Universities. Pamphlets, including Josiah's *1d. Vegetarian Cookery*, had been made available. The society had cooperated with the Congregational Union (who owned the Memorial Hall) in providing dinners for poor children. Meetings utilising a number of speakers had brought new recruits, and future plans included an annual mission week, like those held by Christian organisations, using every available hall or room in each district. Each evening there would be meetings - at least one, and sometimes up to four, where different vegetarian arguments would be presented by speakers including Ernest Axon, Henry Salt, John Mayor, Josiah Oldfield, Howard Williams and C.W.Forward. Such a week had taken place in Oxford in November, attracting over 250 people to a free vegetarian dinner at the Clarendon Assembly Rooms on the Wednesday, and another 200 to a breakfast the following day. Arnold Hills presided (and paid?) at both events. Oxford now had its own vegetarian society, although as yet no vegetarian restaurant.

The wealthy Arnold Hills, who had been at Oxford University at the same time as Josiah's brother William, was the owner of the Thames Ironworks and Shipbuilding Company, and was a well-known philanthropist and temperance supporter. He used non-Union labour but introduced profit-sharing and an 8-hour day for his work force, and in 1890 it was agreed that his pamphlet *Individualism and Socialism* would be distributed by the London Vegetarian Society. Hills probably had some connection with the Farringdon Memorial Hall, and the Dietetic Reform Society. He joined the Manchester-based Vegetarian Society in 1885, but it seems likely that he was the instigator of the new London group. It was not until his death in 1927 that the rumbling feud between London and Manchester finally came to an end.

At Canning Town he sought to improve his workers' recreational facilities: the firm's football team, on whose ground he is said to have spent £200,000, would ultimately become West Ham United. Hills himself had played for England against Scotland. He was anxious to prove that a vegetarian diet led to fitness and vigour, and promoted the growth of cycling clubs whose feats and activities were regularly reported in vegetarian magazines. Arnold Hills was a good and persuasive speaker, and also wrote articles, his rather dense prose being generously interspersed with biblical quotations, verses of hymns, and scraps of Greek and Latin - like Josiah he was an unorthodox Anglican. His paper 'Vital Food' was read at the Vegetarian Congress in Chicago in 1893, and a lengthy series called 'Liberty in Unity' ran to more than 32 parts in *The Vegetarian*.

His assets were frequently called upon by his fellow-vegetarians. In October 1890 he agreed to return to his former position of simply doubling the total subscriptions up to £50, and no doubt it was his money that allowed the London Vegetarian Society to print and send out no fewer than 10,000 circulars in December to subscribers to various charities. Junk mail is not new! Another of his charitable works was the provision of two Scholarships, each worth twenty pounds per annum for five years, at Chigwell School. He would later become a Justice of the Peace and Deputy Lieutenant of Essex.

Arnold F. Hills, President of the Vegetarian Federal Union

The London Vegetarian Society had its own magazine, *The Vegetarian*, which styled itself a weekly paper of progressive thought. Financial backing was again provided by Mr Hills, who set up the 'Ideal Publishing Union' for this purpose. Its first Editor was J.Newton Wood, but very soon Josiah was appointed to the post, writing many of its articles himself. His subjects were diverse: medical topics such as influenza, ringworm, tuberculosis, cholera, or 'What are ptomaines?' reflecting his growing interest in medical matters. Some of these had previously been given as talks and would later be published as pamphlets. Discourses entitled 'Life and Death' or 'Are Animals Immortal?' (a qualified yes), 'Hypnotism in Church' (he found current Anglican services distinctly soporific) and a series on the Christian Brothers hark back to his first, theology, degree. The items on the history and work of the Brothers were apparently prompted by a visit he paid in June 1890 when called upon to take part in the 'Examination of Tooting College'. Tantalisingly he does not specify what type of examination, but Father Fegan, who ran orphanages for the Christian Brothers at this period, was a vegetarian who expected his charges to enjoy the same diet... As is to be expected there were features in the magazine on the superiority of the vegetarian diet, on the horrors of abattoirs and slaughter-houses, on the dilemma faced by those seeking non-leather footwear (Josiah had experimented with rubber and asbestos soles) and similar topics.

There were also suggestions from Josiah, not always practical. The idea that railway companies should plant fruit trees rather than thorn hedges alongside their lines seems a forlorn hope. Another proposal was that a 'Book of Golden Deeds' be opened, with readers earning points according to the work they carried out on behalf of the vegetarian movement. Examples of such 'deeds' might be lending a drawing-room for a meeting, delivering 500 handbills, or writing a letter to a newspaper. The points earned would count towards a full subscription to (presumably) the London Vegetarian Society.

Josiah utilised the pages of the magazine to help in his researches, inviting readers to respond to a questionnaire about the vegetarian diet and its effects on their physical and mental powers; their ailments; their resistance to infection, heat and cold; their happiness and their passions. What exactly was included in their diet? How long had they practised it? Did they exclude tea, coffee or condiments?... How many people responded is unknown.

One of Josiah's pieces, published in 1892, is worth quoting in full. Entitled 'The Cost of Living', it was written in answer to an article on 'The Income and Expenditure of the Working Classes' which had postulated a stoker earning 21/- per week, paying 3/6d rent for his room, and spending 12/7d on food and 1/3d on heating and lighting. Josiah scorned these amounts, writing:

> 'Except during severe frost, for a man neither very old nor ill, a fire is a luxury, not a necessity. I speak from the experience of winters spent in rooms at Oxford and in London, and therein of long evenings spent in study, when the cold made itself felt most keenly, but seldom so severely but that an extra coat, or a newspaper over the knees and feet, prevented any unpleasant sensations... I should not allow more than 3d. for fuel, and as to light, another 3d. a week quite covers it.'

Josiah went on to say that rather than spending 5/- a week on meat, 1/- on tea and 10½d. on beer, the imaginary stoker should adopt a vegetarian regime which would only cost him 7/- a week. He could then afford a day's holiday in the country every couple of months, and also be able to invest in an annuity for his old age.

Gandhi joined the London Vegetarian Society, and, encouraged by Josiah (by now editor of *The Vegetarian*), soon found himself on the Executive Committee. It was unfortunate that the first meeting he attended was rocked by dissension. Arnold Hills was a puritan, and could not countenance the use of artificial methods of birth-control as taught by Dr Allinson to his working-class patients. He moved a motion 'That in view of the deadly poison of licensed immorality conveyed in the teaching of "Protective Checks and Artificial Prevention of Conception" it is resolved that the London Vegetarian Society leave no effort unmade to dissociate Vegetarianism from this defilement, and so long as Mr Allison identifies himself therewith his name be excluded from all connection, either by advertisement or otherwise, with the work of this Society'.

**Josiah (in white) and Gandhi (on his left)
at a meeting of Vegetarians in London in 1890.** (Copyright)

After some discussion Mr Hills withdrew the motion - but Dr Allinson resigned. As Gandhi and no doubt the other committee members realised, the society's very existence depended on the financial backing of Arnold Hills, so that they literally could not afford to disagree with his views. Many were 'more-or-less his protegés', as Gandhi recalls in his autobiography.

The same book tells how Gandhi always felt tongue-tied and was shy about speaking, although he did write numerous articles on nutrition, the social system and Indian festivals for *The Vegetarian*. Josiah had said to him 'You talk to me quite all right, but why is it that you never open your lips at a committee meeting? You are a drone'. Despite this comment Gandhi was one of the speakers when both he and Josiah attended the annual May meeting of the Vegetarian Federal Union in Portsmouth in 1891. Gandhi and Oldfield together had started a Vegetarian Club in Bayswater, of which Sir Edwin Arnold, the poet, translator

20

and theosophist (his *Light of Asia* had been a bestseller in 1879) had agreed to be Vice-President. It flourished however for only a few months after Gandhi left England.

In its article on Gandhi the *Encyclopedia Britannica* sums up the milieu in which he lived while in London:-

' In the vegetarian restaurants and boarding houses of England Gandhi met not only food faddists but some earnest men and women... The English vegetarians were a motley crowd. They included socialists and humanitarians like Edward Carpenter ('the British Thoreau'), Fabians like George Bernard Shaw and Theosophists like Annie Besant * Most of them were idealists: quite a few were rebels who rejected the prevailing values of the late Victorian Establishment, denounced the evils of the capitalist and industrialist society, preached the cult of the simple life and stressed the superiority of moral over material values, and of co-operation over conflict'.

Most, if not all, of these characteristics can be ascribed to Josiah.

Membership of the London Vegetarian Society had made a deep impression on the young Gandhi. In a 'very graceful but somewhat nervous' speech at his Farewell Dinner he 'spoke of the pleasure it gave him to see the habit of abstinence from flesh progressing in England, related the manner in which his connection with the London Vegetarian Society arose, and in so doing took occasion to speak in a very touching way of what he owed to Mr Oldfield'. Gandhi was called to the Bar in June 1891, and left England a few days later. Josiah's call to the Bar took place the following year.

*In November 1894 the LVS purchased 500 copies of one of her pamphlets.

Chapter 3

Medical Student - St Bartholomew's Hospital

Josiah's interest in diet and medical matters had obviously been growing even before he completed his law terms, for in March 1892, just before being called to the bar, he signed the student register at St Bartholomew's Hospital, giving his address as 32 Brunswick Square WC. At this time the cost of lectures and instruction in hospital practice for medical students was £150.0s.0d., which Josiah chose to pay in four annual instalments. Until 1892 a professional qualification under the regulations of the Royal College of Physicians and the Royal College of Surgeons required four years study, (of which only thirty months had to be spent at a hospital medical school), but after that date five years was more usual. Josiah Oldfield qualified in 1897 with the 'conjoint diploma', i.e. as a Member of the Royal College of Surgeons (MRCS) and a Licentiate of the Royal College of Physicians (LRCP).

The origins of St Bartholomew's Hospital lie in the twelfth century, and as early as 1662 medical students were in training there, 'walking the wards' behind the surgeons and doctors in order to learn their trade. Lectures to students had begun about 1720, but the formal foundation of the Medical School is dated as 1822 when John Abernethy, an Assistant Surgeon, persuaded the Governors that this would be of benefit both to students and to staff, who could call on them for assistance. It was at this time that the lecture theatre was rebuilt.

When Josiah began his studies the hospital had four 'wings' set round a central courtyard with a fountain. Three of these wings provided the ward blocks, the fourth the administrative offices. Surrounding this group of buildings were the surgery and associated casualty wards, a range of living quarters for medical staff, an out-patients' department and pharmacy, the library and teaching areas, and the church of St Bartholomew the Less.

22

The Courtyard of St. Bartholomew's Hospital

There were also a fives court and a quoits ground. The hospital was immediately opposite Smithfield Market, and Josiah later wrote that while he was dressing for the surgeon Howard Marsh, a man from Smithfield with a badly-gashed hand, on being asked where he came from, jerked his head across the way and said "from the other meat shop over there".

Of the hospital's 746 beds in 1892 349 were surgical and 227 medical. A convalescent unit at Swanley, Kent, accounted for a further seventy, while the remainder provided fifty beds for syphilitic patients, 24 for 'diseases of women' and 26 for ophthalmic cases. In that year almost six thousand in-patients were treated and more than 160,000 attended the out-patient department. Almost all children were born at home at this period: doctors from St Bartholomew's oversaw the delivery of 1772 babies in 1892. Josiah as an 'extern' student of midwifery liked to prescribe oranges or orange-juice to his slum mothers if their babies were weakly or anaemia was present, and as a result was chaffed unmercifully by his colleagues and Medical Officers, who told him the mothers would get belly-aches. By the 1930s he was able to write 'Nearly every doctor today is a disciple of the method I then taught and practised.' But whether all his slum mothers could afford fresh fruit is dubious.

St. Bartholomew's Hospital

The study and practice of midwifery, though, was not undertaken until students were halfway through their five-year course. Before that the first and second examinations of the Conjoint Board had to be passed. The first of these was in four parts; elementary anatomy and elementary biology taken at the end of the winter session; chemistry-and-physics and practical pharmacy in July. Students were able to sign on at any point in the year, so Josiah may have started with the summer session. If so he would have been expected to attend lectures on physics at 10.00 on Wednesdays, and on chemistry at the same time on other days. The Hospital Calendar lists the names of the lecturers in each subject (usually members of the permanent medical and surgical staff, who numbered 39) together with a resumé of the content of their course. Some lectures were not restricted to Bart's students - the fees payable for attendance by outsiders were noted.

With only a few weeks of instruction behind him Josiah had begun writing papers on medical subjects for *The Vegetarian*. One, entitled 'The Influenza', recommended prevention by such habits as deep breathing through the nose,

24

fresh air, moderate daily exercise, a daily rub-down with a rough towel, a tepid bath at least once a week and frequent changes of sheets and under-linen. A diet of fruit, bread, eggs, milk, porridge and plain salads was to be accompanied by pure water, barley water, lime juice or cocoa. There followed a history of the disease, and descriptions of the symptoms both in medical and in lay terms. The benefits of vegetarianism were reiterated, and finally patients were urged to keep going (unless aged or delicate) rather than allow themselves to give way.

The second year of a medical student's training concentrated on anatomy and physiology, which were the subjects encountered in the second conjoint examination, taken in March. As well as attending at least two lectures daily students were expected to spend a considerable time each week in the dissecting room (open 8.00 - 4.00 daily) where subjects for dissection were provided 'at moderate expense'. Records of each man's attendance and diligence were kept, and all students wishing to enter examinations were reminded that they were required to attend lectures and demonstrations to the satisfaction of their teachers, and must attend the various class and 'Test' examinations which were held from time to time.

Even before tackling the part II exam, students would have discussed with their tutors the path they planned to follow. Each year more than 900 posts were made available to students. A few of these, such as House Surgeons, were paid and were only open to men who had already acquired some medical qualifications, whether 'in house' or at another institution. Most, however, were for medical or clinical clerks, or for dressers, where appointments were made every three months. The role of a dresser, which Josiah had selected, is explained in the yearly Calendar. 'Each surgeon has eight dressers who attend daily in the surgical casualty department to dress minor surgical cases under the supervision of the House Surgeons. Afterwards they go into the wards each morning to dress the surgical in-patients and take notes of cases. They subsequently accompany the Surgeons [the top men] on their visits to the wards and read their notes to them'. Clerks carried out similar duties with physicians, noting symptoms and recording patient histories and daily progress.

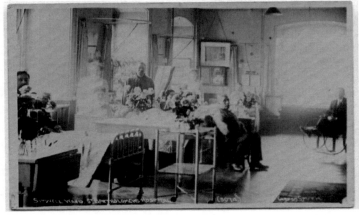

A Ward at St. Bartholomew's

No-one who saw the film '*Doctor in the House*', based on Richard Gordon's novel, will forget the portrait of the irascible Sir Lawrence carrying out a ward round accompanied by a small flock of nervous students. Richard Gordon's model was medical student life at Bart's half a century after Josiah completed his training, but the essentials remained the same.

The list of lectures for third year surgery is as follows:-

Disease and injury - Repair - Hypertrophy - Atrophy - Degeneration
Inflammation - Abscess - Ulcer - Mortification
Wounds - Principles of aseptic and antiseptic treatment - Bruises and Sprains - Effects of destructive heat and cold
Shock and its consequences - Traumatic delirium - Tetanus - Hydrophobia
Pyaemia and its allies - Poisoned wounds - Erysipelas - Carbuncle
Tuberculosis and scrofula - Syphilis - Surgical diseases allied to hysteria
Tumours
Injuries and diseases of bones and joints - Dislocations - Fractures
Injuries and diseases of arteries and veins - Aneurism - Haemorrhage
Injuries and afflictions of nerves, lymphatics and glands
Affections of muscles and skin
Injuries of head and spine - Curvature of spine

Affections of face, mouth, tonsils, pharynx, oesophagus and larynx
Wounds and other injuries of throat, chest, abdomen and pelvis
Diseases of rectum and pelvis
Hernia - Intestinal obstruction
Affections of the urethra - Stricture - Extravasation of urine
Diseases of the prostate and bladder - Stone
Diseases of the breast, testes and scrotum
Defects and deformities - Hare lip - Cleft palate - Spina bifida

This seems a formidable list (although the stomach is not mentioned...) and there were also demonstrations of other kinds to be attended - post-mortems, pathology and midwifery. Lectures on insanity, public health and ophthalmic surgery were included in the summer of the fourth year. Dental surgery had to be fitted in. Then came tutorial classes in preparation for the third conjoint examination, in medicine, surgery and midwifery, whose parts could be taken either at the same session or on separate occasions. Finally, in his fifth year, while continuing with clinical lectures and the practice of medicine and surgery, a student would meet vaccination, and also spend some time at a fever hospital and at a lunatic asylum.

At last came the Final Examination, in clinical medicine and clinical surgery. Now aged 34, Josiah passed, although he came only seventy-first of the 81 students who qualified in 1897. Some of his contemporaries, however, did not reach the required standard until the following year. The rather lowly position he achieved is not altogether surprising when the full extent of his other activities is realised, whether or not he took advantage of the sporting and other opportunities offered by the Abernethian Society. The life membership fee of five guineas to this student club covered use of its library and a subscription to the house journal, which Josiah was still enjoying in his eighties.

Of his training at Bart's Josiah wrote later that the study of diet was considered beneath the dignity of a doctor. During the whole time he was a student at St Bartholomew's Hospital he never once heard a physician or surgeon attempt to explain anything about the relation of diet to disease or ever to draw up a dietary for any patient. Feeding was the province of the Sister. Josiah would attempt to remedy this omission when training his own students later.

When Josiah qualified as a surgeon and physician in 1897, he obviously had ambitious ideas, taking rooms at 122 Harley Street. Here his consulting hours were from 3.00p.m. until 5.00p.m. each afternoon. If they preferred, however, patients could be seen by appointment in the morning. He supplied those who consulted him with a specially selected diet card, on the back of which was printed a strict list of twelve rules to be observed by the patient. These were:

1. Eat slowly, chew well. The food may be cold or warm, but nothing must be hot.
2. Breathe through the nose, avoid all close and hot rooms, by day and by night.
3. Be out of doors ... hours daily, wet or fine; if fine only, avoid winds.
4. Take ... hours exercise. Gentle, active, bicycle, walking.
[5. Take very little/no active exercise, lie down in a bed or on a couch in the open air, well covered up with woollen wraps or blankets.]
6. Rub your whole body down every .... with a rough towel till the skin glows with warmth, especially rub your.......
7. Take a cold bath of .... minutes every morning.
[Stand in hot water and sponge yourself down with cold water.]
8. Wash your face, neck and chest, night and morning with cold water.
9. Brush your teeth with .... and rinse out your mouth well with ...... water every ....
10. Wear ... thicknesses of clothing and wear .... next to your skin. Flannel is **not** to be worn next the skin by day or by night.
11. Wear no article of clothing at night that you have worn during the day.
12. Take a hot bath every .... Weigh(t) ....

Beneath the rules space was left for the name of the patient and the date and time of her, or perhaps less commonly, his, next appointment.

Did all his patients return? Or would some of them, like the biblical Naaman when told simply to bathe seven times in the Jordan to cure his leprosy, have decided that such simple orders could not possibly have any effect on their complaint? The diets Josiah prescribed in conjunction with the regime above were also minimal, though not necessarily cheap. The simplest, Diet A, provided little more than half a pint of liquid (equal quantities of boiled milk and oatenade or water) to be taken through a straw every hour between 8.00a.m. and 8.00p.m. This was relieved only by twenty soaked raisins, two slices of dry toast and half an ounce of butter. Those who were allotted diet F had a rather more interesting menu based largely on fruit. Breakfast consisted of 2 oz. bread and

1 apple, pear or plum	10 grapes or raisins
1 banana, plum or slice of pineapple	6 large or 12 small nuts
4 figs	1 tablespoon dry rolled oats
4 dates	a quarter of a pint of milk

which sounds rather like a helping of home-made muesli. Lunch was the same, with the addition of salad and an ounce of cheese, but dinner was extensive. Beginning with a pint of bread and milk and a stewed onion, the patient was then permitted (if still hungry!) omelette or toasted cheese, 2 granola biscuits, four stewed prunes or a pear or two small apples, as well as cream, bread and salad.

When he discussed their pregnancies with expectant mothers, he may have enhanced his reputation by following the advice given to him by a 'wise old physician'. This was to tell the lady that her child was to be a boy, then write 'girl' in the diary (or vice-versa). If the result wasn't as had been predicted verbally, then the written evidence proved that he had been correct in his forecast!

Josiah retained rooms in Harley Street throughout his life although in 1901 he moved to No.30, and by 1903 his address had changed to No.5. Finally No.8 Harley Street would be the letter heading he used in 1950.

Chapter 4

Animal Welfare and 'Animal Rights' - Josiah's Views

The idea that animals were entitled to be treated with care and consideration was recognised by many, not only by vegetarians. Henry S.Salt, whom Josiah knew as a fellow speaker at the London Vegetarian Society, was an early proponent of the cause, and it was his words Josiah echoed when in 1893 he proclaimed 'Today there is dawning the fact that even animals have rights', a conviction which formed a significant part of the argument in his booklet *The Best Way to Begin Vegetarianism*.

Shortly afterwards Josiah was sufficiently incensed by the cruelty to animals destined for food, which he and others had observed, to publish *A Groaning Creation*. This presented a short record of some ways in which the human race inflicted pitiful sufferings on 'sentient fellow-creatures who are lower in the scale of life than itself, for the purpose of obtaining an unnecessary form of food'. It was produced under the aegis of the London Vegetarian Society in Farringdon Street, EC, at 1/- per copy, with illustrations (of dubious merit) by 'a well-known Veterinary and Surgical Draughtsman'. This was Mr R.E.Holding, who added his own description of some of the scenes he had encountered in slaughterhouses.

In fact the same work was published almost simultaneously as a Humanitarian League Pamphlet (No.17), with the title *The Evils of Butchery*. Josiah had previously addressed both the League and the London Vegetarian Society on this topic, and had also written to the Editor of the *Standard* on the same subject. Incorporated with his own thoughts were excerpts from other sources such as the New York Times describing, for instance, the hardships of cattle left out in winter to freeze or starve to death, or, from Ireland, the beatings endured by animals during droving. Particularly moving was an account by Samuel

Plimsoll, M.P., of some of the practices employed on cattle ships. Insurance companies wanted their freight to arrive alive, so that a dying animal would be forced to its feet by such methods as stuffing the ears with hay soaked in paraffin, which was then set alight. Lack of food, water and ventilation during transportation was commonplace.

Nor were cattle the only animals to suffer. Evidence was offered of similar cruelties to sheep, pigs and ducks. Then came blow-by-blow descriptions of the different methods of slaughter employed - the novelist Tolstoy for one had found such killings 'worse than war'. Josiah himself had visited the slaughter-house at Deptford, London's entry point for foreign meat, which was a model of its kind. He used his experience there when presenting a paper, *Tuberculosis: Flesh-Eating a Cause of Consumption,* to the Congress of the Sanitary Society at Portsmouth in 1892. In this address, though, he concentrated on the poor quality of the inspection of the meat rather than the care of the beasts.

Josiah's prefatory chapter had begun by pointing out that meat is **not** a necessity, and then considered the issue of the pain caused by butchery, a practice which degrades its practitioners. We are tempted to dismiss the animals' suffering as short-lived, and to cite 'Nature red in tooth and claw' in mitigation of our activities. Our affection, our powers of sympathy, are very limited in extent, and are capable of being readily exhausted: our love for a pet dog does not extend to a herd of cattle.

The final part of the work was devoted to 'model slaughterhouses', and considered guillotining, electrocution and lethal chambers as alternative methods of killing animals. But discussion of these, though well-intentioned, was really irrelevant. One of the aims of the Humanitarian League, as printed in its manifesto in 1895, was 'the prevention of the terrible sufferings to which animals are subjected in the cattle-traffic and the shambles, and, as an initial measure, the abolition of **private** slaughter-houses, the presence of which in our large centres is a cause of widespread demoralisation.' Josiah's vision went further: while acknowledging the good will of the 'sanitarians and inventors who are doing their best to reduce the suffering of the tortured, slaughtered animals' he saw butchery as a relic of man's barbarous state, and looked forward to a time when the Enmity between man and his fellow creatures would be replaced by a wider Amity. He believed the deliberate infliction of pain and the deliberate destruction of life to be an outrage upon the rights of creation.

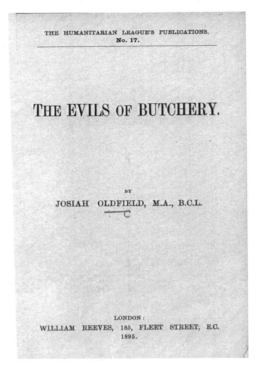

THE HUMANITARIAN LEAGUE'S PUBLICATIONS.
No. 17.

THE EVILS OF BUTCHERY.

BY

JOSIAH OLDFIELD, M.A., B.C.L.

LONDON:
WILLIAM REEVES, 185, FLEET STREET, E.C.
1895.

When Josiah's book was published in 1895 he had yet to complete his Doctoral Dissertation, so was still a **Bachelor** of Civil Law.

It was probably through shared humanitarian ideals that Josiah met Sidney Hartnoll Beard. A year older than Josiah, he was a wealthy stockbroker, who in 1895 had founded the 'Order of the Golden Age'. This was a philanthropic and humanitarian society whose philosophy is set out in its publications. The Order exalted the great Ideal of a coming Era of Peace and Happiness, of national and individual health, of systematic physical and spiritual culture, of kindness, unity and goodwill; and invited all men and women to live a humane, hygienic and beneficent life, so as to hasten its advent. Members regarded animals and human beings simply as different orders of creatures, to be regarded with equal compassion. 'Thou shalt be as a father and as a mother, as an elder brother and a loving sister, as a king and a queen towards all the sentient lower creatures' wrote Josiah in 1897 in *The Voice of Nature*. Half a century later his sentiments were unchanged when he stated 'It is one of the earliest privileges of a man to take up the position of comforter and protector and elder brother to the animal world'. (*The Crown of Grapes*). Like the Hindus, for whom he had much respect, Josiah thought that even the lowest animals should be treated with consideration.

Josiah's crusade against butchery continued with the issue of *The Cruelties of the Flesh Traffic*. The content of this booklet, published by the 'Order of the Golden Age' at 2d. per copy, was an only slightly revised version of *A Groaning Creation*. By 1922, when the fourth edition appeared, it had apparently already sold well over thirty thousand copies. [It is to be hoped that most of these were read: the Library copy of *A Groaning Creation* I consulted retained its uncut pages a century after its publication.]

Another objective of the Humanitarian League was an end to vivisection. It contended that the practice was incompatible with the fundamental principles both of humanity and sound science, and that the infliction of suffering for ends purely selfish, such as sport, fashion, profit, or professional advancement, had been largely instrumental in debasing the general standard of morality. Josiah, after he had qualified as a doctor, was prepared to allow the claim that scientists used vivisection in order to alleviate suffering to both men and animals. His somewhat ambivalent views on this subject were summarised in *The Claims of Common Life, or The Scientific Relations of Humans and Non-Humans*, which cost 1/- from the Ideal Publishing Union* in 1899.

In the same volume Josiah asked 'Do we create life? Have we solved the mystery of vitality?' He considered that there was a finite total of 'vital force', which man had diverted by breeding animals for his own purposes. What would he have thought of cloning, or of genetically modified crops? Perhaps the latter, if leading to greater yields of fruit or vegetables, might have been welcomed if it spared animals from butchery.

An international medical congress in London in 1881 had passed a resolution recording its conviction that experiments on living animals had proved of the utmost service to medicine in the past and were indispensable to its future progress. Therefore, while strongly deprecating the infliction of unnecessary pain, it was of opinion, in the interests of both man and animals, that it was not desirable to restrict such experiments by competent persons. Dr Samuel Wilkes of Guys Hospital reiterated this opinion in 1892, declaring 'We cannot as a body declare our disapproval of the so-called vivisection'. Dr Wilkes noted that hunting for sport, or to supply wealthy women with furs, was tacitly accepted by the majority of the general public - and if such behaviour was considered 'correct' it would be ridiculous to speak of the rights of animals. That such statements were made implies that strong criticism of experiments on living animals, and other cruel practices, were being expressed. It is not clear whether Josiah himself was present on either occasion, but proceedings at both are quoted extensively in *The Claims of Common Life*.

* This publishing house was born in 1893, its directors being none other than Josiah himself, editor of *The Vegetarian* and Charles Forward, who held the same position at the quarterly *Vegetarian Review*. The new company, which was offering 10,000 shares of £1 each, would acquire these two publications, together with plant, assets and goodwill, from A.F.Hills (who would join the Board after allotment), and start another magazine called *Merry-go-Round*.

34

After presenting the generally-held views Josiah gave his own. Man is himself an animal, and although the life of one man might be considered of more value than that of a single sparrow, might it not be equally valid to say that the continued existence of a number of other animals is more important than that of just one man? If so, is it justifiable to kill large numbers in order to save him? 'We believe in the beauty of thought of that next generation of which we are the pioneers, and we believe that such a generation of merciful hearts and infinite yearnings will recognise as an axiom of their creed that...every unit of life has its rights

> 'That nothing walks with aimless feet,
> That not one life shall be destroyed,
> Or cast as rubbish to the void,
> When God hath made the pile complete.'

In other paragraphs Josiah pointed out that man's ability to breed animals did not confer the right to slaughter them for meat nor use them for experimentation, and repeated his conviction that cruelty of any kind degrades the perpetrator. He also contended that evolution chiefly had its most stable basis in corporate co-operation and not in antagonistic warfare. Survival of the fittest depended on socialism rather than the individual unit. At this date Josiah saw family life as the 'essence of perpetuation of higher life forms' and concluded that man's higher instincts should rule his actions.

He also referred to his own experience as a scientist seeking knowledge:- 'I never looked with such fearsome eyes on the mysteries of the body as I have done since I tried to dissect limb from limb ...(to) follow the delicate tracery of nerves from the centre of the brain to the furthest periphery... to say that science can harden or degrade man in his relation to animals is to malign the most sacred of studies... Science increases the rights of animals by deepening the rights of man'. This somewhat puzzling statement remains unexplained, although it may be linked to the views he expressed in *The Voice of Nature* in 1897. Young boys may instinctively lust to torture and maim, but the earlier barbarism should give place to a growing revolt against cruelty, killing and blood. Those who continue in adult life (butchers, sportsmen, vivisectors) are but 'cosmic children, having reached the physical form of the complete human, but [who] have not yet attained to the physical stature of a man'.

Josiah would have studied anatomy during his time at St Bartholomew's Hospital, but physiological investigations of living animals might not then have had a place in the medical course. A Royal Commission in 1875 had recommended the use of anaesthetics whenever possible where experiments on animals were deemed necessary, and a law passed the following year prohibited their use simply for the acquisition of manual skills. It was the strong anti-vivisection lobby in England which had led to the 1875 Royal Commission, and in Bromley, where Josiah was later to set up home with his family, there were many prepared to listen. Interest continued in that area, and the *Bromley Record* reported a public lecture on vivisection given by the Rev.Lionel Lewis in November 1913.

Perhaps today Josiah would have found cause for concern in some clinical trials whose main purpose appears to be the academic progress of the scientist rather than the alleviation of suffering. His thoughts on testing cosmetics on animals can be deduced from his attitude towards powder and other beauty aids - 'there is no complexion powder equal to the use of rain-water without soap'.

By 1909 Josiah's position was clear. At the International Anti-Vivisection and Animal Protection Congress held at the Caxton Hall he addressed the 'Medical Anti-Vivisection' division on 'The Principles of Healing and the Practice of Vivisection'. He dismissed as dishonest and misleading the claims of those who stated that it was nothing more than a pin-prick. Vivisection was contrary to the spirit of medicine because it took no note of the pain incurred by the victim. Its spirit was not healing, but killing. Other speakers at the same conference considered the rights of animals: George Greenwood, MP, chose 'Blood Sports' as his topic, while 'Draught Dogs in the Low Countries' was a paper attracting the notice of *The Times* reporter. Had he been alive in

November 2001 Josiah would no doubt have been gratified to find that, while bombs rained down on Afghanistan, the deaths of eleven mice made the front page of the *Daily Telegraph.* They had died during a study of how loud noise strengthens the toxicity of 'speed' - methamphetamine.

Wendy Higgins, Campaign Director of the British Union for the Abolition of Vivisection, said 'These sick experiments are absolutely despicable. Just because people choose to take drugs and go to raves doesn't justify subjecting animals to suffering and death in the laboratory.' The study, at Cambridge University, was headed by Dr Jenny Morton. Of 40 mice forced to listen to 'The Prodigy' at high volume, seven died, as did four of forty made to listen to a Bach violin concerto.

Chapter 5

St John's Hospital for Diseases of the Skin

Even before starting his medical training Josiah had been elected to the Board of Management of St John's Hospital for Diseases of the Skin, his name having been proposed by Mr Ernest Bell, a fellow vegetarian, and seconded by Dr Boothby Dow. This establishment had been founded in 1863 by John Laws Milton, and in its early days was subject to financial difficulties, opposition from other well-established hospitals and public controversy culminating in a libel action, as well as internal conflict. Its premises in 1891, when Josiah joined the Board, were at 49 Leicester Square, London, where both in- and out-patients were treated. The building was far from ideal: complaints are recorded in the minute books of 1894-5 concerning noise from passing cabs and 'the language of the drivers, which frequently lasted till 4.00 a.m.'; of the nuisance caused 'by the keeping of poultry, rabbits, etc. on the roof of the adjoining premises' and, more puzzlingly, by the dancing school next door.

Josiah did not intend to be a sleeping partner, and almost immediately volunteered his services as Honorary Standing Counsel to the hospital. This seems to be the first record of the use of his legal training. By July 1892 he was a member of the Rules Committee, and worked with Dr Morgan Dockrell, of the 'Annual Meeting Subcommittee' on the draft annual report at the end of that year. Josiah seconded its passing, with a flowery speech, in 1893, beginning by mentioning that the cause 'needed not the pathos of a pleader to persuade persons... nor the silver voice of a Siren to gloze over evils'... He pointed out that the large amount contributed voluntarily by out-patients showed how much they valued the hospital, and emphasised the need for teaching others how to treat skin diseases. As a member of the Board he believed that at that time the Hospital was being managed with less friction, more unity of purpose, and better teamwork than had ever been the case.

Leicester Square about 1900
St John's was behind the photographer. The large building on the
right is the Alhambra Theatre

The same report mentioned the several entertainments at the hospital for patients and their friends, 'notably under the direction of Mr Josiah Oldfield'. These included a concert given under the auspices of the Vegetarian Federal Union. Josiah's musical contribution continued; an offer by two of his lady friends to sing to the patients in the wards was accepted a year or so later.

In March 1893 he was elected to the House Committee which dealt with the day-to-day running of the hospital: premises, staff, cleaning, payments and other matters. At once he proposed the formation of two further subcommittees, and became a leading light of both.

The Building Committee's remit was 'to discuss, formulate and carry out such steps as shall seem good to them for the purpose of raising funds for rebuilding, purchasing or building new premises either in London alone or in London and the country'. The previous autumn a small convalescent home connected with St John's, had, after a trial year or so of use, been condemned because of its insanitary condition. (A nurse there had contracted typhoid fever.)

This house, in the Finchley Road, was owned by Ernest Bell and known as 'Bellgarth'. Later in 1893 an advertisement was published in the *Vegetarian* appealing for contributions to fund the 'Shaftesbury Convalescent Home' at Bellgarth... Ernest Bell was willing to take patients from St John's at 10/- per week.

The main building too was under fire, Mr Cheesewright, M.I.C.E., reporting to the House Committee that the house was so dilapidated that no amount of money could make it suitable for hospital premises. St John's hoped that the landlord might be prepared to rebuild at the site if they offered to take a long lease at £550.0s.0d. per annum.

Josiah's other creation was the Educational Committee, with powers to arrange and submit to the Board a scheme for a teaching institution in connection with St John's Hospital. Its first step would be to give facilities to any member of the current medical staff who might desire to lecture during the summer session. Of the five medical staff, two agreed to lecture (at a guinea a time), and the course was advertised in the *Lancet* and the *British Medical Journal*. In addition 250 cards were printed and distributed. The first evening had a mixed reception, for one of the two lecturers failed to arrive, sending a telegram too late for a replacement to be arranged. The lecture room was overcrowded, even though only seventeen students (whose fees went to the hospital) attended. Nevertheless Josiah persisted with his plans, persuading others to approve the award of certificates to students who completed the course, and the Earl of Chesterfield, who had recently joined the Board, to give a Prize Medal. It was hoped that the best students would be prepared to act as dressers for ensuing courses.

From the patients' point of view there were distinct disadvantages to the lecture courses. Evening outpatient surgeries were supposedly open from 6.00 p.m. until 8.00 p.m. but as one complained: 'No-one is seen before 7.00 when up to 60 patients may be waiting. Those seen are lectured on until 8.30, then the rest are rushed through'. His justifiable grievance brought a distinctly sniffy reply from Dr Dockrell, but the hours were altered as a result. Under Josiah's guidance the Educational Committee had already agreed to purchase a 'lantern for oxy-hydrogen exhibition' at lectures, but slides were obviously no substitute for actual cases.

Josiah had some sensible suggestions to put before the House Committee, such as giving out diet sheets to patients, proposing that medical staff be allowed to attend Board meetings, and that monthly 'consultation meetings' be held where all the medical staff would confer over the progress and treatment of any patients who had been at the hospital for three months or more. This last was **not** universally welcome, and one doctor, Mr Milton, preferred to discharge two of his patients rather than allow any interference with his regime. Mr Bell had resigned a few months before this, largely because of the slurs cast upon the conditions at 'Bellgarth', Dr Bowrie left, and his casebooks disappeared with him, and at least one other member of the Board felt that Mr Bell had been shabbily treated and resigned in sympathy. So much for 'less friction, unity of purpose and better dependence on one another'!

His legal expertise was put into practice by Josiah in querying the authority of the House Committee to determine salaries (the prerogative of the Board of Management), in voicing his disquiet when accounts for work done without written authorisation from the Secretary were passed, and in challenging the legality of medical representatives taking the Chair at Board meetings. But when his official advice was urgently needed early in 1894 an outside Counsel had to be employed at a fee of £1.3s.6d. as Josiah could not be contacted in time. This was unfortunate, for Josiah's record of attendance at meetings of the many committees to which he belonged was excellent.

Rules, both written and unwritten, concerning advertising would frequently involve Josiah. The Board declined to accept advertisements for publication in the hospital's annual report, (nor would it permit a would-be advertiser to erect a hoarding on the roof of its premises in Leicester Square). At a Board meeting in July 1892 Josiah raised the subject of Mr Milton's endorsement of Pears Soap under the Hospital's name, deeming it unethical. The medical officer concerned answered that Messrs Pears were

41

merely quoting from a book written several years previously in which he had noted the efficacy of that firm's soap. When Josiah insisted that he should write requiring them to drop the offending advertisement, Mr Milton refused - whereupon Josiah demanded his resignation. The medical staff unanimously rejected this proposal, and Mr Milton, apparently speaking for St John's Hospital, continued to give his approval to soap and other products.

The boot was on the other foot at the end of that year, however, when the Christmas number of *The Vegetarian* carried unauthorised photographs of patients. Josiah took full responsibility for this breach of etiquette, and proffered his apologies. (And only a few months later he was to be in trouble at the Bar over advertising...)

The continual need for funds meant that publicity of all kinds was necessary, and the accounts of the hospital reflect this. In January 1892 the monthly balance sheet showed expenditure of £37.17s.6d. for printing, stationery and advertising, compared to a total wage bill of £55.13s.3d. for two nurses, dispenser and four ancillary staff. Admittedly this was probably rather higher than usual, because advertisements had been placed in the Christmas editions of both *The Philanthropist* and the *Charity Record*. Written appeals were sent individually to possible donors, and obtaining patronage from 'persons of quality' was all-important. The Board agreed to pay a Mr Taylor a 10% honorarium if he could influence Lady Hatherton to make a substantial contribution, while Josiah, via the Education Committee, recommended that the clergy of the parishes from which the hospital drew its patients should be asked to preach on behalf of its Building Fund.

A disturbing event occurred in January 1893 when the magazine *Truth* queried the financial dealings at S t   J o h n ' s. This organ seems to have fulfilled a similar role a century ago to that performed by today's investigative TV programmes, with similar drastic consequences based on sometimes   imperfect or biased research. Throughout the ensuing year   the   'system   of book-keeping was inquired into at great length', and the Board of

Management repeatedly invited *Truth* to inspect its accounts and see that all was in order, but it was a full twelve months before a further article appeared making it clear that nothing untoward had taken place. Even this retraction had a sting in its tail, remarking that patients were encouraged, if not expected, to make a payment if they could. This was the mark of a dispensary rather than a free hospital. Only after the whole matter was settled did the Earl of Chesterfield, an active member of the Board, agree to put his name to a new appeal for funds which Josiah had drafted. *Truth* made a renewed attack in April 1895, its target this time being Mr Dunsford, who was employed **on commission** by the hospital to supply names of worthies who might respond to appeals.

Josiah the Keen Committee Member

Throughout 1894 Josiah's name frequently appeared in the minutes as he volunteered a variety of gifts to St John's - vegetables, sketches to decorate the walls, magazines, books and book-shelves for the nurses, the loan of a microscope... He offered to arrange 'simple Christian services' for the patients (and these did take place for a few months, but not without attracting some criticism); he organised a further concert; he suggested that his brother, by now a Canon, should preach on behalf of the hospital 'if a neighbouring pulpit could be found'.

The Annual General Meeting held on 6th February of 1895 seems to have been a lively one, with far-reaching consequences. Josiah himself was re-elected to the Board of Management, but other elections were not so clear-cut. From accounts of later Committee meetings, it seems that although it was generally realised that new blood was needed, names were being proposed which were not acceptable to the existing Board. A special meeting held immediately after the AGM to consider the rules for convening a 'Special Board Meeting' could not pass an amendment whereby the number of members forming a quorum would be reduced from forty to twenty because a quorum was not present! The matter rumbled on throughout the year, Josiah writing letters to be read at Board meetings if he himself could not attend. The following January, the 'Annual Meeting Committee', under Josiah's Chairmanship, recommended that names of possible candidates should be approved before being offered to the subscribers for election.

The second major change resulting from the 1895 AGM concerned the number of committees to which one person might be appointed. On 12th February, in Josiah's absence, this was set at two: Josiah could no longer remain a member of four different sub-committees. It was also agreed that meetings be held on a fixed day each week, something which Josiah attempted unsuccessfully to rearrange a few months later. Was his presence at almost every meeting beginning to irritate some members? Perhaps **every** working party has a member who always likes to contribute, is constantly querying procedure, and insists on discussing details at inordinate length. But it is often their work which ensures that necessary action is co-ordinated and results achieved. With hindsight we can appreciate that Josiah was learning as much as possible about the management of a small hospital.

The search for new premises to supplement the Leicester Square building, where serious overcrowding was affecting the treatment of all patients, became ever more urgent, and eventually a suitable house was found for in-patients at Arlington House in Uxbridge Road, Hammersmith, some distance away. A grand opening ceremony (chairs for 200 hired at a cost of £4.0s.0d) was held there in early 1896. By this time Josiah was back on the House Committee, querying whether a Committee room would be available at the new site.

In his history of the hospital (1963) Brian Russell quoted Josiah, who wrote in 1897 that the separation of the two departments undoubtedly caused the duties of the medical staff to be doubly heavy - so heavy that the future must bring a time when a single great edifice would be created for St John's within the centre of London. (This never materialised). Mr Russell also notes that in 1893 attendance on patients at St John's was more onerous than at most other hospitals, for each patient was seen **separately** and had the individual care of the Medical Officer on duty. The complete privacy thus afforded was obviously unusual at the time.

Unfortunately the books dealing with affairs at St John's Hospital between 1896 and 1899 are missing, but it seems likely that Josiah's involvement probably diminished as a result of his other activities.

Chapter 6

Growth and Activities of the Vegetarian Movement in London

One of Josiah's particular interests was the London Vegetarian Society, which had flourished and soon spawned numerous sub-groups. Of these Josiah was usually a member, and frequently the Treasurer. They included the Legal Considerations sub-committee, the Organizing Committee for International Cooperation, and the Literary Committee. One of the most important was the 'Health Councils and Entertainment Fund' Committee, whose object was to create a larger and more practical recognition of the value of good health, and to form a bond of union between Temperance, Food and Sanitary Reformers, Trade Unions, Working Men's Clubs, Co-operative and other Friendly Societies. If, in spite of their varied opinions on different subjects, these organisations could be induced to unite in efforts to remove the ignorance which caused the prevailing sickness and suffering, and to teach the laws of life, then the happiness of mankind would be advanced.

In order to achieve this a concert party known as the 'At Home' Company arranged a series of entertainments 'of an unique and popular character - concerts, dramatic recitals, comediettas and operettas (with or without appropriate scenery and costume)'. The six artistes involved included some professional performers: the organiser was Miss May Yates, who also gave recitations. Miss Yates' real name was Mary Ann Yates Cockling, but in deference to her father's wishes she used a pseudonym. Miss Yates was one of the most active workers spreading the gospel of vegetarianism. A frequent speaker, she was prepared to step in wherever needed, as at a meeting held at the Mildmay Radical Club in January 1893. When the expected speaker failed to turn up Miss Yates threw herself into the breach. She resigned as Secretary of the LVS in 1893 to lecture on Bread Reform in America; she was later to advise on the production of bread in Britain during the First World War. In its 'endeavours to

The "At Home" Company.

ARTISTES—

MISS FANNY PERFITT
(From the Crystal and Alexandra Palace Companies).

MISS LOUISE AUGARDE
(From Mr. D'Oyly Carte's Opera Companies).

MISS MAY YATES
(Reciter).

MR. T. C. WRAY
(From the Gaiety Theatre, London).

MR. ERNEST THIEL
(The well-known Pianist).

MR. J. M. GORDON
(From the Savoy and Comedy Theatres, London).

The above Company having been organised by the London Vegetarian Society with the view of popularising the principles which they advocate, are arranging a series of Entertainments throughout London and the Provinces, when Concerts, Dramatic Recitals, Comediettas, and Operettas (with or without appropriate scenery and costume) will be given.

Brochure Advertising the 'At Home' Company

bring the refining influence of high-class recreation within the reach of the poorest' the concert party directed the attention of its audiences to hygiene and food reform by what are described as 'short bright addresses' and by distribution of literature. In a single year they had performed on over 120 occasions, at some 60 locations. In a typical week in January 1893 they entertained at the Upholsterers' Club in Gower Street on the 16th, at Braby's Club, Deptford on the 18th, and at the People's Palace the following day. They also entertained members of the VFU at a conversazione following their semi-annual meeting in 1892 at which a new set of rules had been drafted. Most of the group's engagements were in London, but the remainder seem all to have been in south-west England, perhaps dependent on travel via the Great Western Railway: Andover, Bridgwater, Salisbury, Wells and Weston-super-Mare were just a few of the destinations visited.

47

As well as the lectures and debates arranged by the LVS there were also cookery demonstrations. These tried to extend the use of wheatmeal, oatmeal, barley, lentils, peas, haricots, and other cereals and pulses, nuts, fresh fruits and vegetables. Private lessons in vegetarian cookery were available at the house of Mrs Boult in Torriano Avenue, Camden. But perhaps the most useful and practical work carried out by the London vegetarians at the turn of the century was that of providing cheap and nourishing meals for the capital's school children. A typical meal, which cost a ha'penny, consisted of soup, a slice of wholemeal bread and a slice of raisin pudding. The soup was particularly appreciated, though whether it retained any vitamins is doubtful. The recipe for 'West Ham Vegetarian Soup' was as follows:-

> 'To make one gallon - Take half a pound of grains (wheat, barley, oats, maize, rice), one pound of pulses (peas, beans, lentils) and boil sharply for two hours. Then add one pound of potatoes (mashed) and one pound of mixed vegetables (turnips, parsnips, carrots, onions, &c); these should be grated or cut up small. Boil for another hour and stir well. Flavour to taste with butter, sweet herbs, spices, &c.'

A daily newspaper commented at the time that London's stray dogs would be pleased to regain their bones.

A more detailed account of a dinner for 300 children in 1892 also quotes costs. The soup was made from eighteen pounds each of lentils and rice, eight pounds each of turnips, carrots and potatoes, two pounds of onions and some salt - total cost 5/. Twelve quartern loaves of bread, each providing twenty-five slices, cost 4/6d. Twelve half-quartern loaves of currant wholemeal bread added a further 2/4d. Three-quarters of a pound of butter (for the soup) at 8d brought the total cost to 12/6d, exactly the amount raised if every child was able to pay its half-penny. There might be strings, in the form of addresses to the children, attached to the provision of meals at a school. Sometimes small prizes were offered for the best essay on the subject.

THE FIRST ANNUAL REPORT

OF THE

Educational Food Fund

AND

CHILDREN'S DINNERS.

ORGANISED BY THE BREAD AND FOOD REFORM LEAGUE AND THE
LONDON VEGETARIAN SOCIETY.

**Members of the Vegetarian Movement were early
Supporters of Dinners for Schoolchildren**

These meals were supported by The Educational Food
Fund, a joint venture organised in 1889 by the LVS and the Bread
and Food Reform League. Josiah was the Treasurer, and Miss
May Yates the Secretary. The fund also sought donations (to be
sent to the Memorial Hall) which could be used to make supplies
of pulses and grains more generally available in poorer districts,
to 'aid the toiling millions to obtain cheap, healthy, nourishing
food, and thus help to check the alarming physical and moral
degradation into which such large numbers of our population are
sinking'.

At the end of 1892 Josiah, through the pages of *The
Vegetarian*, was asking for contributions (to be sent to the Editor,
i.e. Josiah) towards the provision of 'Vegetarian Soup Barrows'
which would offer to hungry adults meals similar to those given to
children in school: just over £68 had been collected by January the
following year. Josiah also formed the 'National Food Supply
Association' which apparently duplicated the work of the

49

Educational Food Fund. Why? Such activities would surely not have endeared him to Miss Yates and her fellow-workers. It is possible that this was simply a way of finding out which advertising brought in more money, all of which was used for the same good work. An alternative explanation hints at diversion of donations to less worthy causes. Or perhaps Josiah and Miss Yates did not work well together, and he thought he could improve on her methods. Whichever is the true reason, Josiah's version did not last, whereas the school children's dinner scheme continued successfully until at least 1905.

Vegetarian societies were flourishing in other countries too, and what was probably the first international meeting was a Congress held at Leipzig, in Germany, in September 1889. Did Josiah attend? It seems possible: he would certainly have been involved when the second such meeting took place in London the following year, for by then he was Treasurer of the London Vegetarian Society. By this date the London society, the large Manchester group and other smaller English associations had together decided to form the 'Vegetarian Federal Union' which would send representatives to international gatherings. Arnold Hills was Chairman, the Secretary was Mr O'Callaghan, and Josiah was Treasurer. All but three of the committee of this body were also on the committee of the London group; both associations were based at the Congregational Memorial Hall in Farringdon Street, and their aims were essentially similar.

An important event in the Vegetarian calendar for 1892 was a banquet held in London at the Wheatsheaf Restaurant (in Rathbone Place) to celebrate the birth of Shelley, who was one of the pioneers in abstaining from eating meat. William Axon, Henry Salt and Edward Maitland, some of the best-known members of the Manchester-based Vegetarian Society, were joined as speakers on this occasion by George Bernard Shaw, who as a socialist was beginning to be known as a 'platform virtuoso'. According to the *Vegetarian Messenger* the occasion was reported in several papers - and **mis**-reported elsewhere.

THE VEGETARIAN
MESSENGER AND REVIEW.

VEGETARIANISM (V. E. M.)

THAT IS, THE PRACTICE OF LIVING ON THE PRODUCTS OF THE VEGETABLE KINGDOM, WITH OR WITHOUT THE ADDITION OF EGGS AND MILK AND ITS PRODUCTS (BUTTER AND CHEESE), TO THE EXCLUSION OF FISH, FLESH, AND FOWL.

" *Fix upon that course of life which is best ; custom will render it most delightful.*"

Vol. I. No. I.
(5th Series.) 50th Year.   JANUARY 1st, 1898.   PRICE TWOPENCE.

A Medical Sack Race and Medical Ethics. — A short editorial article in the *British Medical Journal* compares Oriolet Hospital with a sack race. In the sack race, as we all know, the competitors handicap themselves by racing in sacks ; at Oriolet Hospital, according to the *British Medical Journal*, the authorities handicap themselves in the treatment of the patients by deliberately tying their hands and limiting their efforts to a single " fad." Surely the comparison is not a just one. The point is, do patients at Oriolet recover sooner than they would at an ordinary hospital ? If they do, it is evident that the treatment is the right one, and the medical man who confines himself to the right method is doing better service to his patient than the medical man who tries half-a-dozen wrong methods. A doctrine is enunciated in the same article which all laymen must protest against, for the *British Medical Journal* says that " the patient in choosing his hospital *chooses his treatment, which is ethically wrong.*" A patient may possibly be foolish in choosing his own treatment, instead of letting his physician choose it ; but, surely, he is doing nothing " ethically wrong " if he decides to go to a hospital where he

**The *Vegetarian Messenger* was relaunched under
Josiah's Editorship in 1898**

The LVS on several occasions voted grants to the VFU, and their annual meetings took place on the same afternoon at the Congregational Memorial Hall. In 1893 the meetings were timed at 3.00p.m. and 5.00p.m., and were followed by a 'Substantial fruit banquet, with instrumental and vocal music, and a musical sketch by members of the Vegetarian Rambling Club'. Admission to the meetings was free, but tickets for the later Conversazione cost 1/- in advance or 1/6d on the day. Considerably greater numbers attended the evening events than participated in the meetings.

The Federal Union had a slightly wider agenda than the London Vegetarian Society, although cheap dinners for schoolchildren, opposition to vivisection, suppression of the trade in live animals for slaughter, and encouragement of fruit cultivation were common to both. In 1892 two additional topics raised for discussion at the VFU Congress were reform of the penal code together with abolition of capital punishment (a cause dear to Josiah), and the extension of the franchise to women. A brief note in the *Vegetarian Messenger* later that year, however, informed readers that the suggested political programme had, after considerable discussion, been withdrawn on the suggestion of the Vegetarian Society and the Bolton Vegetarian Society.

Members were also concerned with introducing free trade for dried fruits, treating tobacco sales like those of other poisons, and making hare-coursing and pigeon-shooting penal offences. The inclusion of a resolution proposing that international disputes be subject to arbitration would have been fitting for a group comprising delegates from several countries, although whether many of these actually attended is doubtful. In 1893 the representatives at the AGM came from Brighton, Bolton, Croydon, Exeter, London, Northern Heights, Portsmouth, Sheffield, the Vegetarian Society (Manchester), West Ham and Woolwich. A speaker at this meeting was F. Pierce Doremus. An American citizen, and a Quaker, he had been the original Secretary of the LVS (1889-90), then served in the same position for the VFU from 1892-95.

Problems over finance figure regularly in the minutes of the London Vegetarian Society. By November 1891 Josiah had amalgamated the assets of the Educational Food Fund, the Health Councils and Entertainment Fund and the LVS itself in order to save bank charges. In June the following year there was apparently a deficit: Josiah was absent from the meeting but in a letter he suggested firstly that a submission of **proposed** outgoings be made monthly to the committee, and secondly that a 'Guarantee Fund' be set up. Arnold Hills said that he would be happy to guarantee anything he had instigated, and his commitments were detailed at the committee's next meeting. He would provide £50 per month to the London Vegetarian Society and the Health Council Fund, £100 quarterly to the Educational Food Fund and the Children's Dinners, and £50 to the new 'Guarantee Fund'. In addition he undertook to pay all the society's outstanding debts. The other members of the committee contributed guarantees ranging from a guinea to twenty pounds, Josiah subscribing ten. There were more deficits in May 1893, largely because of the expenses involved in paying staff to prepare the school dinners. A year later the 'At Homes' affairs were in a mess, and it fell to Arnold Hills once again to remedy the matter, while the bill-poster was invited to appear before the Executive Committe to explain his account.

Was Josiah at fault? The study of theology, law, and medicine does not necessarily lead to skill in book-keeping and accountancy, and allegations of poor financial management and irregularities in the publication of accounts would arise later in connection with other institutions with which Josiah was involved. It seems very likely, however, that the enthusiastic LVS amateurs promoting their vegetarian creed, secure in the knowledge that Arnold Hills had apparently limitless funds at his disposal, may have simply spent too freely.

**Mr and Mrs Henry Salt
in costume for a performance of *Hamlet***

53

A manuscript note in Josiah's handwriting in the Minutes for November 1895 remarking on the number of members who had not paid their annual subscriptions suggests another reason for the shortfall in funds. Incidentally Josiah had added yet another to his portfolio of Treasurer-ships in 1893, this time that dealing with the Lecture Fund.

Josiah, though, was not the Treasurer of the London Vegetarian Society itself. This was Ernest Bell, M.A., of the publishing firm, who was also treasurer of the Bread and Food Reform Society. He had studied mathematics, but his main preoccupations were with animal welfare; he was the author of numerous booklets concerned with anti-vivisection and similar topics. When in September 1896 he wanted to resign his position in the LVS other committee members persuaded him to continue with at least some of his work (including the signing of cheques) even if he was unable to attend all their meetings. He, like Josiah, who as Vice-Chairman frequently ran the proceedings, had been present at the majority of the monthly meetings.

The Congregational Memorial Hall, Farringdon Street

Chapter 7

Josiah and the Legal Profession

Between 1895 and 1899 London directories give Josiah's address as 1, Mitre Court Buildings, Temple E.C. Was it at this time that Josiah practised on the Oxford Circuit? Apart from Oxford itself the other towns on this Circuit were Hereford, Shrewsbury and Monmouth (Birmingham was added later). Josiah perhaps hoped that in Oxford and Shrewsbury, near which he had grown up, his name might be recognised by those in search of a lawyer, and that this was what prompted him to **advertise** his services - an infringement of legal custom.

The Oxford Circuit Mess Minutes reveal the result. At a meeting held at the Inner Temple Lecture Room in London on 27th April 1894 'the Junior read a letter from Mr Oldfield placing his resignation in the hands of the Mess and expressing his regret for the breach of professional etiquette of which he had been guilty.

Mitre Court

The Leader (Jelf, QC) said that he had received a letter from Mr Oldfield who stated that Mr Spearman having called his attention to certain paragraphs of a puffing nature which had appeared in local papers, he (Mr Oldfield) frankly admitted that he was cognizant of their having been sent, and as he found he had thereby done wrong he put himself in the Leader's hands. Mr Jelf had written to Mr Oldfield advising him to take the course that gentleman had taken and at the same time censuring severely the misconduct he had been guilty of. The relevant paragraphs which were read to the Mess appeared to be a public notification of the fact that Mr Oldfield had joined the Circuit and was about to visit the towns thereon, and laudatory notice of his learning and abilities.'

A proposal that the matter should stand over for a year was put forward, but fortunately for Josiah a colleague named Acland moved an amendment

'That this Mess considers that Mr Oldfield's act was a gross violation of the rules of the Bar, but having regard to his explanation and to his expression of deep regret, allows him to withdraw his resignation'.

After considerable discussion the amendment was carried by 21 votes to 13.

It was probably Josiah who was responsible for a regular column signed 'Lex' in *The Vegetarian* at this period, in which simple legal queries from readers received very brief answers. This might have been an outlet for an otherwise frustrated lawyer, lacking briefs, to give his opinions. Maybe he also posed the questions.

The existing Mess Minutes of the Oxford Circuit begin in 1861 with a summary of the Mess Rules (according to the Recorder, Henry Matthews, earlier records had been lost). Most of the rules are concerned with the purchase and supply of wine, the payment for this due from each member, and fines to be exacted for non-attendance at Dinners. Members were also required to pay for the services of the Circuit Messenger, whose fees varied from 1/- at Reading, Oxford or Abingdon to 2/6d at Worcester, Stafford or Gloucester. Perhaps more important was the rule stating that in every defended cause at the Assizes where the plaintiff was represented by 'two silk gowns alone, a kite must be given to the Junior in Court to open the proceedings.' Intriguingly, Rule 14 says simply 'No Barrister shall travel from one Circuit town to another by Coach'.

A list of barristers according to seniority, with their lodgings, was to be put up by the Circuit Messenger at the principal Inns in each town (although Barristers were not allowed to robe or sleep at Inns). The list was to be revised each year, and the names of gentlemen who had not attended any town on Circuit for two years were to be erased. Their names could, however, be reinstated on their giving notice to the Circuit Messenger of their return to Circuit. There are considerable discrepancies between the general Circuit List of Barristers and the Oxford Bar Circuit List as far as Josiah Oldfield is concerned. In the former his name does not appear until 1910, where it remains until 1934. Then from 1935 to 1949 his Circuit is given as 'Jamaica Bar'. In contrast the Oxford list records his name from 1896 to 1904, in 1912, and from 1919 to 1924.

Every candidate for election to the Bar Mess on the Oxford Circuit had to be proposed and seconded by Members of the Mess, although in March 1893 it was decreed that only one of these members need have personal knowledge of the candidate. In January 1894, with reference to the candidacy of Mr J.Perry Oliver, there was further discussion of the subject, the Leader, Mr Jelf, QC, stating that although there was no rule, it was most unusual for a junior to propose a member. The usual practice was for a member to be proposed by a QC, generally the Leader, since his approval was a guarantee that the candidate's fitness had been ascertained by someone well-acquainted with the rules and practice of the Circuit. Bosanquet, QC, Reid, QC, and Darling, QC, pointed out that it was essential that the Mess should have some information as to **the candidate's social position** (my emphasis), and as to whether he was practising or intending to practise.

One wonders whether there had already been discussion concerning Josiah's suitability; the son of a shopkeeper, and a vegetarian? Certainly the memorandum quoted above implies that he was already a Member of the Mess by April 1894, although his name does not appear in the Minutes as one of those welcomed. But the omission may have been simply because the Recorder forgot to list the new Members on a particular date (the names of those elected in 1897, for example, have been squeezed into the record between other transactions). Or perhaps only the names of those new Members actually present were transcribed. The Members admitted in Winter 1892, i.e. just after Josiah had been called to the Bar, are Bagnoule-Evans, Henry J.Farrant,

H.Neville Monk, M.H.J.Pigott, Watkin Watkins, R.J.Lawrance and L.G.H.Mayer. The penultimate name is of interest as it was Lawrance who seconded the amendment restoring Josiah to membership of the Mess. Acland, the proposer, was more senior: he had in 1886 managed to carry a motion simplifying the election of members.

This was not the first occasion on which Josiah had broken the rules, for the previous autumn, on 3rd November 1893, he had been called before a committee of three Benchers at Lincoln's Inn. Their report reads:-

'Josiah Oldfield, Esq, a barrister of the Society, appeared before the Committee and admitted having written the letter in question. He explained that at the time when he wrote it he was anxious to befriend the plaintiff who was a poor woman in distress, and did not realise the irregularity he was committing. That he had since realised that it was an impropriety, and desired to express his extreme regret and to apologise to the Incorporated Law Society.

The Committee impressed upon Mr Oldfield the grave impropriety of his conduct, and he assured the Committee that he should be most careful in the future to avoid any transgression of the laws of the profession.'

Tantalisingly, no details of the letter are revealed. It seems clear that Josiah's habit of departing from the rigid but often unwritten rules of the professional bodies to which he belonged started early in his career.

Although in theory it was possible for a Barrister to practise without being a member of the Mess, it was very uncommon, and the man concerned would be unlikely to receive many briefs or to rise in his profession. Jelf, QC, who was still Leader in 1899, thought everyone on Circuit should be a Member. It could prove expensive: any Members honoured in any way, being made a Judge, perhaps, or being elected to Parliament, were 'fined', the usual penalty being a dozen of champagne. The same fine was levied on those committing the crime of matrimony! But Josiah's name does not appear as one of the sinners following his marriage in 1899.

Josiah's social gaffe in allowing his services to be advertised was almost - but not altogether - unique. A somewhat similar case arose in July 1897 when a London solicitor wrote to a solicitor whom he did not know in Worcester requesting that the latter would give work to the London lawyer's brother-in-law, who had just been elected to the Oxford Circuit. Mr Jelf's thoughts on the matter are worth repeating: 'Although it would be impossible to prevent a relative, even if a solicitor, asking a friend to give his relative an occasional brief, yet for a relative to approach complete strangers and send them a sort of circular was improper, and not calculated to do any good to the person on whose behalf it was sent.' In this case the Barrister concerned was completely ignorant of the advertisement and escaped censure. But it is apparent that having friends in high places could help to establish a young barrister, and there was considerable truth in the words of the song given to the Judge by W.S.Gilbert in *Trial by Jury*:

> 'When I, good friends, was called to the Bar
> I'd an appetite fresh and hearty
> But I was, as all young Barristers are
> An impecunious party...
> 'I soon got tired of second-class journeys
> And dinners of bread and water
> So I fell in love with a rich Attorney's
> Elderly ugly daughter...

thereby ensuring preferment.

For vegetarians like Josiah and Gandhi the compulsory dinners to be eaten in hall while at Lincoln's Inn (and costing up to 9/-) were largely incompatible with their beliefs, so that they were restricted to consuming little more than bread and potatoes even on occasions when others had some respite from their 'dinners of bread and water'.

Josiah

Many years later Josiah described dining at the bar table rather differently. 'When the allowance to each four diners is a generous two or three bottles (of wine), with beer ad lib., it is a pleasure to me to "pass the bottle", while I sip my half glass and get the fragrance and aroma of a hundred vineyards out of every drop that slowly titillates the tastebuds of my tongue'. This habit caused him to be called a 'vinegary ascetic' by a fellow diner, but Josiah in his turn described his critic as lacking in aesthetic instinct, swilling down priceless vintage port like a sow slobbering in its trough of barley mash.

It appears, in fact, that Josiah used 1 Mitre Court as an accommodation address only. The chambers, on the second floor, were owned by the Honourable Dudley Campbell, but when Charles Carthew visited them in about 1898 he was told that that gentleman was 'presently in retirement, suffering, it is said, from an affection of the brain'. The clerk also told him that Josiah had 'not once been to chambers since his name has been up', and that letters received there were sent on to the Memorial Hall in Farringdon Street. The only apparent connection between Josiah and Dudley Campbell was that both were vegetarians.

Chapter 8

The London Vegetarian Association

In 1894, as membership of the London Vegetarian Society continued to grow, Josiah proposed the formation of separate local groups. Branches were formed in areas such as Clapham and Wandsworth, Bermondsey, Walthamstow and Wanstead. As the number of branches increased it seemed sensible to change the name of the London Vegetarian **Society** to the London Vegetarian **Association**. *The Times* reported the Annual General Meeting of the Society held in January 1897, at which the Chairman pointed out that the original single group had grown to twelve separate branches in London. The number of members and associates had reached 800. There were other reasons too for the change of name. A Mrs Cranston had recently died, leaving a legacy of £193 to be divided equally between the vegetarian **associations** of London and Manchester. Arguments amongst the residuary legatees continued throughout 1898: there was apparently still a London branch of the northern group which was known as the London Vegetarian Association, though it seems that most of the active and influential London vegetarians belonged to both the LVS and the LVA. An impassioned 8-page letter from May Yates, now back in England, condemned the proposed dissolution of the LVS, and suggested instead that it should simply adopt the new name. Whether there was a formal name change, or simply a merger, is not clear, but from this point onwards the London Vegetarian Association was the name used.

For many vegetarians the great event of 1897 was the Jubilee of the Vegetarian Society in Manchester, to which most groups had contributed much time and labour. By 1898 the number of London groups alone reached fourteen, and the annual meetings during the next few years all reported a more general acceptance of the meatless diet and a steady growth in the number of recruits. One discordant element, however, was the refusal of the London School Board to allow further lectures to children during school hours. When the London Vegetarian Association held its annual dinner at the Holborn Restaurant in May 1899 'between 200 and 300' attended, including Josiah. Arnold Hills, in his Presidential address, noted that 'people of all classes had been brought to see that a purely vegetarian diet was perfectly practicable, as had again and again been systematically demonstrated'. The guest of honour, Sir W.Wedderburn, M.P., referred to the 'hardy and muscular peasants of Lowland Scotland who lived mainly on porridge and milk' in his speech, echoing the words of some of Josiah's earlier writings.

The Association's Minutes for 1st December 1899 suggest a cooling of the relationship between Josiah and Arnold Hills, for the secretary was 'instructed to write to Dr Oldfield telling him that by special desire of Mr Hills he will endeavour to be present at Committee'. Recent absences on Josiah's part are understandable, for he had just married, but during early 1900 he did find time to attend four or five of the monthly meetings. In May he put forward a controversial resolution, proposing that the work of the LVA be divided into agreed areas, and that all receipts from these areas be paid into the common central fund. Monies would then be equally divided between local and central work. His resolution was, not surprisingly, vetoed by the local societies. Josiah attended the July meeting, but missed all the autumn dates, reappearing only in January 1901 when he failed to be re-elected to the Executive Committee.

The relationship between the parent association and local societies and their funds occupied many of the Committee's discussions, and some of its members tried to make the LVA more businesslike, proposing an office where local delegates could report in once a week, and the employment of a **paid** secretary. The latter arrangement had been suggested as early as 1894 by Josiah when the Vegetarian Federal Union was under consideration. 'To get a good name as President, influential people as Vice-Presidents and a trusty Treasurer is important, but the **Secretary** is **all**-important, needing to have persistent and tireless energy and good tact. Such a person should be **paid'**. One change which did take place was that local groups were banded together to form districts. The branches at Loughton, Wanstead and Walthamstow, for example, combined to form the 'Northern Heights' district. This cooperation would no doubt have helped when each group held its anticipated annual week-long mission. But every decision was always subject to the approval of Arnold Hills.

As with all committees, there were disagreements between members. Mr O'Callaghan's distribution of circulars was not approved... Mr Theobald objected to the proposed programme, perhaps on financial grounds. A Congregationalist, he was a chartered accountant and had probably succeeded Josiah as Treasurer of the VFU. An unexpected item in the 1901 Minutes is the proposal to start a 'Children's Dinner Fund', but this may be explained by the terse statement at the following year's Annual General Meeting. Mr Hills, in the Chair as usual, told his audience that arrangements for schoolchildren's vegetarian dinners had been taken over from the 'National Food Supply Association' - which had been Josiah's fund intended for the same purpose. This was another sign of the deteriorating relationship between the two men.

Much of the Executive Committee's time was spent on arrangements for social events like bazaars and conversaziones. The Christmas event in 1901, opened by Lady Harberton, a recent convert, featured 'an excellent display of musical drill by girls of the Devons Road Wesleyan Mission Band of Hope', while the 1904 programme included 'selections on Canadian sleigh bells by Mr Duncan Miller, marionettes, and a drawing room entertainment'. The chief organiser of these and many other events for several years had been Miss Florence Nicholson, who had originally been hired as Assistant Secretary of the LVS at 30/- per week. She had held the same position simultaneously in the VFU, and was to run three of the depôts concerned with children's dinners. The number of such meals served in the winter of 1902/3 was 103,207. The cost had now risen to 1d., but

10% were allowed free, to be distributed to necessitous cases at the discretion of a school's managers. Then, as now, care was taken not to 'pauperize' these children.

Arnold Hills continued to dominate the activities of the London Vegetarian Association, speaking at each annual meeting to report growth in interest and membership. The vegetarian movement was spreading in the United States, in India and the Colonies, in Italy, Germany, France and even in Russia. He saw a growing need for an organised vegetarianism, reflecting the fact that the Vegetarian Federal Union was not fulfilling this role (some members had attended a congress in Chicago in 1893 but subsequent meetings were all in London. The VFU finally disbanded in 1910). By 1908 his wishes were met: the first International Vegetarian Union Congress was held in Dresden in that year, and the second in Manchester in 1909. Florence Nicholson and the London Society took a prominent part, but Mr Hills had by now been completely disabled by arthritis and was dependent on an invalid carriage. He would speak from a wheelchair at the launch of the 'Thunderer' from his yard in 1911, and was carried by his servants on a stretcher to a demonstration in Trafalgar Square in 1912.

Chapter 9

The Oriolet Hospital, Loughton

Although Josiah Oldfield did not complete his medical diploma until 1897 he was already utilising his medical training. By 1896 he was registered at Loughton, Essex, where the *Epping, Ongar and Loughton Almanac* for that year records his address as 'Oriolet Hospital'. A short historical report in the *Loughton Review* in December 1986 gives some information about this Hospital. It had been a private house in 1858, and by 1898 the owner, according to the Rate Books, was Arnold F.Hills, and the occupier was Josiah Oldfield. The two men had inspected a number of houses in the area early in 1895, with a view to setting up an experimental hospital where cancer patients and others whose cases seemed hopeless, and who were willing to try any treatment, could be received. They saw it as an extension of the Humanitarian Hospital of St Francis, which anti-vivisectionists would be happy to support. It would remain under the control of the Council of that hospital.

Loughton Village

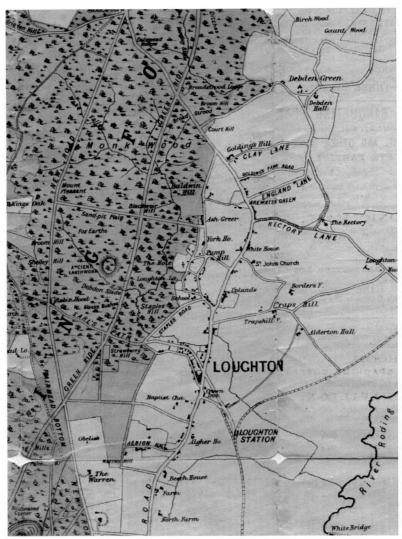

**Map of Loughton, on the edge of
Epping Forest, about 1890**

Kelly's Directory in 1898 extends the description to 'Oriolet Cottage Hospital and Convalescent Home, York Hill: Miss Clark Crowther, Matron'. Loughton had a population of just under 4000 at this time, and York Hill was one of its main streets, with mixed private and commercial occupation. The population of the area was growing rapidly, partly because of the improving railway service - the journey from Liverpool Street took only thirty minutes. In 1899 Loughton's Parish Council was to be superseded when the town became an Urban District.

Josiah himself wrote of the new hospital in the *Vegetarian Messenger* in 1895, describing its well-wooded grounds which were formerly part of Epping Forest, and its large western windows looking out into the sunlit sky, and over the fertile western forest slopes. The garden, orchard and forest provided both occupation and amusement, for they offered 'carpenters' shed, goat-house, fowl runs and houses, lawn, trees and a swing'. As well as three goats there was a resident donkey.

The establishment had two large wards, for men and women respectively, each with five beds. Miss Nind was the nurse in charge of the Men's ward, taking its name to become 'Sister Oroea', while nursing care in the Women's ward was provided by 'Sister Pomona', Miss Pitcher. (Pomona was the Roman Goddess of fruit and fruit trees, 'Oroea' was probably derived from the Greek word for fruitful, 'oraios'.) In these wards the minimum charge was 7/6d per week; there were ten smaller rooms for patients who preferred privacy, the cost ranging from one to three guineas weekly. As well as staff accommodation, there was a room which served as a Chapel, plus bathrooms, kitchen, sculleries and cellar. Treatment was largely confined to the use of diet, supplemented by massage and hydropathy; if patients did wish for medicines they could have them prescribed by the visiting physician at additional cost. (Josiah himself had not yet qualified as a doctor). The visiting Medical Officer was Wilson Aston: in 1896 the matron, whose brother was a doctor, was Gertrude Hick, known as 'Sister Oriolet'. There had been no fewer than seventy candidates for the post. The Sister's uniform, described as a 'true red with white bibbed apron and Sister Dora cap' later attracted the attention of the Princess of Wales during a presentation in connection with the Nurses' Pension Fund.

According to a report in the *Loughton and District Advertiser* in September 1899, the name 'Oriolet' had no more mystic meaning than that there were oriel windows at the rear, and the building was described as a somewhat old-fashioned cottage taken over from a butcher. The paper found this ironic in view of its new use. At the time a new ward was under construction in the garden for use by patients suffering from tuberculosis, other chest complaints, or any form of 'devitalisation'.

Professor John Mayor paid a visit at Christmas, when the general festivities included songs and recitations and the wards were decorated with evergreens. Gifts received included some 'bee appliances' from Fred Oldfield of Bomere, probably Josiah's younger brother Frederick Henry. The professor's contribution, possibly not the highlight of the occasion, was his reading (with annotations) of Milton's 'Samson Agonistes' to the assembled staff. He also wrote a number of German philosophic maxims, with translations, to be put up in the wards...

Professor John Mayor

The hospital was hailed as the first in England to cater specifically for Vegetarians, but the Medical Establishment scorned it. An editorial article in the *British Medical Journal* in late 1897 compared the lot of its patients with that of competitors in a sack race - they were handicapped in that only a single treatment was given, and that a 'fad'. The same article thought it ethically wrong that a patient should, by choosing his hospital, be in effect choosing his own treatment rather than allowing his doctor to decide what was best. There was a swift reply, through the pages of the *Messenger*, probably from the pen of Edwin Arnold. If the Oriolet's patients recovered more quickly than those in an ordinary hospital, then their treatment would have been proved correct.

Josiah was anxious not to antagonise the medical profession in general. When the possible opening of a vegetarian sanatorium in the north of England was under discussion in 1899, he stressed that it should be under careful and skilful medical surveillance, and that it should aim to be self-supporting. It should draw upon the experience gained at Loughton and be in a good style, and not, like many vegetarian enterprises, (Oriolet to a considerable extent included) be run on the cheap. He also reminded his audience that they should not be shocked when visiting such hospitals by bare feet or the absence of hats.

The maladies treated at Oriolet during its first year included indigestion, sleeplessness and general debility; eczema, abscesses, gastric ulcer and anaemia; varicose veins and hernia; locomotor ataxy, rheumatoid arthritis and other more serious diseases. From today's viewpoint it seems highly probable that Josiah's regime would have been just as effective as some of the other remedies in use at the turn of the nineteenth century. Its philosophy might be summed up in the words of Prof. John Mayor following a personal tour: 'A hospital where the physician's aim is to make himself unnecessary by teaching the laws of health'. Professor Mayor was at that time President of the Vegetarian Society. Although not then medically qualified Josiah served as 'Warden', carefully selecting individual diets for the patients, and making detailed notes on their progress. The patients, who might in some cases receive up to fourteen days free treatment if they were considered sufficiently deserving, seemed satisfied with their vegetarian diet.

Another visitor was the Vegetarian Society's Treasurer, William Harrison, who wrote an account of what he had observed. He found a caring institution, where even patients with very serious diseases remained cheerful, 'gathering together in groups, and singing hymns, manifesting all the homely joys of their own fireside'. He himself was asked to conduct the evening service in the chapel on that occasion, although he understood that the local Vicar normally performed this office. At Josiah's request he donned, for the first time, a clerical white gown, for the Warden liked everything done with due ceremony. There were daily prayers at 8.00 a.m. and 8.30 p.m.

Although treatment of certain patients (roughly one third) remained free the charge for ward patients soon rose to 10/- per week. The wealthy Arnold Hills who had so generously 'lent Oriolet to St Francis' had made an endowment to the Oriolet Hospital sufficient to fund it for three years, commencing with £500 in 1895. After that period it was hoped that the hospital would become self-supporting, but Josiah's vegetarian readers were urged to help the infant institution. The details of all the gifts to the hospital are listed in its report for 1896, ranging from Arnold Hills' second donation of £400 down to subscriptions of 2/6d. Gifts in kind are also recorded, and the list makes fascinating reading. It includes:

> Three tins of condensed milk
> A scrapbook
> A valuable old engraving
> Texts
> Italian macaroni
> Two copies each of *Herald of the Golden Age* and
> *The Vegetarian*, and one copy of the *Vegetarian Review*
> A dressing gown (from Lady Coomaraswamy)
> Bibles, hymn and prayer books, given by the SPCK.

The same report also remarks 'We are now training our own servants, and at the close of the year shall be in a position to recommend those who do well to families requiring dependable hospital-trained servants'. In that year a total of 190 patients had been admitted, of whom two died. There was also one birth.

In *The Mystery of Death*, written in about 1949, Josiah wrote that when the first little Fruitarian Hospital at Loughton, on the borders of Epping Forest, was opened, a rumour went round that it was for cancer patients. At that date the word 'Cancer' was scarcely mentionable in polite society. The hospital's 1896 report says 'Special cases of sarcoma, carcinoma and epithelioma are admitted for **observation** (my emphasis) under dietetic treatment'.

Josiah considered fasting to be an efficient way of treating the earlier stages of cancer or syphilis, and looked upon it as extremely helpful in association with other forms of treatment for these diseases. He did not, however, believe that they could be completely cured by eliminative fasting only. Like many ardent disciples of Nature Healing he wanted to show that choosing a fruitarian diet was the best way of **preventing** cancer. The diet is described in the book cited above:-

'Plain herbage like fresh salads, grains like white wheat, soaked or cooked into frumenty; pinhead oats as brose or porridge, a teaspoon of linseed soaked in warm water for an hour; a handful of milled nuts, root vegetables like a cold boiled beet; a dish of braised or fried onions; a clove of garlic rubbed on bread - these are the suitable medicament foods for a diseased or septic alimentary canal'.

Loughton from Earl's Path

71

Josiah would have no truck with beef tea or pasteurised milk, but many of his other recommendations remain valid today. Less acceptable would be his advice to drink only when thirsty and reduce fluids to the utmost. His instruction to increase salivation by masticating dry grains or hard toast he later modified, preferring that patients should chew on a fresh hawthorn or hazel twig to stimulate the salivary glands, and afterwards use the chewed twig to clean their teeth.

Josiah was proud of his achievements at Loughton. Because staff and patients alike abstained from meat, and unusual treatment was used, he knew that if he lost a patient his fruitarian regime would be blamed, for 'if a man pioneers along a non-orthodox line, he sets a whisper going among the stately pillars of the profession... They suggest the word "faddist", which condemns a man for all times as an outsider from participation in the loaves and fishes which are the reward of the faithful'. So after qualifying as a doctor it was with some trepidation that he put patients under anaesthetics, and with his colleagues performed serious operations. In fact the Oriolet's record was better than that of ordinary hospitals for Josiah carried out a thousand operations there without a single fatality.

One case which Josiah talks of in *The Mystery of Birth* concerns a patient suffering from TB caries, whom he first encountered when she was just twelve. He says that he operated on her on average once a month from then until she was seventeen, for abscesses, removal of teeth and parts of the jaw, amputation of fingers and of one foot. She was eventually cured, and later married and lived to be over fifty. These operations must have been carried out at the hospital at Loughton within a few years of his qualification, and demonstrate Josiah's skill and wide range of surgical knowledge - and, of course, the efficacy of his regime.

The *Epping Advertiser* (whose content is largely identical to that of the *Loughton and District Advertiser*) has an account of a visit by members of the Vegetarian Congress to a Harvest Festival celebrated at the Home Farm at Oriolet in September

1899. 'The hospital was once a private country house, but was altered to suit the needs of a modern hospital. We understand that though patients have been admitted at all ages, varying from children born in the hospital to those of three-score years and ten, there has been no instance in which it has been found necessary to vary the rule against flesh food, or the preparation of fish and game, on the premises'.

The celebrations included special harvest hymns, prayers that those connected with the (Vegetarian) movement might be enabled to extend its sphere of usefulness, and addresses by different speakers. Josiah, who had welcomed the visitors, mentioned in his speech that a Turkish bath and a sun bath would add greatly to the hospital's usefulness. Music from the Loughton Military Band accompanied the occasion.

VIEW OF THE OPEN-AIR WARDS AT OUR FRESH-AIR HOSPITAL, LOUGHTON.

The Outdoor Ward at Oriolet

Another Oriolet Festival, at which a new open-air ward was opened, was celebrated the following year in the presence of a large and distinguished party, although some of the anticipated guests, such as Professor Mayor and Sidney Beard, President of the Order of the Golden Age, sent their apologies. A certificate was presented to the senior nurse by Lady Gwendolen Herbert, addresses were given by Josiah and by the Dowager Duchess of Portsmouth; tea (with a silver collection) and a chapel service completed the proceedings. Josiah complained that he had asked 'a well-known Christian man' to lend his carriage to carry the Dowager Duchess to the Festival, but this gentleman refused since he believed vegetarianism to be unscriptural.

A paragraph which appeared in the *Herald of the Golden Age* in 1900 mentioning the addition of the new ward, and also extension of the work of the St Francis Hospital, went on to announce vacancies for at least a dozen well-educated women to undertake training in midwifery with the 'Maternity Society'. The Maternity Society was a private venture of Josiah's and was unknown to the Nursing Council. The only qualifications required were health, strength and intelligence, and a 'heart in the right place'.

When did Oriolet close? Josiah himself could not have operated before 1897, and if he spent five years on the TB case it was obviously still functioning in 1902. At that date, in addition to Josiah, *Kelly's Directory* recorded two further medical officers in attendance, Wilson Aston and Morley Frederick Agar.

The Secretary was Harry Cocking, and a new matron, Miss E.M.Davies, had succeeded Miss Clark Crowther. (Miss Crowther herself cannot have held the position for very long, for according to the hospital report Gertrude Hick had been Matron in 1896.) In fact the whole establishment was about to be taken over by the Salvation Army, whose leader, General Booth, and his wife were both prominent vegetarians.

Of General Booth, who died in 1912, Josiah wrote later 'I remember we met in Magdalen College Hall to partake of that delightful Nature Food repast provided under the will of Lord Crewe, Bishop of Durham. Over plates of strawberries and cream, peaches, cake and bread and butter, with vintage wine and fruit drinks we chatted .... and while General Booth and I were talking he proclaimed in his loud voice, so that in that quiet assembly his voice rang out like a trumpet - "you and I, Oldfield, are the only two here who know how to praise God by Fasting". When the obsequious waiter said - gently - as he offered to the General a tray "Would you like white wine, Sir, or red?", the General snorted and said "Wine, wine - no, take it to the Devil". The Oxford waiter in obedience to his training gently replied

"Pardon me, Sir, but would you show me the way..."'

In 1901 Mrs Bramwell Booth wrote in the *Deliverer*, the Army's newsletter, as follows:-

'We have, for twelve months, with the option of renewal, taken over the management of Mr Hills' Oriolet Hospital at Loughton, Essex, and we are intending to carry it on upon very much the same lines as before, namely as a hospital and home of rest, where the benefits of a non-meat diet and the practice of hydrotherapy and hygiene will be offered to all'. She noted that a new wing had been built. The hospital was still aiding poor patients in 1904, when the London Vegetarian Society collected approximately £180 on its behalf. How long this arrangement operated is unclear: there is no entry for Oriolet in Kelly's 1906 edition, and by March 1912 the hospital had become St Ethelburga's Home, owned and run by the Society for Waifs and Strays.

St Ethelburga's Home, formerly the Oriolet Hospital

William Chapman Waller (1850-1917) was a resident of Loughton whose writings, both in the parish magazine of St Mary's Church and in manuscript notebooks, provide valuable information about the development and growth of the town from 1871 onwards. During the Oriolet Hospital's time Waller lived at

75

Ash Green at the top of York Hill. On 5th March 1912 he describes a tour of the area, beginning near the junction of Staples Road with York Hill opposite the old National Schools. At this point were the 'little buildings put up as sanatoria by Arnold Hills, when he bought the land there... Adjoining them [on the site of what later became York Crescent] is Oriolet, built originally, I think, by Cummins, a verger of St Paul's Cathedral'.

This description, which comes from a manuscript made available by the Loughton and District Historical Society through its publication *Loughton 100 Years Ago* continues with gossip about Josiah and speculation concerning the hospital's closure. 'O(ldfield) was a barrister, a doctor, something in the way of a Volunteer, read the lessons at St Mary's and in the chapel of the hospital, wore sandals, and usually no hat - and of him Mrs Hills once said to me that if he were going to be married, she really thought he would want to perform the ceremony himself. Coming along one Sunday evening, I heard a ripple of laughter and saw one of the nurses dangling his straw hat from the window above where he was sitting below at another. After that I was not surprised when H(ills) questioned me as to whether I had heard any reports, etc. Anyway, not long afterwards, Josiah vanished and we heard he had married one of the nurses - a very good-looking one, if I remember aright. He next appeared at Southwark, and then at Bromley, as head of a Fruitarian Hospital, with no end of fashionable supporters, and there I imagine him still to be. He was in some way mixed up with an impostor called the Swami, but whether by his folly or his fault, I don't know. It does not appear to have done him any harm, though his name appeared in the newspapers - Arnold Hills was thoroughly sick of him, I know'. Arnold Hills had very strict views on morality.

But Josiah's reputation may have affected his chances of achieving success in one field. The *Loughton Advertiser* for 11th February 1899 gives the results of elections to the Loughton School Board, whose deliberations were reported regularly. There were some ten candidates for the seven vacancies: 543 of those eligible cast their votes. The most popular candidate amassed 565 votes (presumably each elector had seven votes), but Josiah managed only 51. All the other candidates gathered at least 270.

Another subject occupying Josiah and almost every other Vegetarian at this period was the issue of vaccination, which had become compulsory. Resistance to the idea of introducing animal matter into those who avoided meat and other animal products had been growing since the middle of the century, and rose to a peak in the 1880s. Dr T.R.Allinson was prosecuted and stripped of his medical qualifications because of his refusal to vaccinate.

Dr Allinson, (1858-1918) had for a short time run a small vegetarian hospital but it closed due to lack of support from fellow vegetarians. Although officially disqualified he continued to practise, and favoured birth control, a practice which had led to his expulsion from the London Vegetarian Society. Allinson's bread appears on supermarket shelves today - the doctor had a large interest in the 'Natural Food Company', which produced whole grain flour and bread.

The Loughton local press at the turn of the century carried several reports of court cases where parents were pursued because they would not allow their children to be vaccinated. At Stratford Petty Sessions in February 1899, for example, an objector was granted a certificate of exemption on two grounds: he believed that vaccination had not been shown to be an effective preventative, and he thought that sanitation and cleanliness were sufficient. In September another father, following a court appearance for the same reason, had to pay 8/- costs. A conscience clause had been introduced in 1898, but it was not until 1948 that the Vaccination Acts were finally repealed. In March 1899 an advertisement had sought support for a proposal, at the instigation of Morland Hickman, for the formation of a local Anti-Vaccination Society, while later in the year the Loughton Debating Society (apparently an active and well-attended body) passed a motion opposing compulsory vaccination, a move which the paper's Editor thought might have influence in higher circles. Since Josiah was firmly opposed to vaccination it is probable that he would have been involved in the contemporary discussion. In 1896 the London Vegetarian Society, of which Josiah was a leading light, had organised a debate on the subject, and the interest was so great that 1000 extra tickets had been required.

The Loughton society had, a few years earlier, held a debate where the motion 'That the adoption of Vegetarianism will conduce to health, economy and general well-being of the Community' failed to gain sufficient support. Instead an amendment proposing 'That man's physical structure being adapted to a mixed diet, a judicious mixture of animal and vegetable foodstuffs is best suited to the requirements of the human system' was passed by a majority of twenty to five. This was before Josiah had moved to Loughton - but at least there had been a few supporters there to welcome the Oriolet Hospital and its regime.

Chapter 10

Relaxations in Essex

While living at Loughton Josiah also acquired some land of his own at Althorne. Evidence for this comes from a letter written to *The Motor Trailer* in about 1949, headed "England and her Love Spots". 'In my early days after I left Oxford the first thing I did was to buy a bit of land in Essex and spend my weekends there in the quietude and peace of Nature'.

Althorne - still completely rural in 1937

He also referred to his field in Essex in a letter written to *The Times* in 1921 on the subject of allotments. He recommended that town families should buy a few acres of country land, where they could experience 'Colonial Life' at weekends. A tent or log hut could be erected, vegetables could be cultivated, and fruit trees planted, so that with a very small outlay and a continual succession of happy holidays a man could build up a valuable homestead for the future. 'When I first came to London this was how I utilized the pennies I saved, and those long days amid the birds and the butterflies - plying spade and fork and saw and hammer with a sense of happy ownership - were full of delight, only perhaps surpassed by the joy of gathering the first apple or digging up and cooking and feasting upon the first potatoes grown upon a field that I had turned into a garden.' This holding was, perhaps, the source of the vegetables he presented to St John's Hospital in August 1894.

St Andrew's Church, Althorne

Josiah had a plan for implementing his ideal of a country plot for even the poorest. This was reproduced in full in the *Daily Chronicle* in 1892, although there is no way of knowing whether the Editor thought it practical.

Josiah's idea was that whenever land came on the market, the Post Office Department of the Government should purchase it, in somewhat the same way as it purchased stock for depositors, and then cut it up theoretically into quarter-acre allotments. If each such allotment were then divided up like a chessboard into squares of a yard each, details being printed in a book, the poorest labourer would be able to go and start a book for any quarter-acre that might be in his neighbourhood. On payment of 2d, 3d or 4d, according to the price given for the land, the Post Office clerk would stamp an appropriate square in the customer's book and he would at once become owner of the first and each following yard of his plot. At this date, of course, the Post Office's activities were largely confined to dealing with the mail and the telegraph.

By 1901 Josiah had been living in Essex for long enough to have finished his log hut, for here he composed the thesis which earned him his Doctorate. 'Today I look with no little pride upon the first of the many books I have written, a book entitled *The Penalty of Death* which Oxford accepted as my Thesis for my Doctorate in Civil Law. This book...is still specially beloved by me because it was written in the little wooden hut that I put up for myself on a country field near Althorne, Burnham-on-Crouch'.

Althorne, with its extensive views over the River Crouch, remains a haven of peace a century later, although its fields have grown larger, and pylons have replaced some of the trees. Close to the station someone still has a 'little wooden hut', complete with curtains and letter box...

A Little Wooden Hut....

Planting trees was one of the recreations Josiah listed in his entry in the *Dictionary of National Biography*, and increasing the number of fruit trees grown was an important element in the way of life practised by members of the Vegetarian Federal Union and by Fruitarians in particular. A VFU resolution of 1892 proposed that the ownership of small tracts of land be encouraged for fruit cultivation, the land to be transferred cheaply. Land would become available if animals were no longer bred for meat. The particular value of English fruit lay in the fact that 'Nature has done to the starch of the apple what we do to the starch of grain by baking it, **and** it has produced an acid antagonistic to the growth of germs'. The fruit of hard wood trees was thought preferable to soft fruits 'which are far less removed from the decaying matter which has been transmuted into them'.

This rather odd statement does not square well with the emphasis Fruitarians placed on grapes and currants. A pamphlet which Josiah issued in 1923 entitled *The Raisin Cure* describes the grape as the earliest of Man's foods. Rich in sugar, its cultivation necessarily meant a life spent in the open air and in healing sunshine. Apparently Josiah modified his views on soft fruit as he grew older, for when the National Farm Survey was carried out at the onset of World War II it recorded a quarter-acre of strawberries at his Doddington Farm. Vegetables such as parsnips, turnips, and carrots too must have had close contact with 'decaying matter', but could scarcely be entirely omitted from the Fruitarian dietary.

Josiah was prepared to offer practical advice on fruit-growing where necessary. In answer to a *Times* correspondent who wondered why cherry-plums were not more widely planted, he replied that the tree flowered early, making it susceptible to late frosts which might destroy the whole crop. In ten years he himself had achieved bumper crops twice, but in other years no fruit at all. He added that the cherry-plum was an excellent stewing fruit.

Some vegetarians consumed only raw food. Certainly it had to be fresh. In an early article (1893) on 'Ringworm and its Spread' Josiah questioned whether the recent prevalence of skin diseases might be related to micro-organisms growing within overripe fruit and nuts. From personal experiment he had found that the result of eating nuts which were mouldy - even in small quantities - was unfortunate. His theory was that the mould plant was often not destroyed by the digestive secretions of the body, but found its way through the tissues to the skin, where it gave rise to tiny pimples or pustules. He was not happy with fruit which lacked true vitality because it had been 'artificially stimulated' (perhaps by the application of man-made fertiliser rather than manure? Josiah could not have approved of 'hoof and horn'...).

There was also a spiritual element to Fruitarian beliefs about growing trees. In a Good Friday sermon printed in 1894, in which he compared the lambs slaughtered at Smithfield with the sacrifices demanded by the Old Testament, now no longer required because of Christ's full oblation offered once and for ever, Josiah concluded with the passage from Revelation, chapter 22, describing the New Jerusalem: 'In the midst ... was the tree of life which bare twelve manner of fruits, and yielded her fruit every month; and the leaves of the tree were for the healing of the nations'.

Apples were especially favoured by Fruitarians. Josiah emphasized the benefits of 'an apple a day', particularly for those whose diet was mainly tinned, processed or cooked food. To ensure digestibility apples (which had to be ripe - sour green apples could cause acute diarrhoea) needed to be grated, pulped or 'completely masticated'. He allowed the cooking of apples for invalids or those with what he called 'febrile wasting disease', probably tuberculosis.

Josiah's idea that bush, pyramid and standard fruit trees should be planted on waste ground close to railways was presented in *The Vegetarian* in 1891. He thought that the railway companies could from their trains 'with ease inspect miles of fences and trees, collect the fruit, carry manure, etc.' Perhaps this idea occurred to him as he travelled down to Althorne, stopping at all stations, though whether he thought passengers would all assist with the pruning or picking isn't clear! Steam trains may have been slow, but hardly that slow.

While at Oxford Josiah had joined the University Corps of Volunteers, and on moving to Essex he became a member of the Volunteers there, enjoying the company and especially the Camps. Many such volunteer movements had originated at the beginning of the nineteenth century, when the Napoleonic wars brought the threat of invasion. Their effectiveness has been questioned, however, by the military historian Corelli Barnett, who wrote that their 'weekend gatherings performed the same disservice to the army as did the Militia in former times by convincing public opinion that 160,000 Sunday soldiers rendered Britain safe'. Like many other ambitious young men anxious to establish useful social contacts, Josiah became a part-time soldier.

Perhaps the Volunteers were merely playing at soldiers, revelling in their smart uniforms*, indulging in mock battles and no doubt sharing convivial amusements after their field exercises, but they continued in being until their reorganisation as Territorial Army units in 1907-8 under Haldane's reforms.

In his manuscript of 1914 entitled *Early Volunteer Movements in Walthamstow and Leyton* James Bird describes the history of the unit he himself had joined in 1864. Volunteers at this time had to attend eighteen drills in their first year, and then nine annually, of which three were battalion drills. For this the Government paid one pound per man to the Corps, with an additional 10/- per man who achieved a certain standard in shooting. Each man was allowed 60 rounds free, but had to pay for additional practice. Arranging battalion drills was difficult logistically, since its units were spread over Romford, Ilford, Barking, Walthamstow, Brentwood, Epping, Ongar, Loughton, Hornchurch and Manor Park, and also included cadets from Forest School and Ongar Grammar School.

Kelly's Directory for Loughton in 1902 reads 'Volunteer Battalion (1st) Essex Regiment (L.Co.), Forest Road. Captain A.Butler-Harris, W.E.Simpson commanding Cycle Co., Jeremiah Sullivan Sergeant-Instructor'. Captain Butler-Harris, M.A., M.B.,was also the Medical Officer for Loughton District, so that it is possible that Josiah and he first met as medical colleagues.

---

*In 1900 Compton Mackenzie's father spent £100 equipping his schoolboy son with uniform for the Bedfordshire branch - scarlet tunic with silver lace, scarlet service tunic, blue service tunic, mess jacket, tight overalls, greatcoat, cape, haversack, waterbottle, half-wellingtons and marching boots.

Since he was also public vaccinator to the district and to Epping Union this may have been a source of disagreement between the two men, Josiah being entirely against what he saw as an invasive process.

The Unit Headquarters were at Church Hill Road (encircled in 1914 by Cairo Road), Walthamstow, eight miles south of Loughton. Here a new Drill Hall had been erected in 1870, on ground given by Mr G. Borwick, free of rent as long as the Walthamstow Company was in being. James Bird cites an 1873 report which gives an idea of the activities practised there. Prizes following an 'assault-at-arms' were awarded for gloves, foils, dumbbells, sticks, sabres, rapiers, feats with sword, clubs and horizontal bar. The unit's armoury was in the old police station in the former workhouse building (currently the Vestry House Museum). The Walthamstow force also had cricket and football clubs and a drum and fife band.

Vestry House, Walthamstow

The activities of different units of the Volunteers were regularly reported in the local press: in May 1899 the 3rd Battalion acquired the North Weald rifle range 'where practice is to be obtained up to 800 yards', while detachments of the 1st Essex and other volunteer forces engaged in a sham fight with about 1200 of the 2nd Royal Fusiliers in Epping Forest. At the end of June the 1st Essex Volunteers, commanded by Col.Garret(t), attended Church Parade at Chigwell. But the highlight of the year was apparently the August visit to Great Yarmouth, when the various battalions of the Essex Volunteer Brigade had a 'capital week', with fine weather, good work and great enjoyment. At such times the members practised drills, marches and formations, and took part in sham battles. Not all members, though, could afford to attend and the local MP, Col.Lockwood, raised in the Commons the hardship of Volunteers working in Government factories, who lost pay if they took leave to go on pack drills.

Chapter 11

The Order of the Golden Age

When presenting their views, vegetarians often quoted a list of famous personalities who practised their regime, beginning with Buddha, Zoroaster and Socrates, and continuing via Newton and Wesley to Benjamin Franklin and Edison. Other well-known names were those of General Bramwell Booth and Dr.J.H.Kellogg (of Kellogg's Cornflakes). These last two gentlemen shared with Josiah both his views on diet and a common publisher in 'The Order of the Golden Age', the humanitarian organization established by Sidney Beard in 1894, which deplored cruelty to animals and their slaughter for use as food.

When Josiah Oldfield addressed students at Oriel College, Oxford, at about this time on 'The Ideal Diet in Relation to Real Life' he incorporated some of these principles in his talk. He contrasted the 'great red cord of groans of slaughter and hideous cruelty' with the 'tiny golden thread of vegetarianism'. Initially the Gods had demanded human or animal sacrifice: the coming of the God of Love had obviated the need for such slaughter, and contact with blood and death tended to degrade those involved. He then produced further arguments in favour of vegetarianism, stating that Man is physiologically a frugivore (dependent on fruit, grains and nuts) rather than a carnivore or herbivore; and cited a vegetarian diet as a cure for gout, dyspepsia and rheumatism. Better education was needed. Josiah pointed out that children were currently taught how to conjugate and parse the verbs 'to boil' and 'to stew', but not how to do so, and that they learned the rules of division and practice, but not how to lay out 6d to the best advantage.

The second half of his paper invited the future leaders of their generation to 'Come and help the poor to live and fill their sphere of life's duties by teaching them from your own example that...he is richest who is contented with least'. Instead of saying to the poor and the unemployed '**You** must do...' those who intended to make footsteps in the sands of time should instead say 'We must..' Class division was a source of discontent for many, but there would be no need for the disaffected to seize the land of the rich if available wasteland and grazing were to be converted to fruit gardens and orchards.

Josiah's peroration, although granting that some might judge his ideals a lost cause, urged the students to take their rightful places in a Movement which had Peace and Life for its end, and Self-Conquest for its means, the 'Order of the Golden Age'. Josiah, with Sidney H.Beard, was at the time joint editor of the movement's magazine, the *Herald of the Golden Age*.

First issued in January 1896, it was largely financed by Sidney Beard, who was listed as a stockbroker in the 1881 census. Born in 1862, just a year before Josiah, he lived with his family in Paddington. His sister Evelyn, who was to become Mrs Perkins, was a supporter of the Oriolet Hospital.

The Idealistic Sidney Beard

The two editors wrote a large proportion of the magazine's contents themselves, particularly the leading articles, and many of these were later published as pamphlets, either separately or in small collections. Examples include *An Unrecognised Deathtrap* of 1903 (The Transvaal War proved that a meat-fed army was not as robust as Caesar's grain-fed troops) and the *Diet for Cultured People* of 1906.

Sidney Beard had married in 1884. Census evidence suggests that he and his wife Martha lived first at Sydenham, where a daughter was born, and then perhaps at Bournemouth, birthplace of their second daughter in 1891. A few years later they moved to Devon, where Mr Beard would compose his *Testimony of Science in Favour of Natural and Humane Diet*. Much of its content reiterated what Josiah preached to the students at Oriel, but it also promoted an open-air existence, and quoted the superiority of physical fitness found amongst vegetarians. One example given was that of a Captain Goddard E. Diamond, who at the age of 106 was teaching physical culture to a class of young men in San Francisco. Several athletic and cycling records were then currently held by those who foreswore meat, and every issue of the *Herald of the Golden Age* carried at least one page detailing their achievements.

When the Beard family moved to Paignton in 1900 Josiah was an early visitor to the new home, Barcombe Hall, which became the Headquarters of the Order until 1909. House-moving is said to be a stressful experience, and it seems that despite his belief that by cultivating greatness of thought, and having a wide horizon of outlook and interest, vision and knowledge would be enlarged so that the minor worries of everyday life could be seen in their true perspective, Sidney Beard was particularly affected. The *Herald* records at the end of the year that Mr Beard would shortly resume joint editorship of the magazine with Josiah, who had been acting alone to give his friend a rest. Beard, in Josiah's words, 'had overworked and overthought... had spent himself to the utmost... and needed quiet communing with the healing forces of nature'.

Sidney Beard, in close association with Josiah, had also been responsible for the almost simultaneous establishment of the Fruitarian Society. Some of the ideas outlined in the previous chapter were incorporated in its ethos, and the *Herald*, as might have been expected, expanded its teaching. According to an advertisement in one of its publications, the Fruitarian Society's 'system of living makes a hygienic and humane life possible, and tends to promote Health, Strength, Longevity and a higher form of

Consciousness...'

In the search for a higher form of consciousness Sidney Beard and Josiah were united. 'The slow march onward of human spirituality... will make possible the contemplation of a human so completely spiritualised and so leavened throughout with the divine Essence that man shall be able to walk with God and share in the blessedness and powers of the Divine' was how Josiah expressed this in *Healing and the Conquest of Pain*. Beard wrote 'True Christianity (not Churchianity) is a great dynamic Ideal - the transformation, or restoration, of mankind from the animal plane of mentality to that of complete and perfect Manhood; from a state of ignorance and elementary development, from mortal consciousness caused by mental separation from God, to one of high knowledge, spiritual realization, divine unity and fraternal beneficence.' Such a state might only be achieved by those who concentrated purely upon God. As Josiah put it 'When you are conveying spiritual currents, how much more essential it is that there should be no alloy in the thoughts, no trace of the baser elements mixed up with the spiritual, no self or selfish strain mingled with the prayer'.

Souls in the lower sphere were to be helped upwards by those who had attained to the higher. 'There is **hope** for every sufferer and **life** for every seeker and **joy** for every sorrowing one who will leave the "lower classes" and seek permission to enter the "higher"' wrote Josiah, and Sidney Beard took this further: 'Only those whose feet are upon the rock of Spiritual Understanding can reach out helpful hands to uplift others from the troubled sea'. Attainment of this higher kingdom meant freedom from egoism, self-assertion and self-idolatry, traits which promoted discordant vibrations that destroyed harmony, unity and peace.

The *Herald* survived until 1918, although by 1903 it was issued quarterly rather than monthly. Its demise was perhaps due in part to Josiah's illness at that date. Another factor may have

To promote obedience to God's Laws of Health on all planes, and earnest effort to further the Divine Purpose concerning the upliftment and evolution of mankind.

To proclaim and hasten the coming of a Golden Age, when Health, Humaneness, and Peace shall reign upon Earth, and when Kindness towards all fellow-creatures shall prevail in the human heart.

To promote the study and observance of those physical Laws which concern the welfare of the human body. To teach that it is both the "instrument" and "temple" of the Spirit, and therefore sacred. To affirm that physical, mental, and spiritual health are so closely related, that *physical* Law concerning the welfare of the body demands reverence from all mankind, as surely as does *moral* Law relating to the health of the soul.

To advocate the universal adoption of a bloodless and natural dietary, for philanthropic, ethical and humane reasons, as well as for hygienic considerations.

The Order is striving to promote a great reduction of human and sub-human suffering, and is working to accomplish this object in a most direct and practical manner.

Instead of advocating palliatives for the *symptoms* of our worst social maladies, it seeks to remove their *root causes*. Disease, degeneracy, pain, premature death, and the consequent national loss can be largely prevented by dietetic amendment and hygienic living; and *prevention* is better than *cure*, either by drugs or the knife.

It demonstrates, by facts, statistics, and full information on the subject, contained in numerous books and pamphlets, that the practice of the unnatural habit of flesh-eating causes a large percentage of the illness, suffering and physical deterioration so manifest everywhere.

The Objects of the Order of the Golden Age

been Sidney Beard's need to devote time to a substantial book which he published in about 1921 called *Our Real Relationship with God: the Lost Ideal of Christianity.* No author's name appeared on the volume, merely the words 'by a Disciple'. The essential Humanity of Christ, the great Exemplar; the 'etheric body' and its reincarnation; the thought that Time is irrelevant, for man exists in Eternity; the belief that Love on the spiritual plane corresponds with Life on the physical - these are just some of the major topics examined. Josiah's theological beliefs were substantially the same, although it was not until he was over eighty that he would expound them in three books concerned with Birth, Marriage and Death. Beard's book clarifies some otherwise puzzling matters, for instance the hostility expressed by Fruitarians towards Roman Catholics. Beard quotes the

Catholic Dictionary of 1884 where animals are defined as 'brutes' lacking souls, and so no more worthy of consideration than rocks. Such a sentiment was anathema to those who recognised animals as fellow-creatures.

An obituary published in the *Vegetarian News* in 1938 refers to Mr Beard, in association with the Hon.Secretary of the Exeter Vegetarian Society, Mr J.I.Pengelly, 'resuscitating the practically defunct Order of the Golden Age' with headquarters at the residence of Mr Beard, 'The Beacon', in Ilfracombe. Sidney's younger brother Percy was also involved with the Order, for between 1910 and 1919 he was listed as its Honorary Secretary at premises in Brompton Road, Kensington, where the organisation occupied numbers 153-155. After the war number 153 was abandoned, and Sidney's name, as President, replaced that of Percy. E.A.Quinnion was Secretary in 1925, but in 1933 had been succeeded by Mrs J.Patterson. By this date Mr and Mrs Patterson were living with Sidney Beard and his second wife Annie at West Hill, SW15.

Other branches of the Order of the Golden Age were to be founded in other countries: by the time of Sidney Beard's death in 1938 there were groups in Burma, Bombay and Pietermaritzburg. His obituary defined the order as a humanitarian and philanthropic society whose objects were to lessen and prevent suffering by practical means and to promote health, humaneness, spirituality and unity. The Order advocated Fruitarianism since its adherents believed that flesh-eating produced malignant disease, and physical, moral and spiritual degeneration.

Chapter 12

The Humanitarian Hospital of St Francis

The idea of a hospital to be run on purely humanitarian lines appears to date from about 1897, soon after the founding of the Order of the Golden Age. A note in the *Morning Post* on 23rd March of that year announced that 'In Commemoration of the Queen's Jubilee the anti-vivisectionists of this country and the Continent have decided to found a hospital...named for St Francis of Assisi. It is meant to be a protest against all forms of cruelty and especially of vivisection.' The proposed hospital was to be built in south London where the need was very pressing. An address to which subscriptions might be sent was appended.

An appeal couched in the flowery terms common to the Order of the Golden Age's publications appeared at about the same time. It requested 'gentlemen and gentlewomen of every race and language, creed and profession to rise in your millions and pour into the crucible of healing your golden rings, and cast into the bitter lake of pain your precious stones and pearls of price'. In this 'fair and beauteous temple of healing' there would be no 'greed of fame or curse of false science', no demand for "material" to sully the beauty of its teaching, no 'haste to pile up huge numbers and gigantic statistics' through the admittance of "interesting" cases rather than lingering ones. The leaflet acknowledged the existence of the Prince of Wales' Fund in raising monies for hospitals, but emphasised the need for a new establishment in the south of London. It concluded 'It is not superfluities that are wanted, but loving lives that will build themselves into every brick and stone and beam and rafter, and will show that they who denounce the wrongs of the conscripted victims of vivisection are willing to offer of themselves, that by fellow-suffering through self-denial they may become saviours of the tormented.' Donations were to be sent to the Treasurer at 6 Southampton Street, Strand, the address which had been given in the *Morning Post*. No names of individuals appeared anywhere.

It is not known how many copies of the leaflet were printed, or how they were circulated, but presumably at least some reached persons of influence. Not all were kindly received, and an investigator from the Charity Organisations Society was sent to carry out some inquiries. Mr Charles Carthew went to Southampton Street, and reported back that he had returned, by appointment, and seen a Mr Povey, whose Bohemian dress did not appeal to the visitor. Mr Povey was unable to answer all Charles Carthew's questions - he said he had only held the appointment of Honorary Secretary for a few weeks. When pressed Povey explained that the project had been mooted about twelve months previously; some donations had been received but nothing practical had been done. **He** thought that the hospital would not be conducted on purely vegetarian or anti-vivisectionist lines (he actually said anti-vaccinationist more than once, but corrected himself). He knew of no connection with the Nursing Council: sisters of the 'Maternity Society' would aid in the hospital. No decision had yet been made concerning a site.

The Maternity Society seems to have had strong connections with the Vegetarian movement. A prominent member was Edith Tegetmeier, a member of the London Vegetarian Society in 1896 who later served on the committee of the Vegetarian Union, and who was also associated with the City of London Lying-in Hospital. One venue for the Society's meetings was the home of William Theobald, who was to become Treasurer of the Vegetarian Federal Union - his wife was a supporter. It is not clear whether the membership included any qualified nurses.

Charles Carthew found this interview unsatisfactory, and, perhaps unduly influenced by Charles Povey's unusual dress, left with a strong conviction that there was something wrong about both the man and the project. Povey had asked him more than once whether any inquiries had been made, and seemed much relieved on learning that they had not. Consequently Mr Carthew returned a fortnight later when a Committee meeting was in progress. Afterwards he met some of its members, including Josiah Oldfield who was the chairman, Mr Povey, and a Miss Dickson who appeared to be the secretary since she had books and papers before her. Also present were another lady and gentleman and 'a young lady taking shorthand'. From them Carthew learned that the idea of a humanitarian hospital had emanated from Josiah Oldfield and some of his friends, and that it had been agreed to take on a seven-year lease the premises in the New Kent Road formerly occupied by the Mildmay Medical Mission (which had recently moved to Bethnal Green). Fees, how the amount payable by poor patients should be assessed, who should be the medical officer, what part vegetarianism would play, were all matters as yet undecided.

The most important point engaging Carthew's attention, however, was the question of subscriptions and how they were being used. Josiah told him that funds were currently about two hundred pounds, and that an account **jointly in the name of the hospital and himself** had been opened at the City Bank. It was hoped that sympathisers who at present subscribed to existing hospitals would switch their allegiance to that of St Francis. Disbursements so far had been small: wages of the assistant secretary, printing and stationery. Correspondence with the Registrar of Friendly Societies had commenced. This information appeared reasonably satisfactory, but further probing elicited the fact that since the Treasurer was currently in Bulawayo (for his wife's health), and the previous Honorary Secretary (who was Treasurer of the Vegetarian Federal Union) was now in the Klondyke, only Josiah could sign cheques for withdrawals.

Charles Carthew was nothing if not thorough. He began to check what he had been told, and the results were not encouraging. The Registrar of Friendly Societies said that he had not had any letters about the hospital. The agents for the premises of the Mildmay Mission had been approached about the lease, the names of Josiah and of the Treasurer, Commander Turner, being given as references, but as yet they had not agreed as they were uncertain whether the rent would be paid! Carthew found out that Josiah was a barrister, was Secretary of the Vegetarian Federal Union, Warden of Oriolet Hospital, Loughton, and on the Committee of St John's Hospital for Skin Diseases in Leicester Square. When he asked some of those who knew Josiah for their opinion several shrugged their shoulders, and the general concensus was that 'there was something not altogether straight about him; at any rate he does not appear to be too scrupulously truthful'. In support of this last statement he cited Josiah's declaration that the Oriolet Hospital was not supported in any way by the alms of the Public - yet its annual report showed that it was. Perhaps, as C.E.M.Joad would have put it, 'it all depends on what you mean by the Public'. Were the donations given only, perhaps, by fellow-vegetarians or members of the Order of the Golden Age?

An appeal in the latter's journal, the *Herald of the Golden Age,* in 1900 urged readers on Hospital Sunday to 'let your church collection plate pass by if you are doubtful whether they are sound on vivisection', instead sending their contributions direct to Oriolet or St Francis.

Carthew's final comment in his report was that although Josiah Oldfield was apparently the leading light, his name never appeared on any printed document.

No doubt the investigations prompted Josiah and the other supporters of the proposed hospital into more decisive action. A new and more prosaic pamphlet appealing for funds was produced, with a list of thirty Council Members at its head. The names include that of Josiah and, significantly, of Gertrude Hick. Philip Tovey and Commander Turner, R.N., were Hon.Secretary and Treasurer respectively. The content of the leaflet dwelt largely on the need for a hospital to serve the growing populations of Camberwell, Walworth, Newington and Bermondsey. It explained that, despite the name, the institution was not Roman Catholic, but would seek the support of all religious bodies. Its mission would be the 'teaching of kindness to all that lives, of the preciousness of lives, of the beauty of relieving pain'. The out-patient department would be open at times when the poor were able to attend. Few in-patients would be treated here, as it was hoped that those needing an extended stay could be sent to the country.

There was an avowed intention not to incur debt, but to carry out only such work as funds permitted until further generous help should permit its expansion. The final sentence of the main text is of particular interest in the light of subsequent events: 'An offer has been made by the Matron of an important hospital to give her services, free of charge, for one year as Matron of the Hospital of St Francis, so soon as such help is required'. The leaflet concludes with the usual appeal for subscriptions and donations to be sent to 6 Southampton Street, or direct to the Hospital itself at 145 New Kent Road. To this has been added in neat manuscript 'when it is opened'.

The actual opening followed shortly afterwards, negotiations for the premises in New Kent Road having been successfully completed. It was, like many other houses built in the nineteenth century in the growing suburbs of London, high but with a comparatively narrow frontage - only about eighteen feet. A staircase at the back of the building led from the basement to the two main floors and the attics above. At some point before the opening of the hospital a single-storey red-brick extension had been erected at the front to provide additional accommodation.

The New Kent Road in the Edwardian period was busy, with a wide variety of enterprises surrounding No. 145 - a bicycle fitting manufacturer and a pawnbroker were neighbours on one side, while coffee rooms and a grocery incorporating a Post Office lay on the other. Today the buildings have been replaced by gardens in front of modern flats, but 'The County' Public House remains. This name may be a reminder that the New Kent Road formerly backed on to County Terrace Street at this point.

The layout of the building lent itself reasonably well to the demands of Josiah and his associates. The extension provided an office, a dispensary, two consulting rooms and a waiting area: steps at the end of its central corridor went down to the semi-basement which housed a dark room for ophthalmic consultations and another larger examination room. Behind them was the scullery, and beyond it a small backyard with a 'lumber-room'. The two main floors each consisted of a single large room with windows looking out on to the New Kent Road, although in the case of the first floor these were partly blocked by the extension. The attic afforded one large room where three probationer nurses slept, and another for the senior probationer. The rear of the building housed smaller rooms with lower ceilings: the kitchen on the first floor, the Matron's room immediately above it, then that of the senior probationer, and finally the servants' quarters. There was, however, no bathroom, and the two lavatories, one inside, one out, were at ground level.

 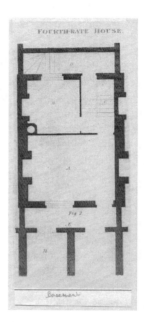

Elevation and Plan of a Fourth-Rate House

Having been much involved with the acquisition and fitting-out of Arlington House, the annexe to St John's Hospital, Josiah attempted to replicate that conversion in his own venture - but with an even more restricted budget. Would the Matron at St Francis' Hospital be entitled to a carpet specified as '4-thread Brussels at no more than 3/3d per yard', as was prescribed for her peer at St John's?

The objects of those reponsible for the Hospital of St Francis were summarised in the opening paragraph of the 'Rules' governing its administration: the Society had been established for the benevolent or charitable purposes of providing medical and surgical treatment upon humanitarian lines, and of disseminating a knowledge of the treatment of disease. The rules themselves dealt first with the number of patients who could be nominated by patrons donating different amounts annually. Thus those subscribing ten guineas were allowed twelve out-patient letters and four in-patient letters. Three guineas reduced this allotment to letters for six out-patients and a single in-patient, while a subscription of one guinea earned either three out-patients **or** a single in-patient a letter.

The major part of the printed rules was concerned with those in charge of running the hospital, which had a Council of about twenty whose names, it was hoped, would attract further patronage, and a rather smaller Executive Committee. Only two of the latter were required to form a quorum; the Treasurer would take the Chair in the Chairman's absence. In fact the Secretary 'who shall furnish good and sufficient security in the sum of £300, or such additional sum as the Council may from time to time order, for the faithful discharge of his duties' appears to have been largely reponsible for the day-to-day running of the hospital. He looked after the cash and the office, and was in charge of the male servants and much else. His hours were from 10.00 until 5.30, or later when evening surgeries were held. His salary was not defined, but he was to receive a generous four weeks holiday.

The Matron, who was also granted a month's leave, was concerned with the nurses (including the training of probationers) and the female servants, and was required to live on the premises. The Dispenser had to 'attend as required...but shall not leave until the work of the day is done'. At its inception, according to contemporary directories, there were several medical officers in attendance: W.H.Freeland, W.M.Leslie, H.J.Paterson and L.A.R.Wallace. But in 1900 none of these gentlemen was listed, and there was another almost complete change of personnel the following year. The Honorary Secretary had also been dispensed with. Had Josiah's ideas proved unpalatable to his colleagues? Or were they afraid that their association with him would harm their chances of advancement?

One of the Secretary's main tasks was the production of 'begging letters' which were written in longhand, not typed, and which were sent to names presumably selected from the pages of directories or the Society pages of newspapers. (The *CETS Yearbook* was one source utilised by St John's Hospital when sending out their 'select invitations' to five or six hundred people). Philip Tovey's standard letter read as follows:-

'Dear Sir,

I am directed by the Committee to ask if you will kindly consent to be a Patron of the Hospital of Saint Francis. Only those who have actually visited this densely-populated and poverty-stricken district can realise the immensity of good done by an institution of this sort in South London. Despite the fact that the majority of our staff of doctors and nurses are working gratuitously, further support is urgently needed to enable the Committee to cope with the many sad cases so constantly brought to their notice. Trusting so good a cause may receive your kind sympathy I am, dear Sir, your obedient servant,

Philip Tovey
Hon.Sec.'

Some of his letters undoubtedly brought positive results, but other recipients, like His Royal Highness the Duke of Cambridge and Alderman Vaughan Morgan, were more careful before committing themselves. On 8th December 1898 the alderman paid a visit to New Kent Road, and reported to His Royal Highness that he had found 'one nurse, two or three empty beds, and no sign of business'. It seems probable that this visit took place just before the first patients were admitted. By 1901, at the time of the census, the Matron was Miss Agnes Boys, and there were three probationer nurses to assist her in the care of eight

100

patients with ages ranging from three months to fifty-three years.

Charles Carthew too continued his investigations, finding that Josiah's address at the Inner Temple did not imply that he was in active practice: evidently the Law was not providing him with an income. Carthew encountered a Mr Welsh, an Inspector under the Adulteration of Food Act, and a vegetarian colleague of Josiah's. Welsh, who had stayed at the Oriolet Hospital in Loughton where Josiah had acted as Medical Officer under the supervision of a qualified practitioner, praised Oldfield, explaining that though he had no private means, he was supported by the wealthy Arnold F. Hills. Mr Carthew also spoke to a Mr Mearns, who presumably was responsible for ensuring that the rent of 145 New Kent Road was paid. In response to his enquiries Mearns said that he knew nothing of Oldfield, but that 'there is something about him which would make him (Mearns) like to get him out of the building, but what this is he is not able to explain'.

The Charity Organisations Society must have been contacted in several instances by those in receipt of Tovey's missives, for it produced a duplicated letter warning against giving to St Francis' Hospital. The letter dealt fairly with Josiah's qualifications, but described the Oriolet Hospital as 'an institution originally provided by Mr Oldfield himself for the purpose of treating cancer patients on a vegetable diet'. It deplored the lack of established Medical Officers and 'persons of influence' connected with the scheme, and also pointed out that the chosen site was too close to both Guy's and St Thomas's Hospitals. The conclusion read 'It is evident that this (St Francis) hospital owes its inception to the private predilections of Mr Oldfield and his friends and, without impugning their zeal or good faith, the Charity Organisation Society would recommend those who seek their advice to reserve their gifts for institutions of a more substantial and genuinely public character'.

Despite the Establishment's opposition the venture went ahead. A press release printed in the *South London Press* of 29th August 1903 reported:

'It quickly became a useful institution, and it is computed that since it was opened over a hundred thousand attendances of patients have been recorded. The admissions to the in-patients' department numbered 428. A small charge was usually made, though no poor sufferer was ever refused treatment or admission through lack of pence'.

But this short notice hides a story. It was preceded by news that 'Camberwell, so long isolated from much-needed hospital accommodation, may soon be specially favoured in this direction. It is understood that the authorities of King's College Hospital have in view a site in the borough...whilst the useful little Hospital of St Francis has already been removed from the New Kent Road to Camberwell Green. This last-named Hospital is not yet actually open, but the Committee hope to recommence the good work of the institution as soon as possible.' It was further reported that the St Francis Hospital had actually closed to in-patients in October 1902.

The main reason for its closure, apart from the small numbers of in-patients using it, was probably a scathing report which appeared in the specialist journal *The Hospital* at the end of July 1902. This is unsigned, but damning in the slant given to its version of the facts. Beginning with the definition of a hospital as a house for the reception and aid of the sick, infirm or poor, it continued 'that being so **we must acquit of actual fraudulent intent** those who describe as a hospital an institution consisting only of a very small house in which a couple of rooms are used for the reception of patients'.

After ridiculing (with some justification) the list of names prefacing the St.Francis Hospital annual report, it described the premises in detail, comparing them unfavourably with those in certain modern hospitals. The fact that one W.C. served all the staff as well as both male and female patients, and also had to be used for disposal of slops, was singled out for special condemnation. In the male ward, which contained three beds and a cot, the writer(s) found the arrangement whereby the lower half of each window was lit and ventilated via the out-patients' department 'most objectionable, and one which ought not to be permitted to continue for a moment in any institution obtaining money from the public on the pretence of being a hospital'. Only the temperature sheets above the beds relieved the poverty-stricken aspect.

Front Extensions to Fourth-Rate Houses in City Road

Moving up the narrow twisting stairs which would 'entirely preclude the proper carriage of a patient seriously ill', the visitors reached the female ward which was granted to be a much more airy and pleasant apartment. This was furnished with three beds, two small cots and a baby's crib. What the report does **not** tell is the number of patients then in the hospital, though it speculated that the average number of beds occupied would be fewer than six.

The article continued by criticising what it considered to be the excessively large staff - matron, four probationers, a porter and a female servant, a dispenser, a secretary and a lady clerk to look after the cards of the out-patients. It discounted these patients, although if the newspaper item quoted earlier is to be believed, there would have been more than five hundred of them each week.

Their payments were assumed to help subsidise the treatment and care of the in-patients, which, from the financial details given in the annual report, the author(s) calculated to be £6 15s. each.

This figure, in their eyes, was 'a sum for which any hospital in the neighbourhood would have been delighted to receive them. Thus, even were this institution properly fitted for the work it has taken upon itself, which it is not, this work would be better and more economically done at existing hospitals. There is no place for it, and no excuse for its continued existence'.

Poor Josiah! What must have been the feelings of the idealists who had set up the St Francis Hospital with its humanitarian principles and desire to help those in need? There is no hint in the report that any patients were asked for their views: one feels that the visitors did not care to spend long in what they called a 'wretched, grubby little house in the New Kent Road'. Did they ask whether the patients were cured, or at least relieved? How did cross-infection rates compare with those in hospitals with thirty or more in a ward? Were there many deaths? (Presumably not, or the number would have been quoted with relish).

Their prejudices appear more clearly in the concluding paragraph. They conceded that although they did not approve of the possibility of treating disease on a non-meat diet there was a case for a well-conducted trial. But apparently some of the medical officers **had** ordered meat, so invalidating the 'vegetarian' claims. (Was this disagreement with Josiah's strongly held views a reason for their departure?). The final sentences read 'we may well believe that (the Hospital's) present wretched condition is due to the fact that the prospects of the institution have been sacrificed to the ambition of those in power on its council to be able to say that there is at least one hospital in London which definitely excludes vivisection... It is to those "anti-vivisection methods" which have become such a byword that we must attribute the attempt to make the subscribing public believe that the institution...is worthy of the support of the charitable'.

Following the publication of this report it seems likely that many of those listed in the annual report as Vice-Presidents ('from Dukes downwards'), Lady Patrons, Council Members, or those holding honorary appointments as chaplains, legal advisers, architect or auditor, would have hurried to sever their connection with the Hospital. Its income would have dropped dramatically, and although few potential patients would have seen the report, gossip would spread the word, and closure would have followed swiftly.

There had originally been plans to acquire the house adjoining 145 New Kent Road in order to enlarge the Hospital, but instead, as mentioned earlier, new premises had been purchased at 34 Camberwell Green. £2000 was needed to open what was to be known as The South London Hospital, a daunting task in view of the adverse publicity of 1902. This lack of funds, rather than the decision of King's College Hospital to build nearby, was probably the real reason why the Camberwell site was sold. According to a letter from Hugh Fickling in March 1903 it had cost Oldfield £4000. It is not clear for how long it played a part in serving patients, although at least one early brochure for Margaret Manor, Sittingbourne, implies that it was then operational. Patients intending to spend time at Margaret Manor were 'advised to see the visiting Doctor in London before coming down... poor patients must send a Doctor's Certificate, or be examined at Lady Margaret Hospital, Camberwell Road, S.E. (Tuesdays, 6-8, Saturdays, 6-8) before admission.'

Mr Fickling appears to have succeeded Charles Carthew as the investigator concerned with Josiah's enterprises. He discussed them with the Secretary of the Camberwell Provident Dispensary, who thought that they could hardly be regarded as charities, but rather private undertakings primarily for Josiah's own benefit. Fickling paid a visit to the New Kent Road, where he found that out-patients continued to be treated at what had been re-named 'The Margaret Dispensary'. They were usually charged 3d. or 6d., although it was claimed that no poor person was ever refused treatment. The dispensary was not self-supporting, but a few subscribers enabled Josiah to keep on with his beneficent work. The caretaker told Mr Fickling that Josiah came from Bromley most evenings, but had few patients.

Dispensaries provided poorer patients with a source of medical care, but Josiah was scornful about some of the doctors who treated such patients. He attacked the much-vaunted panel system whose practitioners' first question was 'Which medicine shall I prescribe?' Josiah thought drugs like aspirin, morphia and strychnine to be 'indigestible poisonous substances which tend to hide symptoms and produce greater evils. Drugs out of a bottle are the very last thing a sick person should take'. Such pills were marketed by the unscrupulous. (With the benefit of hindsight we might well agree with his condemnation of proprietary remedies, with their extravagant claims to cure almost any ills). The wise physician would ask whether it was necessary or wise to give ANY medicine. Fasting and a healthier diet should be tried in the first instance. Reginald Payne grew up in a vegetarian household which subscribed to the same view: 'the treatment of illness was the reduction of food to a minimum'.

A study of Post Office directories implies that the St Francis Hospital still occupied the premises in New Kent Road in 1903, although Josiah's name is missing. But the following year the entry has been replaced by 'The Margaret Dispensary, Josiah Oldfield, Physician'. Another reason for the disappearance of the St Francis Hospital, and the absence of Josiah's name in 1903, is undoubtedly connected with his new ventures, the Fruitarian Hospital at Doddington, near Sittingbourne, in Kent, and the Lady Margaret Hospital, Bromley.

The 'Margaret Dispensary' entry persisted in directories until 1909, but in 1910 it had gone. Only 'Josiah Oldfield, Physician' now appeared. When Hugh Fickling paid his last visit to the premises, possibly in late 1905 because of some recent letters of complaint, he found it to be the home of several different organisations. These were The Vegetable Oil Co. Ltd., Millennium Ltd., The Fruitarian Society, The Society for the Abolition of Capital Punishment, and The Orange Flour Company. A card in the window announced that a Sale of Work was to be held in January, but Mr Fickling did not record which of the above groups would benefit from it.

An indenture of 15th January 1906 in the London Metropolitan Archives [A/KE/245/4] shows that the trustees of the National Anti-Vivisection Hospital (later Battersea Hospital) received a conveyance in trust of Darenth House, 34 Camberwell Green, the grantors being the **Trustees of the Hospital of Saint Francis**. The two institutions were effectively merged. The National Anti-Vivisection Hospital, which had fifteen beds, had been founded by Mrs Theodore Russell Munroe in 1896: its trustees included Ernest Bell, who had introduced Josiah to the Board of St John's Hospital. Its policies precluded the uses of remedies obtained as the result of experiments on living animals, such as the Pasteur anti-rabies serum, and no staff who had practised vivisection could be employed.

Chapter 13

Josiah's Companies

The note by Hugh Fickling that the premises in New Kent Road housed several different organisations in 1905 opened another line of inquiry into Josiah's multiple interests. Initial interrogation of the computer records at Companies House revealed no trace of the Orange Flour Company, Millennium Ltd or the Vegetable Oil Company. There was a brief reference in the Committee Minutes of the London Vegetarian Association to a transaction in June 1900, when it was resolved that the Secretary be authorised to write and accept a share of the 'Vitol Oil Company', the certificate to be made out in the name of the Treasurer, Mr Theobald.   That a certificate existed certainly implied that such a company was in being.

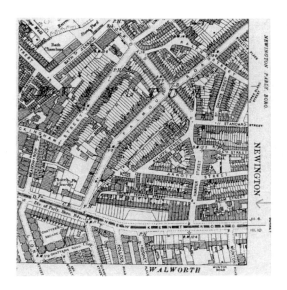

Newington, South London in 1894. New Kent Road
forms the boundary between Newington & Walworth

108

But it was the chance discovery of some stationery in an attic at Doddington which revealed further details of such enterprises. One sheet of paper was headed 'Memorandum from the Vytalle Oil Co., Ltd., Proprietors of:- "Vytalle Oil", "Lady Margaret" Lime Juice Cordial, "Sunlight" Olive Oil, "Nuttalle" Oil, "Castralle" Oil, "Brahmol" Soap, and the "Vytalle" Pillow of Sleep'. (Since it involved the slaughter of living creatures vegetarians shunned fish oil. Instead of taking 'Cod liver oil for coarse stomachs', they could buy 'Vytalle oil for dainty digestions'.) Such concrete evidence prompted another visit to Companies House, where probing elicited the fact that at least the Vitalle Oil Company and Millennium Ltd were authentic. But unfortunately all the physical records had been eliminated in about 1985 when electronic storage of information began to replace piles of paper.

The address for the various companies cited was 145, County Terrace Street, London, S.E. This street is shown on early maps of London, running parallel to County Terrace itself. The two lay adjacent to New Kent Road (then known as Greenwich Road) between St George's Street and Harper Road, and opposite Rodney Road. It had disappeared by 1913, though County Terrace lasted longer. It seems probable that the 'lumber-room in the back yard' mentioned in the description of the premises of the St Francis Hospital actually fronted on to County Terrace Street, and constituted the headquarters of the companies. Such a union was certainly true in the case of No.149.

Josiah's Solution to Punctures

The County Terrace Street address appears also on a postcard for the Millennium Company, whose main product, it stated, automatically closed all punctures. 'Millennium' was available at 1/6 per tube. Josiah himself used a bicycle and would have experienced the inconvenience caused by punctures incurred when riding over the unmade roads of his times. He, as one of many humanitarians seeking to find an alternative to leather for shoes, had an additional interest in rubber as a possible replacement, and in 1893 had been searching with 'deep earnestness' to find something which would oust leather from its place of importance in the domestic economy of the day. At least one manufacturer of footwear attempted to fill the gap, for in 1905 Richard Hall was offering 'Vegetarian shoes made of improved Pannus Corium and vulcanised vegetable fibre' at 17/6d a pair. Mr Hall claimed that the material looked like leather, was softer than kid, took a polish with blacking and was as waterproof as leather of a similar substance.

The postcard also features a number of other products: 'Darlene' - to replace Lard and Butter, 'Orange Blossom Honey', 'The Margaret Conserves', and a series of 'Piper's Penny Jams, Honies, Mustard, Spice and Pepper'. The last-named came complete with caster. As well as the Brahmol soap (no animal fat) advertised by the Vytalle Oil Company, there was 'Cayler's Cat Soap - 1d. and 'Tab' o' Cat', at which the mind boggles, until one realises it was probably what is now known as Catsup or Ketchup! Darlene was 'a pure white tasteless fat from the cocoanut (sic), containing very little water and costing in bulk a little over 6d. /lb', which in 1907 was apparently used by the hundredweight at the Lady Margaret Fruitarian Hospital both for cooking and eating. Such lists hark back, perhaps, to Josiah's childhood and his father's grocery store: he presumably retailed the products rather than manufactured them.

The inclusion of pepper and spices is interesting in view of the opinions Josiah later expressed about the use of condiments, referring to them as 'the pickaxes which help to dig the grave of youth... Condiments came into fashion when bad cooks were born... The continued use of such things destroys all the delicate sensitiveness of the nerves of taste and digestion... It is artistic to add the delicate fragrance of mint to your dish of early peas, but it is boorish to sprinkle cayenne pepper upon a freshly laid egg...

So soon as a man tells you that without salt or pepper or mustard or spice his food is tasteless, you may be sure that the deadening changes of old age are as surely beginning to creep on as when his eyesight commences to be dim or his hearing to be dulled. Avoid the salts and peppers in your youth and you will enjoy the singing of the spices in the later days of life'. All these are quotations from *Eat and Keep Young* (1928). In the same chapter Josiah also talks of 'the coarse blatancy of curry', although it might be thought that he would have learned to enjoy this while travelling in India in 1901.

Chapter 14

Josiah's Marriage

On 29th September 1899, after banns, Josiah was married in Wakefield Cathedral to Gertrude, daughter of Matthew Bussey Hick, Chemical Manufacturer, who lived at 8 Bond Terrace in Wakefield. This was in quite a smart area, not far from the Court House and County Hall. On the marriage certificate Gertrude's profession is given as 'Nurse': since September 1897 she had been Matron at Kettering Hospital. She had trained at Whitechapel Hospital, and before her Kettering appointment had nursed at Loughton (she was listed as Matron of the Oriolet Hospital in 1896) - which may explain how the bride and groom met. William Waller remembered her as 'very good-looking'.

Gertrude had at least two sisters. One of them, Ethel, acted as a witness to the marriage, the others being her father and Trimbakrai Jadavrai Desai. On the certificate Josiah's address is given as 122 Harley Street London, his profession as 'Physician', and that of his father as 'Gentleman'.

Additional details about the wedding are to be found in the report published in the *Wakefield Free Press and West Riding Advertiser* of September 30th. It was a quiet ceremony, with only immediate family members and a few friends present, although the proceedings were watched with interest by members of the public seated in the nave of the cathedral. The bride, who wore a grey corduroy coat and skirt and a white hat trimmed in grey, was attended by her young niece, Naomi Bannatyne, in white dress and hat trimmed with ostrich feathers. Mr Desai, a medical student from near Bombay who was Josiah's best man, was perhaps the most colourfully attired, in cream silk coat and trousers, blue sash and green turban. The same report also goes into considerable detail in describing the numerous handsome gifts to the happy couple from the London Vegetarian Society. These included an oak settle, cutlery and other silver, and an illuminated address with 300 names attached.

In the account of the wedding printed in the *Vegetarian*

Messenger Mr Desai (whose first names are here spelt as Timbakrai Jadaviaia) is said to hail from Limbdi State, Katiawar. He and Josiah had known each other for several years, possibly through meeting at St Bartholomew's, although Desai was not registered as a student there. On 30th May 1893 Mr T.J.Desai had been the speaker at a London Vegetarian Society meeting when his subject* had been the social prejudice encountered by Indians in contact with the British Raj.

The officiating Minister at the service was pillar of the Vegetarian Society the Rev. Professor John E.B.Mayor, MA, DD, DCL, assisted by Josiah's brother William, by now a Canon and Prebendary of Lincoln Cathedral. It is perhaps slightly surprising that Wakefield Cathedral was chosen as venue, for Mr Hick had for many years been connected with St Michael's Church, Westgate Common, latterly as Churchwarden. After the service the bridal party joined in a 'repast in keeping with the vegetarian principles of the bride and bridegroom' at the Bull Hotel, and the couple later left for a honeymoon at Whitby. Josiah, many years later, told his daughter Josie that each thought the other was packing the luggage, so they both turned up empty-handed.

The 1881 census tells that Matthew Bussey Hick, of Cliff Terrace, Wakefield, was then both a copperas manufacturer and an insurance agent. He had from 1857-60 been a member of the Wakefield City Council and was noted for his charitable

---

* 'Mr T.J.Desai gave a graphic account of the unfair treatment of his countrymen by ours in Hindustan. Colour prejudice, he asserted, went so far as to make Englishmen forget the courtesy, justice and self-restraint which they practised in their own country. From the moment they landed in Bombay they gave themselves up to a line of conduct which must of necessity alienate those whom it was their obvious duty and policy to conciliate. The effect was fatal. It was only natural that the 'natives' should judge of a country by the individuals it sent out - ostensibly as its representatives - and when they saw the higher posts reserved, and only subordinate ones open to them, when they saw that they were excluded from social rites, scholastic honours and official posts - for colour alone - it was hardly to be expected that content should be the order of the day.

113

activities, including being a Governor of a local hospital. Earlier his profession had been that of a chemist and druggist, but contemporary advertisements reveal that his stock included tea and coffee, pickles, soda water, fruit jellies, cattle medicines, and paints, so that it cannot have been greatly different from that of David Oldfield's business in Condover. Mr Hick's son, also Matthew, was a solicitor; his eldest daughter acted as housekeeper, a niece aged 21 lived at the same address, and they had one 14-year-old servant.

Gertrude was not living at home in 1881, but had joined her 27-year old brother Henry, who is described as a surgeon, at an address in Wortley in Bramley. This is now a suburb of Leeds, lying some twelve miles north-west of Wakefield. She was then aged nineteen, and was no doubt helping her brother with the care of sick patients: they kept a servant (who was older than Henry) for domestic duties. Their immediate neighbours included a Catholic priest, a rag merchant, an estate agent and a railway fireman, so theirs was a distinctly mixed neighbourhood.

Chapter 15

Josiah's Fight for the Abolition of Capital Punishment

One cause dear to Josiah's heart was the abolition of the death penalty, a subject which had inspired him to considerable research since beginning his study of law at Oxford. In the course of this he had written to **all** the English judges and bishops requesting their views, but had found only two who favoured abolition. It is to be expected, therefore, that he would have seized the opportunity to join the Romilly Society, whose inaugural meeting had been held on 12th May 1898 at Essex Hall, just off the Strand and close to the Royal Courts of Justice.

Sir Samuel Romilly (1757-1818), who was of Huguenot descent, had been influenced by the revolutionary ideas obtaining in France, becoming involved in philanthropic and humanitarian movements such as the ending of the slave trade. He had begun to consider the amendment of the criminal law early in the nineteenth century, and in particular sought the end of capital punishment for trivial offences. His Bill to remove the death penalty for those convicted of stealing 5/- or more from a shop was defeated in 1810 by 31 votes to 11. There is a bust of Romilly in a prominent position in the Public Record Office at Kew.

The Romilly Society's stated aims were the improvement of the criminal law, the abolition of barbarous punishments, the creation of a Minister and Department of Justice, the securing of the right of appeal on questions of fact as well as of law in all criminal cases, and the reform of prison regulations. But Lord Justice Vaughan Williams, presiding at the inaugural meeting, remarked that he himself, as a member of the Council of Judges, could not support the penultimate objective, and pointed out that not all of those attending the meeting would necessarily agree on all matters of penal reform. He was, however, convinced that nothing but good could come of more openness where the treatment of prisoners was in question: he had found official prison visitors to be useless.

The eventual wording of the motion officially establishing the Society (proposed by Mr C.H.Hopwood, QC, and seconded by Mr M.Crackenthorpe, QC) was:

'That it is desirable to establish a society to be named the Romilly Society having for its objects the amendment of the criminal law and its administrations, the reform of prison regulations, the reclamation of offenders, the abolition of cruel punishments, and the prevention and redress of miscarriage of justice'.

The other speakers named in *The Times* report are Rev.Douglas Morrison, Judge French, QC, Mr Douglas Walker, QC, and Mr J.H.Levy. Although Josiah is **not** mentioned, the addition of 'the reclamation of offenders' to the society's aims suggests that he may have been present, for this is one of the reforms he would recommend in his DCL thesis.

By the time of the Annual General Meeting in 1901 several other distinguished names were associated with the Romilly Society, including those of Earl Russell and Sir John Brunner, MP, who acted as Chairman. The final resolution on this occasion contained the clause 'lenient treatment and sympathy are more effectual than severity to reclaim offenders'. The society offered its support to humane judges, and 'would encourage juries to rise superior to the law when it became necessary and just to do so'. This expression reflected the difficulty felt by some jury members when confronted with cases of infanticide. They thought the law was wrong and savage, and were therefore unwilling to return a 'guilty' verdict. Earlier discussion had approved the enlightened system of a Californian prison, by which industry was rewarded with better food, and members hoped to persuade the British government to adopt a similar arrangement. Again the views of the Society are in accord with Josiah's thinking, so that it is not clear why he decided to found his **own** association at this time. One reason may have been that it was in 1901 that Josiah's thesis, entitled *The Penalty of Death*, which earned him his Doctorate of Civil Law, was published.

Prisoners at work at Bhownagur Jail

During a tour of India in 1901 Josiah paid a visit to a jail at Bhownagur, writing a detailed analysis of the buildings, the type of prisoners kept there, their diet and work and also of how the death penalty there was carried out, a very rare occurrence. Some prisoners guilty of capital crimes and sentenced to death by high court justices had their sentences commuted by the Maharajah to imprisonment, or were even pardoned and set free. Josiah questioned whether such criminals ever committed a second murder, and was told that none had. The jailor told him, in answer to further questioning, that murderers were by no means the worst class of prisoners, and in fact were generally very good and well-behaved, since murder was usually the result of some temporary passion. Prisoners there were well-treated, and the work which they produced, including sheets. towels, bedspreads, carpets and basketwork, was of a very high standard. Misdemeanours led to loss of privileges like smoking.

Josiah's new group, entitled 'The Society for the Abolition of Capital Punishment', had its headquarters at Margaret Chambers, New Kent Road, i.e. at the same address as the St Francis Hospital. Josiah took the Presidential role, and by 1909 Sir Edmund Verney was its Treasurer and Carl Heath its Honorary Secretary. The stated aims were to obtain:-

117

1. A more rational treatment of crimes of murder by the immediate adoption of a gradation of such crimes as proposed by the Legal commission of 1864
2. The consequent exclusion of various forms of homicide from the category to which the death penalty is applied
3. The ultimate complete abolition of capital punishment.

As a means of spreading the message Josiah published a booklet in that year entitled *Hanging for Murder*, in which he suggested that criminals should be trained to want to be good, to develop into a higher and nobler life, not be punished after they had already grown bad. He remarked that if **any** were to be put to death, it should be the criminally insane, since they were incapable of being reformed. Many murderers were not a danger to the general public - indeed they were far less so than some brutal men or callous mothers who had not yet been convicted of crimes but who nevertheless were guilty of cruelty toward others. He reminded his readers of how the mark of Cain, implanted by God, had shielded this murderer from injury by other men. As a Doctor it was not for him to question the power of God's arm, and so he 'lived to heal, and loved to cure, and joyed in freeing from pain', however great a villain his patient might be. The pamphlet, which cost just a few pence, concluded with the drafts of Bills on the subject which had already been submitted to Parliament, and one which Josiah himself hoped to submit.

Perhaps Josiah reasoned that the abolition of capital punishment was not the Romilly Society's prime concern. In 1902 that body's annual meeting dealt with the imprisonment in civilian jails of debtors and of soldiers on military charges; with recommending the appointment of female prison inspectors; and with the new Borstal system by which prisoners might learn a trade. Two years later the chairman, Sir Ernest Flower, MP, reported that there had been some progress with prison reform, but many other matters, such as the judicious modification of sentencing by magistrates, called for attention.

The first direct pointer to Josiah's involvement with the Romilly Society is a notice published in *The Times* in April 1908. This invited those requiring tickets for a forthcoming conference on Capital Punishment to apply to its Honorary Secretary, Mr C.Philipson, at 1 Mitre Court Buildings, Temple - Josiah's address in the then current Law List. The meeting, to be held on 18th June, promised prominent speakers, and was arranged by the Romilly Society 'with the co-operation of the Humanitarian League, the Howard Association, the Medico-Legal Society, the Society for the Abolition of Capital Punishment, the Penal Reform League, etc.'.

Early in 1909 the society expressed regret that the clause in the Children Bill providing for the abolition of capital punishment in the case of infanticide by the mother had been thrown out by the House of Lords, and begged the Home Secretary to take steps to amend the law at the earliest possible date. Later that year the Council was saddened by the death of the eminent criminologist Professor Lombroso, who had 'made the conception of curative treatment scientifically possible and logically wise in the case of all criminals'. This meeting was held at Mitre Court buildings.

From this date onwards *The Times* carries no further reports of the Romilly Society's doings, but in 1908 the death penalty had been abolished where the offender was under sixteen. By 1910 Josiah Oldfield was the Society's Chairman, having recently published his book *Hanging for Murder*. Little further progress was made for several years: abolition in the case of infanticide was not achieved until 1922. Josiah never gave up the cause, and would continue the fight in old age.

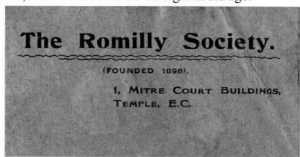

This writing paper was discovered after Josiah's death in 1953

Chapter 16

Josiah's visit to India 1901

Josiah's humanitarian concerns extended beyond Britain. In the winter of 1901 he visited India, with two main purposes in view, to find out whether complaints about the treatment of the native peoples under British rule were justified, and to determine why the efforts of Christian Missions were of limited success. It is tempting to think that this visit was partly inspired by his friendship with Gandhi, who for some years had been leading a crusade in South Africa against the inequalities imposed by white men on those of Indian origin. The experiences of Trimbakrai Desai would also have made Josiah eager to see for himself how discrimination affected the people of India. In fact he had been commissioned to pay a professional visit, and travelled in the company of the State Secretary to one of the Native States, who had come to London for health reasons and had been recommended to visit Josiah in Harley Street.

William Oldfield

Josiah's second objective, to find out why Christian Missions had been unsuccessful, was perhaps inspired by his elder brother William who had been in Belize, British Honduras, from 1881 to 1886, and who had recently gone out to Egypt to work among the Copts, where he remained until 1904.

William's well-argued book *Missionary Failures* would be published in 1908, and would draw partly on Josiah's findings. In fact the title referred to failures on the part of those preaching the Gospel as well as to those of their converts. William explained that missionaries were blamed by traders for 'spoiling the natives', who on becoming Christians rightly learned to have a greater self-esteem, to ask for greater personal consideration, and for higher wages. 'Thus if we expect subservience, and find independence, we call it impudence: if we expect work done for nothing, and find a fair wage demanded, we call it a grasping, greedy nature'.

At this period plague was rampant in India - 236,000 deaths were recorded in the Bombay Presidency alone during 1901. While en route to Bombay Josiah had been required to go before sanitary authorities at both Port Said and Aden when rejoining his ship after venturing ashore. Another routine medical inspection was carried out by a doctor during the night as a train carried Josiah from Bombay north through Ahmedabad and beyond. Third class passengers were all required to leave the train, but Josiah and his companions in a superior sleeping car were merely woken to have their pulse checked in situ. Further examinations were made next morning and at mid-day.

Josiah's natural curiosity prompted him to inquire why the sick were not removed to isolation units to prevent the spread of the disease. He was told that the Government had attempted to enforce such segregation, but that people refused to be separated from their families. In one enlightened Native State 'a deputation of the chief men of certain classes came up to the palace bearing fires upon their heads, a sign of matters of the greatest urgency'. They told their ruler that they would rather die than be segregated, and would close their shops and businesses if the ruling were enforced. The Secretary of State who was Josiah's informant related how His Highness turned the tables on them, saying that he himself would go to the special camp, where those preferring to stay alive could join him, and that he would send soldiers into the city to make sure businesses **stayed** shut until he

121

rescinded the order.

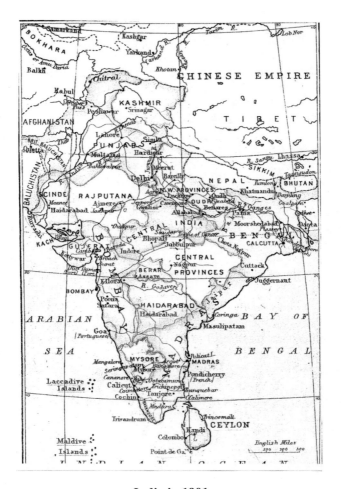

India in 1901

How long Josiah's visit lasted is not certain, but he travelled extensively through many parts of India (learning as he went to associate different places with differing flavours of water. Such nuances could only be fully appreciated by those with 'healthy, sensitive taste-buds'). In an article published in the Unitarian Church's *Hibbert Journal* in April 1903, but probably written in 1902, he outlined the area. His first intention was to visit a patient in a 'first class Indian state' in the Kathiawar peninsula, (from which his friend Trimbakrai Desai hailed) but he also travelled and made inquiries throughout large parts of the Bombay Presidency, Rajpootana, Punjab, the Central Provinces, Indore and Baroda. At Sihor, some sixty miles south of Agra, he visited a 'guest house for tramps' Built by a pious Hindu to accommodate about 200 guests, with rooms according to their caste, it allowed those staying to come and go as they pleased, to bathe, cook, and consume the food they had begged. He was struck by the contrast between it and the casual wards of Christian England.

During his travels over hundreds of miles Josiah had much intercourse with cultured representatives of Indian thought. By conforming to the habits of the highest Hindu castes, and by demonstrating fraternal sympathy with their thoughts and aspirations, he also obtained entrance to the homes and hearts of many natives. Throughout the whole of his stay in India he never once accepted European hospitality. From some of those Indians of the lower castes he learned how they feared that conversion to Christianity might mark them out (because it would demonstrate independence of thought) and that they might suffer as a result. Josiah would entitle his article 'The Failure of Christian Missions in India'.

Some of his early impressions of India are recorded in an article published in *Leisure Hour* in 1902. The food and drink on offer to travellers at stations seemed very strange - trays of spices like aniseed, cloves, cardamom, coriander and sliced betel nut - and milk or water also spiced and sweetened. Sometimes tea, more refreshing, was provided, but no drinks were served after sunset. Since he was travelling with a fairly important personage, there were usually groups waiting to receive the party at each stop on the journey, and sometimes they would be invited to a magnate's guest house to rest. The bareness of such houses struck Josiah forcibly, and he found it slightly unnerving to be placed on a verandah open on three sides to the gaze of crowds below.

Greetings in the form of nosegays or necklaces of flowers were offered to the travellers, but in Josiah's case his 'solar hat was very large, so that the necklaces would not go over it, but remained in the form of beautiful white puggarees' [light scarves worn round the hat to keep off the sun].

When they reached their destination the welcoming party included the Prime Minister, the Chief Revenue Officer, the Chief Justice, the Chief Medical Officer, the Inspector of Police and the Inspector of Education, together with a 'sea of turban-crowned faces'. He noticed that such crowds were entirely composed of men, all dressed in white, more important personages at the front, peasants behind. They remained quiet and orderly, and there was none of the jostling and commenting which an English crowd might have displayed in similar circumstances. A week later he had seen thousands of people and was struck by the absence of guns, remarking 'India is a disarmed people, with no soldiery outside the British and British armies: there are no Volunteers'. He discovered that gun licences were scarcely ever granted to the native population.

The impact of his experiences was still strong ten years later when he described getting up early in the village homes of India to find the housewife busy grinding the corn in her primitive stone mill before baking it into 'muscle-forming, nerve-building cakes' for his breakfast. It was from a Hindu lady with whom he stayed that he learned a simple cheese recipe:

> 'Put a pint of fresh milk on the fire; meanwhile squeeze the juice of a lemon or two in a cup, and when the milk commences to simmer empty the contents of the cup into it and give it a stir. In three minutes the curd will separate from the whey. Pour the contents into a piece of muslin and hang it up for an hour'.

Josiah declared that he had travelled thousands of miles on this form of cheese. After visiting an Indian jail, he noted that the physical conditon of prisoners was much improved after their enforced stay, although they were given only two meals a day, and their diet contained no meat.

The Indian diet had other benefits. Having examined some thousands of children's mouths Josiah ascribed the good dental health and freedom from caries of Hindu children to the fact that they ate food free from decaying animal fibres, practised good mastication, and flushed the mouth afterwards. This practice led to 'sanitation of the alimentary canal'. He also studied the Hindu practice of prahnamin, which involved breathing alternately through each nostril. In *Get Well and Keep Well* he described another custom which he observed amongst intelligent Hindus, and one which interested him very much. This was the habit of drawing up water through the nostril and spitting it out through the mouth in order to cleanse the nasal passages. It is possible that he himself adopted the practice, for he was observed in later life using what a witness described as 'something like an inhaler'.

In a rather different environment, while Josiah was dining with some high Indian officials, they began to discuss Christian missionaries, whose social life puzzled the Hindus - their own spiritual leaders were not expected to attend balls, play tennis or indulge in worldly pleasures as the foreigners did. Instead they devoted their lives to spiritual study and exercises, and earnest communing with the great Spirit of All. One of Josiah's hosts told him 'Your missionaries are extremely nice fellows, jolly to talk to, courteous, kindly and gentlemanly - but I should no more think of learning spiritual truth from them than I should go to an English military officer and ask him to do a surgical operation simply because he happened to be courteous and gentlemanly.' It was back in England that curates could win hearts through their skill at tennis and small-talk.

Another subject of conversation was the antagonism the Indians observed between missionaries of different branches of the Christian church; Roman Catholics, Anglicans and others. Many were narrow-minded, ridiculing the Hindu scriptures which contained much sublime teaching; unprepared even to entertain the ideas of men like Darwin or contemporary philosophers. Such closed minds were not likely to influence those Hindus who knew, and had studied far more deeply, the

125

religions and philosophies of the west as well as their own.

A topic which William emphasized in his book, but which Josiah also raised in his article, concerned the 'so-called converts from the lowest classes, who, having received a smattering of Sunday School instruction, have been baptized'. Their behaviour gave cause for concern, but such people might not be truly representative of the progress made in conversion. It tended to be these who were observed by travellers who visited only large towns - would an Oriental visiting England gain a true picture of her moral climate from what he saw in London? William added that those same travellers did not visit Mission Stations where the real work took place, where the natives were not only clothed, but in their right mind, gentle, peaceable, industrious and leading godly lives, a description that reminds us that the Oldfield brothers were born in the mid-Victorian period. There would always be a percentage of 'missionary failures', for even in England few were willing to evangelise even in their own neighbourhood. A century or two, not just a generation, were needed for Christianity to reach natives properly and bring them into submission to the Gospel of Christ.

William went on to explore the reasons for the early Church's success, comparing the conditions of the years just after Christ's life on earth with those of the late Victorian era, and pointing out St Paul's differing experiences with the Galatians and the Corinthians.

Josiah found other reasons for lack of success in India. Those seeking to convert often offended by failing to observe customary niceties like washing and donning clean clothes before participating at a meal, nor did they abstain from meat. 'India, without flesh-eating, has more of the gentle spirit of Christ' than England, he wrote. If Jesus were to return to Earth He would find many ready to follow Him in India.

Josiah was greatly impressed - and influenced - by some aspects of Hinduism, particularly the asceticism which appeared to lead to a higher degree of spirituality. In *Fasting for Health and Life*, written in 1924, he refers to 'the gentle, tense and vibrant talk of that emaciated salmon-robed Hindu monk of India, as with clasped hands and far-off seeing eyes he sat on the ground under a banyan tree and discoursed to us sitting upon the brown earth in front of him...' Josiah apparently lived for a time in solitude in a 'Yogi's cave', perhaps seeking there the basis of universal spirituality which was one of the ideals of the Order of the Golden Age. The Vedic seers he encountered were spiritual explorers who discovered and employed well-defined yogic disciplines to raise human consciousness from terrestrial turmoil to transcendent tranquillity.

In his discussion in 1924 of the philosophy of fasting Josiah stated that it altered the relationship between sensations and realities, so that all experience gained by previous continuity of connection became, for the moment, valueless. In dreams memories were freed from the 'repressive coordination of waking educated experience'. Fasting leads to a somewhat similar state, a condition which may well explain the visions of saints and mystics. Man's belief in life after death, according to Josiah, stems from visions prompted by memories, a belief supported by the book of Esdras from which he often quoted.

Josiah was probably already familiar with some of the ideas he encountered in India. As well as Gandhi and Trimbakrai Desai, his best man in 1899, he probably knew Edward Maitland and Anna Bonus Kingsford, who strongly believed that a vegetarian diet made its followers sensitive to 'messages from beyond'. Maitland and Kingsford had been President and Vice-President respectively of the London Lodge of the Theosophical Society in 1884. Theosophists believed that God must be experienced directly in order to be known at all. Their aims were three-fold: to study and compare different religions, philosophies and branches of science; to investigate the unexplained, both within man and in the natural world; and to form the nucleus of the 'universal brotherhood of humanity'. Josiah and several of his friends, especially Sidney Beard, found much in common with these ideas.

Ananda Coomaraswamy (1877-1947) who was Anglo-Sinhalese, was also known to Josiah: his mother Lady Coomaraswamy had made a gift to Oriolet Hospital in 1896. He grew up in England, and is remembered today as someone who taught the west to approach and understand the arts of India, believing that 'Each race contributes something essential to the world's civilization in the course of its own self-expression'. Sir William Earnshaw Cooper, one of Josiah's benefactors, who had helped to found a tannery on the banks of the Ganges in 1882, may also have influenced his ideas. Earnshaw Cooper was the author of several books, including *Socialism and its Perils*. There were undoubtedly others - Josiah in 1903 talks of mixing with numbers of Hindus who were spending years of study in the Christian land of England. It was probably largely through his experiences in India that Josiah came to the conclusion that it was better to be a good Hindu than a bad Christian.

As a conclusion to his article Josiah wrote that rather than sending out as missionaries to many parts of the country men who would 'degenerate into elementary schoolmasters and managers of outcast children's homes' it would be better for a dozen spiritual men to settle at one place. Here they should emulate the saintly lives and ascetic practices of the early fathers of the Christian Church, in order to convert, intellectually as well as spiritually, a single devout Brahmin who had nothing to gain by his conversion. This man would spread the news that the 'kosmic forces of the world beyond were changing their focus, and that it is now through Christianity that the closest kinship to the Divine Centre can be obtained'.

Fifty years later, the *Hibbert Journal* would carry a review of Josiah's last book, in which it would describe his theology as 'rather arbitrarily eclectic...'

Chapter 17

The Lady Margaret Hospital, Bromley

After his marriage late in 1899 Josiah Oldfield required a family home, which he found at 'Carn Brae', in London Road, Bromley. He took up residence in 1900, and it was from this address that the announcement of the birth of twin daughters, Irene Dorrien and Josie Margaret, on 9th March 1902, was made. (Bromley Record, April 1902) The twins were baptised at the Church of SS Peter and Paul, Bromley, the following month, 'Dorien' being spelled with a single 'r' in the baptismal register.

London Lane, Bromley

During the first years of their marriage Josiah's wife Gertrude was involved with Josiah's activities on at least two fronts. She was active in promoting the 'Hospitals Working Guild' which had apparently been in existence for some five or six years in aiding Humanitarian Hospitals. It seems possible that it developed from the Maternity Society mentioned earlier in connection with the Hospital of St Francis. In a letter published in the *Vegetarian Messenger* early in 1901, addressed from Carn Brae, Gertrude sought volunteers of different kinds - those who could make donations of money (1/- upwards) to buy materials, others who would undertake to give two items each year, still others who would make up materials to the patterns supplied. 'Cast-offs' of suitable garments were equally welcome. An earlier report in the *Herald of the Golden Age* remarked that the Annual General Meeting of the Guild had taken place at the Congregational Memorial Hall, with Josiah presiding.

The *Herald* at this period was issued monthly, and usually included a page headed 'Household Wisdom' made up largely of simple vegetarian recipes. In 1900 Gertrude's name appeared several times as the contributor: Daisy Whiston was another who supplied material.

In 1903, because of his principles, Josiah was up before the Bench at Bromley when he refused to allow the twins to be vaccinated. He argued that they were of Fruitarian stock. The introduction to human systems of products derived from the blood of a cow would lower the sanctity of the bloodstream of the human race. The Chairman regarded this as a conscientious objection, which should, however, have been submitted before the children were four months old. Josiah was convicted, with fines and costs amounting to nearly £5. His plea was subsequently adopted by other Fruitarians: two years later at the same Court Mr Charles Nye successfully applied for vaccination exemption since he objected to his baby's blood being contaminated by animal blood.

In 1902 Josiah had acquired the premises next door to Carn Brae known as Holmby House, a good-sized double-fronted house which also featured a large single storey extension connected to the main building. Since 1890 this had accommodated Bromley Park School, run by H.C.Bond, M.A. Josiah successfully converted it to a small hospital, initially with twelve beds and four cots, which took its first patients in May 1903. In the main house the attic, formerly the boys' dormitory, provided sleeping accommodation for the nurses. The well-ventilated bungalow section, previously a large classroom capable of being split into three by means of folding partitions, was lit by electricity and warmed by hot air, and it now housed the main ward, Other small classrooms became a dispensary and an operating theatre. The Lady Margaret Hospital was in being.

Inspection of the 1901 census return for 31 London Road, Bromley (Carn Brae) suggests that nursing had already begun at this address. The exact complement is enumerated as:-

Josiah Oldfield	M 38	Physician/surgeon/barrister	
Edith Oplin	S 20	Servant	Nurse (Hospital)
Frances M.Humphrey	S 22	Servant	Cook (Domestic)
Harriet E.G.Browne	S 34	Servant	Nurse (Sick)
Mary Woodall	S 32	Visitor	Living on own means
Emma Shaw	S 32	Visitor	Tailoress worker
Betsy A.R.Slaser	S 16	Visitor	
Margery B.Siers ?	S 4	Visitor	
Francis G.R.Samson	S 4	Visitor	

Gertrude's name is missing, a fact which might be thought significant.

As with the St Francis Hospital, brochures setting out the aims of the new venture, together with the advantages it offered, were sent out in search of subscriptions from the great and good. On this occasion the committee of sixteen, which included Josiah's wife Gertrude, boasted no earls, dukes or even 'honourables', but links with the 'London Centre in the New Kent Road' were explained. The Lady Margaret Hospital at Bromley would demonstrate three things: the value of fresh air and sunlight; the value of pure and natural food; the feasibility of connecting a London Centre with a Country Hospital. 'Barely half an hour' separated the crowded and bad-smelling homes in hot and stuffy blocks from 'a ward where trees shelter the view in place of brick walls, where a sunlit garden takes the place of a stifling court, and where the fragrance of flowers replaces the smell of drying clothes or frying fish'. In this apparent paradise those who were whole learned how to remain well, and those who were ill were taught how to win their way back to health through pure air, sun baths and a Fruitarian diet. 'Frugal and natural foods from the vegetable kingdom have been proved again and again to have a great effect in removing uric acid and

131

allied poisons from the tissues and restoring vitality and strength to bodies that have been injured by over-stimulation'. Medicines or surgical treatment would also be available, adapted to individual needs.

In order to make these facilities accessible to the patients who needed them, donations were sought. Five shillings entitled the giver to a letter for patients coming in for trivial operations which did not entail an overnight stay: half a guinea allowed an admittance for two or three days (or a week at reduced fees). But what Josiah and his associates really needed were more generous sponsors, who might name a cot (twenty-five guineas) or a bed (fifty guineas). Not long after this appeal was circulated the hoped-for monies began to be subscribed.

Tea in the garden

A new hospital ward, named after her late husband, was opened in November 1903 by Lady Julia Lyveden. She was by that date Treasurer of the Hospital Committee, and had given two hundred guineas towards the project.

The official opening ceremony was reported at length in the *Bromley Record*. The doctors attended in their academic gowns, the Mockba Silver Band from Sydenham played, trees were planted, and the invited guests, including civic dignitaries and local residents, contributed a further £20 to Hospital Funds. In her speech Lady Lyveden hoped 'that all the patients who come within (the ward's) walls may therein find health and healing and comfort for body and mind and spirit'. The expected bouquet was then proffered by Master Stephen Chase, and 'Mrs Oldfield's little twin girls presented purses'. The wording of this clause is unusual: why not **Doctor** Oldfield's little girls?

The Chronicle carried a similar report, but also included much of Josiah's speech, in which he outlined his aims for the hospital. In his opinion it was essential that every medical man should have the opportunity of being attached to a hospital so that he might be familiar with the very latest and best techniques, always learning from his colleagues. There he might 'do his work under the eyes of a constant criticism,* that he might have the best resources that could be supplied to him for the treatment of poor patients'. Under the present system only a limited number of doctors in every town had these privileges, and Josiah felt that it was for the benefit not only of the doctors themselves, but also of their patients, that these advantages should not be restricted to a few, but should belong to all. He considered that the system was far preferable where every doctor in a neighbourhood could have the privilege of sending in his poor patients, and that they would not then be lost to him, but that they should remain under his own care while in the hospital. It was upon these lines the Lady Margaret Hospital had been founded, and his wards and the theatre were open to every medical man who wished to utilise them.

Alderman Dr Price moved a vote of thanks, saying that he himself had regularly attended the weekly operating sessions, and had observed the skill and courtesy of Dr Oldfield. He welcomed the opportunity now provided for local doctors to consult with visiting London specialists like Mr Fedde Feddow, senior anaesthetist at St George's Hospital, who attended whenever his services were needed in particularly critical cases.

*Was it the 'constant criticism', perhaps not always favourable, which had led to the frequent changes in medical staff at the St Francis Hospital?

The hospital would stand well in today's League Tables, for at the annual meeting in 1905 it was reported that there had been only one death out of 171 cases admitted during the previous year. This was attributed by Josiah, in his capacity as Chief Medical Officer, to the 'entire banishment of all fish, fowl and animal flesh from the dietary'.

Charles Carthew, however, preferred not to rely on brochures and glowing press releases. He was particularly interested in the financial arrangements, reporting that the late Treasurer, who was also a Probationer, had resigned because she was leaving the locality. A gift of £210 which she had donated to the hospital in memory of her late husband had been invested in stock. A new Treasurer was to be sought at the approaching Committee meeting. Carthew found it difficult to reconcile what he saw with what the brochure offered. The leaflet spoke of private rooms, which could only have been in the main house. This, Josiah said, was run as a nursing home 'conducted as a private undertaking by Mrs McCowan, accepting patients from other local doctors', but it did not pay. Carthew probed further, eliciting the fact that Mrs McCowan was financed by Dr Oldfield.

There was certainly some attempt to put the financial affairs on a regular footing. A 'Memorandum and Articles of Association of the Margaret Nursing Home, Limited' was printed in 1904, in which the 'Subscribers', each taking one £1 share, are listed as

Louisa Sharpe (Spinster) Seddlescombe, Battle, Sussex
Frederick Henry Oldfield (Farmer) Red House, Stapleton, Salop
Olive Frances Goodyer (Nurse) 8 Woburn Square, W.C.
Eleanor Hannah Roberts (Spinster) Highfield, Oswestry, Salop
Mary Ellen Oldfield (Spinster) Ryton, Dorrington, Shrewsbury
Douglas Crofts (Land Agent) The Broadway, Tooting
Hattie Ellen Gregory Browne (Secretary) 2 Hardy Road, Blackheath

The share capital was to be £5000, and the company's declared object was 'to acquire and take over as a going concern the business of a Nursing Home and the employment of Nurses now carried on by Josiah Oldfield, under the name of "The Lady

Margaret Home", at No.33, London Road, Bromley...' It foresaw the establishment of other similar concerns and forecast dividends of 6%. Although the Company's Incorporation is recognised at Companies House, its records have been destroyed.

Interviewing the auditor, a Mr Smith, Carthew learned that the Hospital had an account with the Bromley branch of the London, City and Midland Bank, and that cheques were signed by Josiah and Miss Nye, one of the secretaries. The receipts from the nursing home did not come into the accounts of the Hospital. One feels that Carthew was still unhappy about the intricacies of Josiah's finances, but could not put his finger on any definite misrepresentation. Some months after his visit the 'St James's Gazette' reported in November 1904 that four cheques received by the Lady Margaret Hospital included one for fifty guineas from Lord Llangattock.

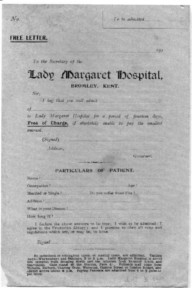

Patrons were able to give 'Free Letters' to Deserving Cases

Contemporary town directories state that medical and surgical cases were admitted to the Bromley establishment, and fees were charged according to the means of the patients. Some, if very deserving, paid no fees at all: this was at the discretion of the Committee. Cases involving infectious disease were not treated, but operations were performed, on Saturdays at 10.a.m. As one might expect the hospital was strictly fruitarian, and one of its aims was to demonstrate the part played by fresh air and sunlight in the healing process. A former nurse recalled Josiah's successful treatment for ulcerated legs. The patient would be out on the lawn, the ulcers having been sprinkled with boracic powder and covered with dry gauze. This was in contrast to the usual method, whereby the sores were kept wet; healing under these conditions was painfully slow.

Not everyone was happy about the treatment at Josiah's hospitals. An unsigned letter was received by the Charity Organisation Society in February 1904 which accused him of being very rough when extracting teeth, leaving his patients at the Margaret Dispensary with 'lacerated jaws'. At this period Josiah came down from Bromley most evenings, though he found few patients awaiting him. There was little activity at the Dispensary in the mornings either. The anonymous writer had also been to Bromley, where he had expected to meet 'Lady Margaret' and so was annoyed that 'Mrs Oldfield put on nurse's attire to represent Sister Lady Margaret'. The correspondent then referred to Josiah's connection with 'the ICKE [iKES? hICK? hILLS? HENICK??]- the writing is illegible] and the Swami case of about two years ago', but gave no details. The letter prompted a visit to Bromley by Hugh Fickling, who found seven patients in residence, all female. There were four nurses, of whom two were probationers. Josiah told Fickling that, on average, two operations were performed each week.

One person who did trust Josiah's dentistry, and his general surgical skills, was Mohandas Gandhi, his former colleague. Gandhi came to England for six weeks during the autumn of 1906 as one of a deputation opposed to the Asiatic Registration Act about to be introduced in the Transvaal, then a Crown Colony.

His colleague was a Moslem businessman named H.O.Ali. On 27th October Gandhi wrote to Josiah at the Lady Margaret Hospital about the possibility of minor surgery on his nose:

'I think I mentioned that, when I was in Bombay, I had lost my sense of smell... I have chronic catarrh. Of course I do not know whether you have made a speciality of throat diseases. If not, and you think it is worth while, you can put me on to a specialist again. I think it was when I was carrying on a fruit-and-nut diet experiment that I damaged my teeth. I believed that I had permanently damaged two molars and I thought that I was going to lose one of them on board... Friends though we are, if you are going to attend to either of the two complaints, you must do so professionally if only because whatever you receive, I know, goes to a humanitarian purpose...'

Gandhi then suggested that, as he was so busy with interviews, Josiah should offer him a choice of appointment times. He also referred to a telephone call from Mr Ally (sic) who reported that he felt much better. H.O.Ali was having treatment at Josiah's Bromley hospital, though for what is unknown.

Correspondence between Gandhi and 'My dear Oldfield' continued. On 11th November Gandhi gently chided his friend, writing 'Mr Simmonds attended yesterday to take down the article you were to have dictated. I suppose you were unavoidably detained'. (Two articles by Josiah on 'Indian Parents' Duties' were subsequently published in *Indian Opinion* in January 1907). He continued 'I had hoped to be able to undergo the operation tomorrow and to pass with you from Saturday to Monday. I see, however, that I must not do so for the present... I must keep myself busy with Deputation work... I may be ready for treatment Saturday week.' A further short note four days later dealt with a legal matter: a law student sought remission from his Terms on the grounds of his father-in-law's insanity, and Josiah was asked by Gandhi to provide a certificate attesting to this.

The next communication first enquired of Josiah 'whether Mr Ally's parcel has been sent' and requested the balance of Mr Ally's account. Gandhi then went on 'My teeth are more shaky than when you saw them and yet I am afraid that I will not be able to undergo the operation at the hospital either for the teeth or the nose'. This letter brought an immediate reply from Josiah offering to carry out the necessary surgery at the Hotel Cecil in London, where Gandhi was staying. This was agreed, providing it could be done late in the day, after 8.00 p.m. if possible. Or 'On Tuesday do you mind coming to the hotel at 5 o'clock or even at 4.45?... You may come up to room No.256 and await my arrival... You can have tea and then perform the operation...' This letter was dated 27th November. But on the 28th Gandhi was at the House of Commons, and met Winston Churchill, while on 29th he held a farewell breakfast for friends and sympathisers at the Hotel Cecil. Presumably, therefore, no date and time convenient for both doctor and patient could be found, for there is no record of any operation taking place before Gandhi's departure from England on 1st December.

Chapter 18

Domestic Crisis?

From this date onwards there is no further reference to Gertrude, or the twins, in connection with Josiah. It seems that he and his wife may have separated, an arrangement which was to become permanent. There are several small pointers as to what may have happened to cause the rupture. First, perhaps, is Josiah's lengthy visit to India in 1901 without his bride of less than two years. From what Josiah wrote later in *The Mystery of Marriage* it can be deduced that he had discovered, too late, that he and Gertrude were not ideally suited. Some collected quotations printed in the *Herald of the Golden Age* in 1912 lead to the same conclusion: an example is 'If love is recognized as the moral ground for making a marriage, want of love should logically be recognized as a moral ground for unmaking it'.

Other clues are more speculative. Why was Gertrude not at Bromley on the day of the census (Sunday March 31st) in 1901? Inspection of the appropriate census data shows that a Mrs Gertrude Oldfield, a nurse, born in Wakefield in 1862, was at Brightlingsea in Essex. This appears to be the only record which fits all the available information about Josiah's wife. The actual entry reference is RG13/1703, and reads:

69 Tower Street Brightlingsea

124	George H. Peggs M 60 m.	Head Oyster merchant	b. Brightlingsea Own acct.
	Ellen Peggs F 48 m	Wife	b. Wivenhoe
125	Gertrude Oldfield F 39 m.	Boarder Sick nurse	b. Wakefield Own acct.
	Henick? Borgstrom? M 27 s.	Boarder	b. Finland? Own means

139

Unfortunately the handwriting is difficult to decipher, but it is evident that Gertrude was acting as nurse to a single man while both were boarding at the house occupied by an oyster-merchant, his wife and family. This may have been a perfectly reasonable arrangement, for nurses were frequently sent out to look after patients in their own homes or while convalescing. The Essex coast would have provided a suitable venue. But did the relationship go beyond that of nurse and patient? The twins were born in early March 1902, so that they were conceived in the summer of the previous year - of which Josiah spent a lengthy period abroad. Is this the explanation for that throwaway line 'Mrs Oldfield's little girls presented purses'?

The next 'sighting' of Gertrude I have found was her attendance at her father's funeral in Wakefield in November 1905. Josiah did not accompany her. As yet I have not discovered where she went following the marriage break-up, nor whether Josiah supported her and the twins financially. There were apparently no long-term effects on her physical health, for she outlived her husband, dying at the age of ninety-eight in London, in St John's Wood. Her unmarried daughter Josie Margaret was with her. Josie Margaret was a witness at the marriage of her twin sister Irene Dorrien in 1929. By this time Irene, aged twenty-seven, was a qualified dental surgeon, living at Tickhill in Yorkshire. Her husband Robert Ball, a resident of York, was a bank official a couple of years her senior. The marriage certificate gives the bride's father's name as 'Josiah Oldfield', so contradicting any speculation about the paternity of the twins.

What had Josiah been looking for in a wife? His attitude towards women would have been shaped by his early life. It is tempting to picture the new-born Josiah as the centre of attention in an admiring circle of female adorers - mother and three older sisters - and to offer this as one possible reason for his later views of woman as subservient to the male: in *The Mystery of Birth* he writes 'every woman must seek a man higher and better than herself' as a partner. At the time of his birth his two eldest sisters, Julia and Sarah, were aged nine and ten repectively, and were very probably expected to help in caring for the new baby. By the time he was a toddler even Mary Ellen, four years his senior, would have been old enough to help.

Once he had left home, Josiah had moved into a series of environments where men were dominant, and most of the women whom he encountered would have been servants. At Chipping Campden there were four, of whom three were female, in attendance on Joseph Foster's family and the boarders. Although at Oxford in the 1880s a few women were allowed to attend some lectures, provided they were accompanied by their chaperones, there would certainly have been none in the Schools of Theology or Law. It has been suggested (in a newspaper report many years after Josiah's death) that he was aware of these young ladies, and that the existence of their college, Lady Margaret Hall, influenced him in the choice of the name 'Lady Margaret' for his establishments. But since the same newspaper paragraph contains two glaring errors of fact about Josiah's time at Oxford, the reporter's source is decidely suspect.

The Inns of Court did not admit women until the twentieth century. Perhaps it was not until he began his medical studies that Josiah began to view females, whether as patients or nurses, with new eyes. In *The Mystery of Marriage* he refers to 'the girl who has slipped off her silken nightie and jumped into a cold bath and has then towelled herself into rosy glorious beauty', comparing her charms with those who disguise their natural odours with synthetic scents. Another passage in the same book reads 'Blessed be this characteristic of the woman's character which makes her to be like gold. In spite of all the drosses and quartzes with which it may be intermixed, gold still remains precious gold. So woman in spite of all her tricks and deceits and vanities and prevarications and variabilities has always a heart which makes her not only indispensable to the human race as a sex, but makes the individual woman a precious necessity to the individual man'. *The Mystery of Birth*, written at about the same time, contains an even deeper purple patch: 'The young females must be ready and fit, and progress, like Cinderella, from the home-making, nest-building, cultured modesty and glory of the kitchen, into the heritage of the radiant Venus who is ready for the coming of the great Prince Charming'.

His idealized view of woman is thus coupled with his expectation that she will also excel in both the 'traditional' woman's role and in other fields. In one of the two essays which make up *Myrrh and Amaranth* (published in 1905) he recognised that washing dishes, clothes and babies with no prospect beyond was drudgery, but recommended women whose lot this was to recognise that labour is divine, and as nothing compared with the work Christ did in saving mankind.

Soon after the birth of the twins the following list appeared in the *Herald of the Golden Age*, of which Josiah was then Editor:-

What our Daughters should be Taught

How to prepare food which will not give dyspepsia to those who eat it.

To wash, iron, darn stockings, sew on buttons, and make their own dresses.

To spend within their income: to keep their accounts, to know where their money goes, and to have something to show for it.

To wear a calico dress which is paid for, with more comfort than a silk one for which they still owe.

To always have a bright face, which is better than any cosmetic, and that if they want fair complexions, clear skins, and rosy cheeks, they should take plenty of out-of-door exercise.

To use good common sense, self-help and industry, which will make them independent and useful.

To marry an honest man - for to wed a husband without principle, conscience or religion, is like putting to sea without a compass, or chart, or rudder.

To like music, painting and other accomplishments, but to have a certain amount of good reading daily. In reading good books there is education, development, and often solace and comfort for weary, lonely hours.

To mind their own business, and to avoid gossiping as they would an infectious disease. A gossip has a perverted mind and an empty head.

To know that matrimonial happiness depends, not on wealth, nor on appearance, but on good health, good manners, good principles, and personal character.

Sidney Beard also had daughters, Elizabeth Catherine and Margaret, who were at that time aged about fourteen and twelve respectively. Did he and Josiah sit down together to compile the list? They certainly shared similar views on marriage, and Beard too may already have been experiencing matrimonial difficulties. He would later express his opinion that love in a marriage was essential, not just the mundane provision of necessities. 'Many women manifest no affection and sympathetic consideration towards their husbands, so as to strengthen them in any hour of temptation'. In early 1911 his wife Martha entered a plea for a judicial separation on the grounds of her husband's adultery with a lady called Grace Hawkshaw: Sidney was then living in Kensington and Martha in Bournemouth. Temptation had won...

If Josiah discovered that Gertrude fell short of **his** expectations of the ideal woman, he himself can hardly have been the perfect husband. Indeed his many other pursuits can have left little time for relaxation together - although had they truly loved one another perhaps he would have found it. A major preoccupation must have been the Fruitarian 'colony' he was planning in Kent.

Chapter 19

A Flourishing Establishment : Bromley 1905-18

Today, when hospitals grow ever larger and more specialized, it seems strange that units with only twenty or so beds could offer such a variety of treatment and care. There was by no means always a resident doctor, and the Matron was not necessarily a fully-trained nurse. When Gertrude Hick had accepted the post of Matron at the new Kettering Hospital in 1897 her reward, apart from food and accommodation, was £45 per annum and her uniform. In exchange she was housekeeper, accountant, dietician and budget-holder; she trained the nurses and managed the ancillary staff; and she was 'Responsible to God for the moral atmosphere of the institution'. She apparently fulfilled her duties conscientiously, reporting fortnightly to the House Committee.

By coincidence the report on the opening of the hospital at Carn Brae in 1903 is flanked by one dealing with the finances of the Bromley and Beckenham Joint Hospital Board, whose establishment was apparently one of the largest and most efficient in the country. From this we learn that the cost of a new diphtheria ward there was £1500, and that the annual income was just under £10,750. Expenditure was detailed as:

Working expenses	£2927 9s 2d
Establishment expenses	£662 11s 10d
Maintenance of patients	£1717 12s 5d
Interest & repayment of loans	£1571 19s 3d
Alterations & additions	£3788 17s 0d

The Lady Margaret Hospital's working expenses would have been considerably less, for the nurses also carried out the domestic duties - and were unpaid. In 1905 160 patients were admitted to its wards, and 120 operations were carried out. Receipts were reported as £500. A local Ladies' Committee held an 'At Home' on the first Tuesday of each month, which no doubt helped to raise subscriptions, but by 1907 the hospital had attracted some wealthy patrons such as General Sir Edward Bulwer and the Hon.Canon Lyttelton, Headmaster of Eton, who were both Governors.

There was also in Bromley at this time the Phillips Homoeopathic Hospital, whose origins lay in a former dispensary held in a room of the 'White Hart'. From 1889 it had occupied a pair of houses, but in 1900 an imposing new building had been opened in the centre of Bromley. No doubt Josiah had similar expectations of his Fruitarian establishment. The advertisements for the different hospitals in Bush's *Budget and Directory of Bromley* in 1911 are revealing. The Cottage Hospital lists more than a dozen members of its medical staff, the Homeopathic lists three, but the Lady Margaret instead quotes the names of its numerous titled patrons. These included the Countess of Derby, Lady Margaret Campbell, the Countess of Kinnoull, the Viscountess Vallefort, the Countess of Yarborough, Lady Louisa Fielding and Lady Margaret Rutherford. Sir William Earnshaw-Cooper and Lord Llangattock were other generous supporters. Titled names no doubt helped Josiah to recruit nurses from the higher classes.

Josiah surrounded by some of the Staff at Bromley

145

During its tenure of the premises in London Road special occasions at the Lady Margaret Hospital were advertised, and frequently reported at length, in the local press. The bazaar of November 1905 was no exception. 'Artistic and fancy articles were there in abundance, and as the prices were low and the workmanship good and the articles eminently useful, the various stall-holders did a brisk trade.... Another great attraction was the demonstration of fruitarian cookery by two of the sisters of the hospital staff.... The sausage rolls and rissoles and potted meats and savoury sandwiches secured much appreciation, and a large number of fruitarian cookery books were purchased'. Those attending the bazaar were assured that 'no dead animals' were used in the preparation of these refreshments, but no details of their replacements were given. The report concluded by inviting any who wished for cards to attend the New Year Reception, at which another new cot would be named, to apply as soon as possible.

Josiah featured in other circumstances too. The *Bromley Record* notes that 'a very largely-attended meeting of the Bromley Women's League was held on February 10th 1903 at the artistic house of Mrs Heywood ... to hear an address by Dr. Oldfield, of Carn Brae, on "Aesthetics in Food"'. The following year Mrs Heywood's home (The Old Summer House in Burnt Ash Lane) again provided a venue for Josiah to speak to the Women's League, this time on 'Humanitarian Ideals'. His speech covered man's gradual emergence from cruelty to universal mercy, considered pain - 'a transient evil whose infliction when necessary is to be regretted, and when unnecessary is a crime'; mentioned war 'ever to be looked on as evil', sketched the line of evolution through which Isaiah's prophecy would be fulfilled, dealt rapidly with his future conception of the function of the church in its dealings with criminals, passed on to the race's attitude to blood sports and vivisection, and finally condemned butchery and its attendant evils. Not surprisingly, the lecture was followed by animated discussion.

146

Josiah's fame was beginning to spread. In June 1908 he received a letter from a medical man in the Antipodes, Dr Abramowski, to which he replied:

'I am very much interested in your letter of 10th February to know that you are carrying out similar experiments in Australia to those which I am doing here, and that you find the Fruitarian dietary is so valuable in your hospital. I have had a very little experience in typhoid cases myself, but we have a great deal of surgical work here, and my experience is that one gets a smaller amount of shock and less amount of inflammation, and more rapid healing, and more complete restoration to the original vitality than one gets on a meat diet.

'I should have no objection to your quoting this statement of mine before your Medical Congress, as I make it with the experience of having done over 2000 operations on patients treated on the Fruitarian dietary, and I have come to the conclusion that to obtain the best results it is well to put the patient on a Fruitarian dietary a month before the operation. In abdominal and rectal and internal cases the benefit of having a clean aseptic condition of the bowels is of the greatest importance. I have lost only one case after operation during the last ten years.'

A new brochure-cum-annual report for the Lady Margaret Hospital appeared in 1909, this time with Josiah's name on the front as founder. The usual long list of patrons preceded a brief report on recent events, including the number of cases admitted (163), whose length of stay ranged from a few days to a year. 125 operations had been performed, including mastectomy, hernia, removal of adenoids and the amputation of a hand. A **very** brief summary of accounts for the years 1906, 1907 and 1908 followed, and it was noted that the nursing staff carried out **all** the work of the hospital - no ward-maids, servants or cooks were employed. An entry in the *Charities Digest* for 1910, under the heading 'Suburban and Cottage Hospitals', amplifies this information, announcing that management was by Monthly Council, and that income from charitable contributions had been £366 while patients' fees had amounted to £225. The Treasurer was Stanley Churton. 2900 Outpatients had been treated during the year, the Outpatient Department address being given as New Kent Road.

But there was other interesting news; the foundation of 'The Margaret Lectureship' was announced. Recognising the immense value of dietary in the causation and cure of disease, Josiah felt that it would be of the greatest importance if the subject could be studied scientifically by those who took up the profession of healing. This scheme had been very warmly taken up by the Jains of India, who, through Mr Labshankar Laxmidas, contributed the sum of £50. It was not, however, until a Miss Walker had generously interested herself in the matter that it became possible to confirm the foundation of a scholarship. Miss Walker had given Consols to the value of £850, and Lord Llangattock made the sum up to £1000, so that interest of £40 per annum was available for a 'Margaret Scholarship in Humane Dietetics', open to medical students and qualified medical men. The paragraph concluded with Josiah's hopes that others would augment the funds...

Unfortunately the exact date when this brochure was first published is not clear, for in December 1908 Lord Llangattock had heard 'disturbing reports' and contacted the Charity Organisations Society asking whether they could shed any light on them. These may have been about the involvement with the Swami already mentioned, or they may have been of much more recent origin. The Society's file includes a letter dated February 1910 from a Mrs Owler in Hampstead, who wrote on behalf of a young woman who had been employed by Josiah at Bromley for seven weeks as a 'secretary and general factotum'. The letter accused Josiah of paying starvation wages, and of 'fostering immorality' : the young woman concerned had already contacted the editor of *Life of Faith*, the magazine in which her post had been advertised, and her local police. The letter-writer understood the residents of Bromley to be uneasy about Josiah's activities, and wrote 'He is clever in involving servants in his schemes so that they will get into trouble if the truth came out'. Mrs Owler was astonished that such a hospital should figure in the *Charities Digest.*

These allegations were immediately investigated by Hugh Fickling, who met with Dr Bateman, of the Medical Defence Union. This gentleman had nothing but contempt for Josiah, and for vegetarians in general. His notably biased view was recorded by Fickling verbatim: 'You can't trust a fellow who lives on nuts - it only makes them more and more earthy'. Bateman also remarked that although Oldfield was married his wife would not live with him, that he was a crank, and, 'like most cranks, a sexual pervert. He got hold of a lot of silly foolish women and could do what he liked with them. Fifteen years ago there was a fearful scandal down in Essex and charges of the greatest immorality were brought against Dr Oldfield in connection with the Matron and nurses'. Dr Bateman did not remember how the affair had ended but thought that the Matron had resigned and that all had been hushed up. He had heard nothing definite, but had no doubt that many shady things were going on still. He 'would not recommend any decent woman to have anything to do with Oldfield. She had better go and seek her living on the streets at once'.

There is a suggestion that Josiah and his exploits may have inspired *The Jacob Street Mystery,* by R.Austin Freeman, published in 1942 but set in 1930. The book is partially set in Loughton, and in it the Divisional Surgeon who examines various corpses is called Dr **James** Oldfield, of **Saint** Margaret's Hospital. Dr Thorndyke, Austin Freeman's detective, who figures in a whole series of stories, has qualifications in both law and medicine. But he does not seem to have any other characteristics associated with Josiah.

Much of the book's plot is concerned with a missing wife and whether her death can be presumed after several years. Of her it is said 'I don't think her husband was unfriendly. The position seems to be that they had separated by mutual agreement and gone their separate ways, simply ignoring the marriage. On the few occasions when she referred to him, she did so without the slightest trace of animosity'. Might this be a veiled reference to Josiah and Gertrude? The husband ultimately turns out to be the villain of the piece, having spent some time successfully posing as a woman, undetected by the coloured gentleman who seeks to become 'her' lover. The introduction of a 'coloured gentleman' who was a barrister of the Inner Temple (but hailed from the Gold Coast) may perhaps be connected with Josiah's friendship with Mr Desai, who had acted as Best Man at the Oldfield wedding.

The reference in the story to Sir James 'bustling out to his waiting car' may be an indication that Josiah relied on chauffeurs rather than driving himself. The real Josiah rode both a horse and a bicycle, but evidently did use a car at times. In a paragraph which makes clear to the readers of *The Mystery of Birth* that the author is a person of note, he wrote 'I well remember an old millionaire patient of mine with whom I was breakfasting...who offered me a cheque for £10,000'. Josiah considered the gift overnight, then turned it down, on the grounds that he was rich enough already to eat the food that he needed, to drink as much as was good, to dress as badly as he liked, and to order a car or carriage when needed.

Hugh Fickling's own views following the meeting with Dr Bateman are not recorded, nor is it known whether Josiah himself was made aware of the accusations. Certainly they do not seem to have impeded the further growth of his hospital, for in June 1913 the foundation stones for a new children's ward were laid. The ceremony took place in the setting of a garden party attended by some two hundred people. There was musical entertainment arranged by Mrs Perkins, (described as 'sister to Mr Sidney Beard, the founder of the Order of the Golden Age'); silver cups and certificates were presented to some of the nurses, and purses were presented to the treasurer. Further funds were raised via the sale of work stalls and those dispensing fruitarian refreshments. The proceedings closed with Compline in the chapel, at which the preacher was the Rev. Richard Lloyd Langford-James, DD. Vicar of St Mark's, Bush Hill Park, Enfield, he had ministered both in South Africa and in Cannes, and was the author of a *Dictionary of the Eastern Orthodox*

Church and of *The Church and Bodily Healing.*

Mr Gordon Allen, who acted as honorary architect to the hospital, had prepared the plans for the new ward, which would be 40' long and 15' wide. A start had already been made on the brickwork: as the *Bromley Record* puts it 'A portion of one of the walls was put up a year or two ago by patients, who will also help to build other parts'. The ward faced south-east and would have folding doors on that side; the roof would be of pantiles. But money remained a problem. A golden boot strategically situated beside the cot of the first patient, a small girl with a diseased hip, collected pennies, each of which purchased one brick. One particularly generous donor was Mr T.W.Rundell, who followed his purse of fifty pounds in June with a cheque for fifty guineas in August. Josiah took care to report this gift in the *Record* as 'an expression of approval of the hospital refusing to go into debt even for building purposes'.

Another gift became the subject of publicity material, in the form of a leaflet which would fit neatly into a small envelope. Entitled *A Legacy*, it acknowledged the generosity of Miss C.A.Cousins, who, having been a regular donor to the hospital for several years, had 'passed on to another world where the gold of earthly commerce is not current coin'. Her legacy to the hospital of £30 had been bequeathed because there was no vivisection there and because it refused to go into debt. Recipients of the leaflet were encouraged to follow her example. A collector's card from the same era has space for some twenty names: any collector whose subscribers' contributions amounted to a guinea or more was entitled to become an 'Annual Governor' while twenty-five guineas allowed the collector to name a cot. A list of subscriptions received printed on the back shows that these normally ranged from a shilling to a guinea.

The Matron at Bromley in its early years was Miss Louisa E.Sharpe, but in 1913 that position was filled by Miss Daisy E. Wilkins. Miss Wilkins was also Treasurer of the 'Margaret Samaritan Guild', which apparently succeeded the similar organisation promoted by Gertrude Oldfield several years earlier. Its aims and rules were almost identical, but the list of articles needed was wider. Tray cloths and small tablecloths were requested as well as more prosaic items such as bed-linen, towels, overalls and theatre stockings. There also existed at the hospital a 'School of Embroidery and Art Needlework'. By joining this poorer patients could help to earn their keep, producing fancy articles for sale at the bazaars or 'At Homes'.

The 'School of Embroidery'

Two years later only Josiah's name, in his capacity as senior honorary Medical Officer, was included in Kelly's listing of the Lady Margaret Hospital, but it is not clear whether this was for reasons of space in the directory or because there was a temporary vacancy for a Matron. By 1918 Miss Sharpe, together with the Hon. Florence Colborne, was acting as one of the hospital's honorary secretaries.

For those wishing to offer their services in a voluntary capacity Josiah had prepared an agreement. In consideration of the experience they would gain each volunteer would undertake to carry out loyally and faithfully all orders given by the Warden or any member of staff appointed by him, would not disclose any information about patients or staff, and in the event of death, disease or injury, would have no claim against the hospital or its staff. The period of service could be terminated by a week's notice on either side.

A rather more formal agreement was made between the Margaret Nursing Home Limited and its resident nurses. An account of what it was like to be trained as a Nurse there is contained in a short pamphlet, *Bromley Local History No.1* (1976). Mrs M.K.Batten was only twenty when she entered in 1915, and on arrival was given a new name, Nurse Beatrice, at Josiah's whim. The Lady Margaret Hospital by this time had 40 beds and cots. There were apparently no other doctors, nor was there a Matron, but it was staffed by two Sisters re-christened Celia and Rosamond, and several other young girls, two of whom had been renamed Pomona and Ceres. The other staff consisted of a paid Secretary, an elderly Irish cook and a gardener. At this time Josiah, now in the RAMC, was stationed in Norfolk, but occasionally he spent time in residence at the Hospital: on these visits he would say grace in Latin before meals.

The four-year training was not only in nursing, but covered also cooking, secretarial duties and household chores. These were carried out by the nurses in rotation, two to four weeks at a time, for the only paid help was a charwoman who came in one day a week and a boy who did odd jobs. Mrs Batten remembers no salary, and if a trainee opted to leave before her course ended, she was liable to pay £5. (A copy of an agreement I have seen gives the penalty as ten guineas - but it also stipulates that a trainee would receive a payment of £5 at the end of the first year, £10 on completion of the second and £15 at the conclusion of the third. This agreement probably dates from about 1904). Nurses were also required to supply their own thermometer, scissors, handbook of physiology and uniform, the most memorable item of which was a dark green cloak with cape attached at the shoulders, all piped in scarlet.

Sleeping accommodation was in the attic, which had been divided by wooden partitions into cubicles, furnished with beds made of straw, and these were refilled by the gardener when necessary. The fruitarian diet was strictly observed, but this does not appear to have been the main reason why many of the trainees 'escaped' as soon as possible to orthodox hospitals with a recognised Nurse Training School. (Such schools only accepted

153

girls who were over 21.) In cookery at least the training was adequate, for at the 'Universal Food Cookery Exhibition' held at the Horticultural Hall in 1913 nurses from the Lady Margaret Hospital were awarded two silver medals, one bronze, and two certificates in the sections devoted to 'Fruitarian Dinners' and 'Fruitarian Invalid Trays'. The report in the *Bromley Record* adds that this was the fourth year in succession that Margaret nurses had secured high awards. What it does not tell us is how many other establishments entered these classes... Apparently most of the patients were meat-eaters when admitted at Bromley, but with few exceptions they found the food supplied to be quite acceptable.

The Refectory

Had they not done so, they would have gone hungry. The third of the 'Rules for patients' says 'No patient is allowed to bring or to accept or receive in any way any article (however small) of food, or drink, or sweets, or fruit, or tobacco without the Sister's permission'. Nor could they try to augment their diet from any local shop, for rule 2 reads 'No patient is allowed outside the grounds except for very special reasons, and then only with the Sister's permission'. The remaining rules referred to visiting, confined to Wednesday and Sunday afternoons, with no more than two visitors on one day; and to what was to be brought in by the patient. This list was short, comprising clean brush and comb, a towel, a pair of slippers, and two pairs of socks or stockings. Such rules sound draconian by today's standards, but similar restrictions lasted in most hospitals for another fifty years.

As well as the public wards there was a private nursing home in the same part of the building as Josiah's own living quarters, where a large number of rooms, extensive gardens and lawns (including one which was secluded so that patients might go walking barefoot) were available at fees from two guineas upwards. Nurses were also sent out to attend private cases at their homes, but if they found such work more to their taste than the regime at the hospital the agreement which they had signed when entering Josiah's employ forbade them from taking permanent posts with such patients for at least two years after leaving the Lady Margaret Hospital. From Bromley patients often moved to Doddington to convalesce, and after 1920 all cases were treated there. The Bromley establishment was closed down when its premises were taken over as a club for ex-service men. 'Carn Brae' became a boys' preparatory school.

The fact that Josiah's entry in the Medical Directory for 1921 continues to show one of his appointments as 'Senior Medical Officer and Warden and Walker Lecturer on Dietetics, Lady Margaret Hospital, Bromley' illustrates that reference books cannot always be relied upon for accuracy. The Duke of York opened the Bromley Ex-Servicemen's Club on 18th November 1920: a photograph of this occasion is on display at the Club today. The title of 'Walker Lecturer in Dietetics' is intriguing, for this must surely be the 'Margaret Scholarship in Humane Dietetics' endowed by Miss Walker in about 1908, open both to medical students and to qualified medical men. Was Josiah the only holder?

The former Lady Margaret Hospital, Bromley
Now the United Services Club

A central feature of the hospital at Bromley, and later of that at Doddington, was a Chapel. At Bromley it was positioned between the women's and the men's (later babies') ward, and was probably built early in 1909. News of an 'At Home' in May that year, hosted by Mr and Mrs Stanley Churton, two of the hospital's most generous friends, mentions the 'beauty of the little chapel just erected'. Mr Churton, of Grove Park, who was then Hon. Treasurer, presented an organ, formerly at Borden Church. He died soon afterwards, and a tablet to his memory was erected in the chapel in 1911.

A feature much prized by Josiah was the new chapel's stained glass window, based on his own plan, and designed and executed by Mr Len Howard. An article in the local *District Times* in 1920 reads:

'The "Margaret" window is allegorical of the triumph of Nature's healing powers over the evil forces of disease. Just as the saint slew the dragon of sin by the cross-hilted sword of redemption, so the lady of healing slays the dragon of disease by the spear fashioned from the succulent stem filled with potent juices, and tipped with

156

an apple-shaped head, symbolical of the vital force embosomed in the ripened and kindly fruits of the earth... The main drawing is surrounded by rich detail work typifying the light breaking upon a dull world, the wisdom of the East being taught to the children of the West, and the glory of the garden of Ardath, where the prophet fed on fruits and flowers, and so prepared for communion with the Divine'.

The window was dedicated by Rev. R.Lloyd Langford-James on 28th June 1913.

The windows of the Chapel have now been bricked up

Josiah composed his own Evening Hymn for use in the chapel, but the only extant copy is much torn and stained. I have guessed at the missing sections, (bold) but hope that the sense is maintained:

Peace of the night has come
Even is here
Now is the sense of home
Freedom from fear.

Rest ends our weary **toil**
Sleep gently f**alls**
Cleansed be **all who dwell**
Inside **these walls.**

Safe then in God's own arms
Pillow thy head
Safe from all wild alarms
Rest in thy bed.

Angels shall guard thee here
God's name be blest
Spirits of love are **near**
Sleep sound and rest.

Josiah's Evening Hymn

Chapter 20

The Fruitarian 'Colony' at Doddington

Although adjacent to Epping Forest, the Lady Margaret Hospital at Bromley had restricted grounds of its own. Josiah now found space to expand his vision at Doddington in Kent, which was completely rural.

The Main Street at Doddington

The hamlet of Greet, where Josiah had bought a former farm and associated buildings, lay an isolated further two miles from that village's centre and here he foresaw a 'Fruitarian Village' with bees, poultry, fruit, vegetable and flower farming. On these 200 acres, available for rent at £1 per acre, a small community of like-minded people would be established. Cottages would be put up to suit tenants, or alternatively pioneers could acquire land freehold at £5 per acre on which they could grow crops or keep their hens or bees. No doubt Josiah aimed to make Doddington largely self-sufficient. 'Single rooms and bungalows may be hired from 2/6d per week' reads an early announcement. He achieved some success: a photograph, undated but probably taken before the First World War, shows an entire field devoted to lavender.

159

The Lavender Harvest at Doddington

Gritt (or Greet) Farm in 1881 had been occupied by William Clifford and his three sons, who presumably also worked on the farm. But by the time of the 1901 census the farm was empty, although Gritt Cottages were home to several agricultural labourers and their families. Little Gritt had its own fields and cottages: there were two other farms in this agricultural community which made up the area called 'Doddington (detached)'.

When Josiah first acquired Greet Farm the Oasthouse, which had an open front where farm carts were stored, was almost derelict. This structure was to become the hospital. A new front wall with a large window was built, and Josiah named the building 'Ellen's Court', possibly in honour of his sister. The reconstruction, and much subsequent building work, appears to have been carried out by workmen whom Oldfield recruited in London - skilled men who were genuinely out of work. Another building on the site, confusingly named 'Oriolet', was advertised as a 'quaint old-fashioned oak-timbered farmhouse, very attractive and quiet for artists and students'. There were also rooms available at 'Margaret Cottage - a charmingly appointed villa, a delightful restful home', and 'Margaret Lodge' - a bungalow.

A handwritten report by a Miss Hanson on pages from an

exercise book describes what she saw and heard on a visit to the 'Margaret Lodge Colony' in 1908. She met a foreman, who was 'one-eyed, he has left a drunken wife and goes by an assumed name', and two other bricklayers, a carpenter ('a drinker by nature, he gives way in London'), and a gardener. The conditions under which they were employed stipulated cleanliness in habits and ways, no meat, and no drinking or swearing while at work. The men had to be single, widowed or separated - there was no accommodation for families. Their quarters were clean but sparsely furnished, the beds consisting of wooden platforms with the chaff mattresses favoured by Josiah. They worked from 9.00 until 1.00, and from 2.00 until 5.30 (4.00 on Saturdays), and apart from their board and lodging they were paid 5/- weekly, of which 4/- was banked for them to collect on their return to London.

No books or amusements were provided, although 'Mr Warden', as Josiah liked to be known, said that he was quite pleased for them to have books and papers. 'Not novels, but he did not mind books on astronomy, or physiology, or geology (or any other -ology?), and he would always be glad of people to lecture to them'. Otherwise the men could occupy their free time by bringing in wood or other odd jobs... 'always a pleasure to them'. The employment of such men seems a good example of Josiah's usual mixed motives: a desire to refine and enrich their characters, thus advancing the coming of the Golden Age, while simultaneously getting work done for very little expenditure. One wonders how long men from Southwark would have wished to stay when they realised the extent of their isolation.

The original farmhouse had been pulled down, but the farm itself was under the direction of a local man, assisted by his 16-year old son and three other men who lived nearby, who received 15/- per week. Of its 200 acres only 40 were arable, the rest providing grazing for a small dairy herd (8 cows, 5 calves and a bull), 20 donkeys which were also kept for milking, pigs, and chickens. The well was worked by horse-power. Fruit, vegetables, eggs and milk were supplied to the hospital at Bromley, and also to 'a Convalescent Home at Broadstairs'. But why pigs at a farm owned by a strict vegetarian? Perhaps these were kept on land which had been sub-let.

At the time of Miss Hanson's visit, arrangements were being made 'by which an isolated bungalow and some woodland shelter will be devoted to the treatment of consumptive patients on Fruitarian lines, and also another house where, with plenty of sunshine and farm occupation, inebriate patients can be dieted, as experience proves that a right Fruitarian diet is one of the most important methods of combating the drink crave'. The only patient accommodation that Miss Hanson saw, however, was in a bungalow known as 'The Lodge', originally a pair of cottages. Now one half provided the kitchen, a nurse's room and a small adjoining apartment for a single patient, while the other half housed Dr Oldfield on the occasions when he stayed (generally Wednesdays), and three Londoners. The other workmen lived at a cottage on the other side of the farm. The Lodge had a glass-roofed verandah at the rear, so it was probably this which would house the consumptive patients when they appeared.

Miss Hanson was somewhat shocked to find that the Nurse was 'the only woman on the place - she looks after things generally, including any patient'. Her duties presumably included preparing meals for all the men, although they were expected to do their own mending. Even though each nurse stayed only a few weeks before being replaced by another 'from the Hospital', she must surely have found those weeks lonely and depressing, particularly in winter.

It was not only men, but boys too who came from London to work at the Colony. Organisations such as the Women's University Settlement would arrange for boys from the slums to spend time in the country to take advantage of fresh air and healthy outdoor exercise, and on paper at least Doddington sounded an ideal venue. But Miss Hanson wrote 'Boys get very ragged and neglected working at the colony due to lack of supervision... The committee of the Women's University Settlement had a boy there three months. He came home clean, but not neat. They would not send other boys under the present arrangement. Other committees sent boys who came home ragged and dirty.'

The Oasthouse, later known as 'Ellen's Oast'

Miss Hanson does not mention the oasthouse in her report, dated 22nd April 1908, unless this, rather than the establishment at Bromley, is what she meant by 'the Hospital'. Her remark about a single nurse implies that Ellen's Oast was not yet completely ready for use as a hospital.

Writing advertisements and brochures was one of Josiah's strengths. One dating from 1913, but still in circulation after the war, extols the virtues of Doddington's 200 acres, where 'pony and trap, riding horses, cows, goats, sheep, fowls, etc. are kept' and 'a number of houses and bungalows on the estate are let to nice tenants. Wooden huts, tents, hammocks in a wood etc. can be hired, with use of house for meals etc., from 10/6d per week inclusive. Board and residence can be had in a charming well-appointed villa from 30/-. Every comfort for an invalid from 2 guineas.' He went on to describe it as 'a lovely place for a real, restful, idle, hayfield holiday, or for those who are run down and want to get strong and well'. No doubt this was the country paradise imagined by those at the charitable organisation in Islington when they paid for a slightly tubercular patient named Mrs Sullivan to spend some time at Doddington. The reality was somewhat different. Mrs Sullivan returned to London

163

complaining that food and accommodation were bad: her sleeping quarters were in the middle of a field. 'The building was wooden and looked like an old barn - I thought they were taking me to a cowshed'. She was given a 'bath' which consisted of a quart of warm water in a bowl, the towel being hastily improvised from a nearby table cover, which was replaced, unwashed, after use! Her first meal consisted of tea, boiled onions and bread and jam.

Although Mrs Sullivan could see the funny side once she was back with her family (she had six children) in London, her story led to a full investigation. Sister Julia of St Silas's church enquired about "Sister Francesca, who had written to the Vicar offering to take in poor women for rest and change at 17/6 per week", a charge raised to £2.1s.0d. because of the tuberculosis. Hugh Fickling visited Mrs Sullivan and elicited further details of her stay at Doddington. Meals were never regular, dinner being served at any time between 12.00 and 1.30. Cooking was done over a wood fire, so that everything was smoked. Josiah's brochure had promised 'a plentiful dietary of farinacea, vegetables, fruit, milk, butter, eggs, and farmhouse produce'. That experienced by Mrs Sullivan and her fellow-guests reads more like the diet served to nineteenth century prisoners... Breakfast consisted of bread and margarine, porage oats, jam, tea or coffee. Dinner was boiled potatoes with 'some coloured stuff - very nasty - thrown over them'. Tapioca was coloured similarly. The stewed rhubarb was cankered and inedible; other puddings were made of 'bread, jam and spices'. There was little fresh green food, although supper might include some half-cooked peas or a small square of cheese. Not surprisingly, the patient failed to gain strength on this regime, and she was then given a glass of milk twice daily and some fresh eggs to supplement the usual food.

Perhaps Josiah should have introduced scriptural readings to accompany the meals. Writing in the 1920s *Eat and be Happy* he recalled the monastic tradition where 'the refectory was a place of mental peace, for one of the brethren would read aloud during meals so that those listening found it difficult to swear at lumpy porridge or burnt soup while they were listening to the voice of a saint...' He knew that a calm mind aided digestion.

Preparing a Salad

Can there be any excuse for such a regime? Josiah himself believed that many people ate far more than they needed, of the 'wrong' foods, and he himself probably thrived on the pulses, grains and vegetables on offer. The poor cooking is more easily explained, since it was done by two, perhaps freshly-recruited, 'nurses' probably more used to some form of stove rather than a wood fire.

Josiah advertised Doddington as a place where 'delicate boys who **want to learn farming** and girls who want to **learn fruitarian cookery** or nursing or dairying' would be welcomed, with the implication that they would pay for the privilege.

As well as Sister Francesca, who was in charge, and the two young nurses, those staying at Doddington in August 1913 comprised Mrs Sullivan and another consumptive patient, an alcoholic woman, a girl with nervous trouble who cared for a small boy who suffered up to twenty fits each day, two girls aged 12-14, two younger boys, an old paralysed woman who was confined to bed, and two or three other women. The accommodation ranged from Sister's relatively luxurious quarters in the Manor House (probably the building previously known as 'The Lodge') to a canvas tent and the wooden huts mentioned earlier. That occupied by the TB patients had 'a sort of zinc covering over each bed, but the rain came in', so that it was necessary to make use of an umbrella. Sanitary arrangements were extremely primitive, slops simply being thrown on the flower borders. This again would be in accordance with Josiah's beliefs. Mrs Sullivan remarked that there were plenty of fleas, possibly because of the chickens which wandered in and out of the buildings at will.

Josiah himself rarely appeared, perhaps once a week, for at this period he was preoccupied with the hospital at Bromley, and with his Territorial commitments. On a Sunday evening he gave the address at a short service, held in a room where there was a piano - presumably the Manor. Sister Francesca also took part. There were few other amusements; no books or papers, and magazines were passed on only after Sister had finished with them. For 'Townies' such deprivation may have been hard to bear.

Mrs Sullivan didn't like Josiah's looks: 'Too deep for me', she thought. Perhaps the dislike was mutual, for while he had a lot to say to some of his patients he dismissed Mrs Sullivan as 'too far gone - better at home'. Medical treatment was minimal, since Josiah had no faith in drugs, considering rest and fresh air beneficial in themselves. His attitude towards his poorer patients, though, does suggest that perhaps his ambition to be a gentleman and move in aristocratic circles might have begun to outstrip his early ideal of a golden age where men and women of all classes, having adopted the Fruitarian regime, would strive together to attain a higher state of being.

Chapter 21

The Fruitarian Philosophy

The Fruitarian Society's aims appear on the opening page of a booklet entitled *Fruitarian Diet and Physical Rejuvenation* by the Australian practitioner Dr.O.L.M.Abramovski*, a contemporary of Josiah. This was available from the 'Essence of Health Publishing Company' in Natal, South Africa, and although the text dates from about 1908, this particular edition was certainly produced after 1946, and possibly as late as 1974, when it reached the British Library's shelves. Its author, like Josiah, was firmly in favour of raw food, stating that cells need **vitality**, which can only come from living material. He advocated what he called rational assistance to Nature, in the form of fresh air whose oxygen was needed to convert food to energy, and free internal and external use of water and fruit juices. These acted as carrying and dissolving agents for impurities, and sometimes it was as well to abstain from solid food altogether to promote the cleansing process.

Another proponent of a similar healthy vegetarian regime was Dugald Semple, who in his book *The Sunfood Way to Health* of 1956 provided detailed menus based almost entirely on raw food. His suggestion for an evening meal consisted of a green salad of lettuce, cress, tomato and sliced raw onion plus some milled peanuts or hazel nuts and a few dates or raisins. This might be varied with a few ounces of flaked oatmeal or whole wheat, taken with dried currants which had been soaked overnight.

*Abramovski was only in his late sixties when he died in 1911, and there were plenty to conclude that his change to a Fruitarian diet at the age of fifty contributed to his decline. His widow was anxious to discount such claims, writing 'Inadequate support of his ideas and his 'Sanitorium' [near Melbourne] resulted in a severe financial failure, quite unexpected and unprovided for by the sanguine Doctor, whose every thought was but the benefit of humanity at large'. Having had to abandon his work [he had a Fruitarian hospital at Mildura], he lost interest in life and neglected himself.

167

The Fruitarian Society.
(FOUNDED 1900)

155 Brompton Road,

S.W.

Dear Sir,

There is an immense scope just now for the advocacy of Natural Living and for the extended use of Natural Food, and I am anxious to organise all those whose faith is strong in the rightness and the wisdom of living upon fruits, grains, nuts, vegetables, milk, butter, cheese and honey, so that their influence may be focussed upon a people that is asking how best to live and how best to help their country in its time of need.

It is important that simple recipes, plain rules of health, and commonsensed information about food and feeding should be widely spread.

We have a number of excellent Cookery Books from 1d. upwards, and leaflets also, but we want a greater variety to meet all needs.

How can you help?

1. You may give the weight of your name and nothing more. This will be helpful and will be welcomed.

2. You may join the Council and give advice when it is required.

3. You may write a leaflet or compile personally tried recipes or write a cookery book.

4. You may purchase and distribute copies of either leaflets or 1d. and 6d. cookery books.

5. You may write letters to newspapers or to clergy, heads of schools and colleges, or guardians, etc., pointing out the importance of a wisely selected Fruitarian dietary for the health of those under their care.

6. You may offer personal services in copying letters, packing and despatching parcels, etc.

7. You may send a subscription or donation.

Will you help under one of these headings?

If you can say, "I am satisfied that most people would be better if they ate less meat and more fruits and garden produce," you are eligible to join the Society as a supporter.

May I ask for the favour of a line in reply in any case?

Yours faithfully,

Josiah Oldfield

President.

168

Those who wished to add potatoes to their diet might try grating them raw and mixing them with flaked peanuts, though Semple did acknowledge that baked potatoes were more palatable.

But he did not lay the same emphasis on apples as did Josiah and other Fruitarians, recommending only an occasional fruit meal. Where he and Josiah did concur might be summarised in his statement 'Woman must no longer be the slave of the kitchen range, but the free partner in man's higher progress to heights unknown. She must have more leisure to devote to the rearing of her children, and fuller opportunities to develop her own intellectual and artistic self-culture'. Today the Fruitarian Society's heirs also stress the importance of 'Raw Energy'. Modern equipment makes the preparation of fruit and vegetable juices a simple matter, and the time saved by eliminating cookery is valued by many a busy woman. The regime is also favoured by those seeking to lose weight...

'FRESH Network' is one example of a successor to the Fruitarian Society, the initials standing for 'Fruitarian Raw Energy Support & Help'. Founded in 1992, it is based on the idea that 'eating raw, unprocessed food is the fastest way to increase your intake of vital nutrients, many of which are destroyed by cooking and processing'. The recommended diet entails selecting from fruits, nuts, seeds, vegetables, legumes, grains and leaves: although Josiah had never heard the word 'detox' (nor would he, as a scholar, have cared for it), he would have concurred with the network's suggestion of a 'cure' to revitalise a sluggish system. Like its progenitor, FRESH offers speakers and events, produces pamphlets and cookery books, and a quarterly magazine giving details of local groups and advertising where specialised products can be obtained. Not all modern Fruitarians are as extreme in their views as the character in the film 'Notting Hill' who believes that since fruit and vegetables have feelings, cooking them is akin to murder.

Josiah's own efforts to promote the Fruitarian Society were life-long. An undated letter sent out in its name and signed by him announced that he was 'anxious to organise all those whose faith is strong in the rightness and the wisdom of living upon fruits, grains, nuts, vegetables, milk, butter, cheese and honey, so that their influence may be focussed upon a people that is asking how best to live and how best to help their country in its time of need'. The letter emphasized that simple recipes and plain rules of health (as prescribed to his patients), and commonsense information about food and feeding should be widely spread. Practical support of all kinds was sought. This might be given in the form of subscriptions or donations, by writing letters, leaflets or cookery books, by helping to pack and send parcels, or merely allowing their name to 'add weight'.

The exact period when copies of this communication were circulated is difficult to determine. On it the date of foundation of the Society is stated as **1900**, and the address given for reply is 155 Brompton Road, S.W. Post Office directories show this to have been occupied by the Order of the Golden Age between 1910 and 1939. The letter may have originated during the First World War, but the shakiness of the signature suggests that Josiah could have sent out copies when war once again threatened food supplies in 1939-45.

Henry Cocking

During the time he spent in London as a young man Josiah would have been familiar with the problems caused by excessive drinking, which he was quick to realise was often caused by the need for oblivion in the face of poverty and hardship. He and many other vegetarians pointed out that adoption of their diet could help to tackle drunkenness: grapes and apples replaced the craving for beer and whisky. Henry Cocking, a fellow-Fruitarian and close associate of Josiah, was the author of a pamphlet published in the 1890s by the Order of the Golden Age entitled *The Drink Problem and How to Solve It*. The booklets (even that called *Christmas Dishes)* which Josiah wrote at the same period do not mention alcoholic drink.

In a lecture given in 1913 Josiah challenged anyone to find a Vegetarian drunkard. As a practical exercise he had helped some men who were alcoholics by offering them work at Doddington, where they were able to take advantage of the Fruitarian regime

When lecturing on dietetics in the same year, Josiah had announced that as a Fruitarian he recognised three aspects of diet; sustenance, sufficiency and pure pleasure, represented by grain, oil and wine If the people of England were to live on grains and oil for six days they could drink wine on the seventh, enjoy it and feel all the better for it. But he considered that 'Spirits entirely, and wines and beers to any large extent, should be abstained from until we are over fifty', and he was entirely against the consumption of cocktails, especially by young women. Young ladies who indulged in this habit were to be regarded with suspicion.

What were the alternatives he offered? One was fruit juice, which he likened to the sap which gives life to plants. His assertion that 'There is food for the muscles in a magnum of fruit juice' is dubious, but what it did contain was vitamin C. The antiscorbutic properties of fresh fruit and vegetables had long been recognised, although the term 'vitamin' only came into use at the beginning of the twentieth century. Tisanes, prepared by simmering the fresh green parts of any edible plant (e.g. nettles, dandelion leaves, celery tops or spring cabbage) for half an hour in water, were another valuable source of vitamins, but in this case a wineglass of the liquor each morning was his recommendation. Chopped carrots could be treated in the same way.

171

For a longer drink Josiah gave his instructions for preparing 'Wheatenade'. A quarter of a pound of crushed wheat (or other grain) was to be sifted slowly into a saucepanful of boiling water and simmered for half an hour or so, stirring occasionally. Then the heat was to be increased until the liquid reached the consistency of thin starch. After straining 'the liquid, when cool, will form a rich jelly; mixed with water it will form a splendid nutritious drink'. For those with a slightly more ambitious palate it could be enlivened by the addition of a little lemon juice, and perhaps a little sugar or spice, thus providing something like proprietary lemon barley water. 'Apple tea', which was apparently particularly good for the kidneys, was prepared by pouring boiling water over a pound of chopped apples, then adding four cloves and an ounce of sugar. It is not clear how long the apples were to remain immersed - or whether they were to be eaten after consuming the liquor.

The last recipe comes from a pamphlet entitled *Apples and Health*, one of the 'Best Food' series written by Josiah during the 1930s and published in association with Gaymer's Cyder. Apples and water could be rather more appetising when fermented, but the sponsors, who held a Royal Appointment, were anxious to point out their product's medicinal value, in a text which, if not written by Josiah himself, certainly represented his views:-

'The action of cyder on the digestive organs is most beneficial, exercising a favourable influence on nutrition. Apples contain more phosphates than any other edible garden product. They also contain cane and fruit sugars, and a considerable amount of vitamins B and C. The acids of the apple, notably malic, are particularly valuable in eliminating noxious matters which lead to jaundice and certain skin diseases. Cyder may be therefore a preventative of those complaints which are due to a deficiency of potassium salts in the body.

'Under medical advice Gaymer's has been used with success in cases of Stone, Gravel, Diabetes, Scurvy, Dyspepsia, Constipation and Biliousness. It is an economical substitute for champagne, when this type of stimulant is advised for prostration following Influenza and Gastric Catarrh.   That obstinate complaint Rheumatoid Arthritis has been relieved by its regular use.   It has been specially advised to sedentary workers as the free phosphorus of the apple is available in its most easily assimilable form'.

According to a final paragraph the same very dry brands produced at Attleborough had been 'consistently prescribed for many years by the medical profession as antidotes to Gout and Rheumatism'.   Josiah was certainly responsible for the opening pages of the booklet, where he explained that consumption of apples could help to stem the craving for beer, for the malic acid they contained satisfied this unrealised need for acid. 'It is largely owing to the increased use of fruits, and especially of apples, amongst all classes of people during the last twenty years that the immoderate use of alcohol has so largely diminished', he wrote. And although he did not state as much, Josiah implied that the Fruitarian Society was largely responsible for the change. (Perhaps the licensing laws too had some effect).   There followed a paragraph or two referring to the story of Eve and the apple as a scientific allegory, rather than a myth, portraying how the fathers of the race progressed from brutish ignorance to human intelligence by selecting a Fruitarian Dietary of which the apple was the chief item.

Returning to the promotion of his sponsors' product, and suggesting that cyder might replace tea and coffee as a daily drink, Josiah pointed out that residents in cyder-making areas were largely free of kidney stone.   Apples lost their indigestible cellulose when converted to cyder, and he thought that the alcohol produced by fermentation helped the absorption of potassium salts and vitamin C. Cyder might well benefit those whose rather vague symptoms had been diagnosed as 'low vitality' or 'nervous debility'

The malic acid contained in apples apparently had a further effect in that it prevented clogging of the liver and fatty deposits in the blood vessels: apples prevented the 'stodginess' often encountered in those of declining years.   Josiah's frequent references to stemming the onset of old age led to reports of his lectures and speeches in newspapers abroad as well as in this country. The *New York Times* printed his prescription in 1919 of a diet including 'dandelion leaves, fowls' eggs, grapes, lettuce, cows' milk, watercress, honey and salads (uncooked)', and finished its report with the words 'Dr Oldfield considers that a normal person, rightly fed, should live from 90 to 105 years of age'.

The same paper, a few years later, carried another short summary of one of Josiah's London lectures, this time with the headline 'Ale as help to Longevity'. This was soon after the introduction of Prohibition. 'Life to the age of 150 years is within our grasp' it began. Perhaps the reporter felt that Josiah's view - that the consumption of home-brewed ale as part of his recommended diet, though not essential, was a potent factor in attaining long life - might help to rescind the veto on alcohol. Josiah had asserted that the vitamins in the barley of old home-brewed ale were responsible for the vigour of the English of the last five centuries. In Tudor times, he wrote, men oppressed by a monotonous rich diet of salt meat and cheese and rye bread had demanded the 'trifles' found in sprouting barley, and by regularly getting drunk on strong home-brewed ale, had saved their lives and kept up their stamina.

Chapter 22

Josiah's Military Career

During the period 1907-8, and in the light of what had been learned from the Boer War, major changes to the country's Volunteer soldiers had taken place. The whole force re-enlisted, and units were reorganised into a new Territorial Force. Josiah had become a Captain, second-in-command of a Company which had evolved from the Essex Volunteer Infantry Brigade Bearer Company. Originally formed in 1897 at the time of the South African War, it had a strength of 230 of all ranks ten years later.

In spite of all his other commitments, Josiah retained a keen interest in the Territorial Army, and on 6th January 1910 he was promoted to the rank of Major. It was in this capacity that he presented two papers to the United Services Medical Society, which met monthly. The first, published in April 1913, was entitled *Regimental and Field Ambulance Training in the Territorial Force*. At this period doctors could either become regimental medical officers, whose army service was largely confined to work with the sick and injured of the unit to which they were attached, or they could join a Field Ambulance. In his paper Josiah questioned whether regimental medical officers were being adequately trained in time of peace to perform their duties in a war situation. For officers attached to combatant units the first year's training consisted of eight days either at an RAMC(TF) school or a selected military institution, **or** at camp; fifteen days at camp in subsequent years, and one further RAMC(TF) course before promotion to Major. In practice these officers did not always attend an annual camp, so lacked the opportunity to learn the practical organisation of such basic elements as sanitation and disposal of waste, or the training of stretcher parties.

An RAMC Field Ambulance,
showing the uniforms worn by different ranks

Josiah took pains to summarise the **duties of the regimental medical officer,** 'the pivot on which the health of his unit depends, the right-hand man of the Commanding Officer...'

> To be responsible for medical and surgical stores, and for the proper discharge of their duties by the RAMC attached to the unit.
> To inspect the sick, knowing the routine for dealing with infectious diseases, and with accidents of varying severity.
> To assess the fitness of men for camp training.
> To train his staff in first aid to those injured in engagements, and in the rapid transfer of these cases to the Field Ambulance.
> To have a knowledge of map-reading, and the ability to select sites for aid-posts, with cover for the wounded.
> To be capable of judging time and distance accurately, and of understanding and transmitting orders.

Josiah's paper emphasised that when a doctor first attended a camp he scarcely had time to grasp how the army functioned before it was over. Since it was run largely by Army veterans the arrangements were all in place before the Battalion arrived, and the new recruit's attempts to learn might be thwarted. This suggests that Josiah had suffered personally, for he wrote 'Since he has no trained knowledge (the medical officer) does not know when to assert himself and when not to do so, and not infrequently the keen man gets snubbed into apathy because he either meddles at the wrong time, or with the wrong person, or with the wrong thing. Some permanent officials of a camp may think it easier to work without a trained medical officer, and therefore he may be encouraged to spend his energies on stretcher drill and seeing the sick, rather than on examining tents and lines, canteens and cookhouses, and putting stress on that pioneer form of drudgery which men naturally like to shirk'.

One can empathise with the feelings of men with many years of service to their credit, who had perhaps lived under canvas for months in South Africa, encountering a strange officer peering into the simmering porridge or measuring the length of the latrine trenches. One of Josiah's duties at camp was inspection of the men's rations, and his mention of tomatoes à propos of this in an article written in 1900 is an early reference to the fruit, not then commonly eaten.

According to Josiah's paper the regimental medical officer was much sought after when his services were required if a man fell sick or when an accident happened but was a 'nondescript' on parade. In contrast the officer commanding a Field Ambulance was a doctor amongst doctors, keen to train his junior officers to a peak of efficiency in all fields. These men were required to do thirty drills in their first year, fifteen in subsequent years, before going to camp, whereas a regimental MO need do none. The skills needed by a doctor in the army included riding: a field ambulance MO had to obtain a riding certificate, but the regimental MO, although allowed a horse, did not have to know how to ride it! Medical gentlemen attending a camp as part of a Field Ambulance would experience 'a delightful change - some hospital work, but a much larger amount of open-air exercise, drilling, teaching, inspecting, advising, horse-riding, the selection and pitching of camp, and the responsible control and administration of batches of men, and a position of weight and dignity'.

A more exact picture of a Field Ambulance was given by the newly-promoted Josiah when he was interviewed in Spring 1915:-

'When I was given this command my duty was to select and train nine officers, of whom at least seven must be doctors, and two hundred and nineteen soldier-nurses, and to take charge of and train the transport section. The transport of a Field Ambulance includes ten officers' chargers, ten ambulance wagons, six ordinary wagons, three carts, three water carts, and about thirty horses'.

Before the outbreak of war Josiah had recommended the 'delightful holiday'* enjoyed at camp, and the Territorial Movement generally, to the worried mothers who wrote to the Editor of *The Herald of the Golden Age* in 1912, fearing that their lads would be corrupted in such an environment. He assured them that the Territorial Army did not foster Jingoistic pride of race, creed or colour, and that the RAMC fought disease, pain and death with no distinction between friend and foe. They need have no worries about immorality at camp for a man was under constant observation, beginning with bugle-call at 5.30 followed by an hour's drill in the open air, 'learning to appreciate the smell of the dew-tipped grass as he crushes it under his feet...' Lectures and instruction filled the afternoon, while games or a sing-song occupied the evenings. Even if they visited local towns for entertainment men were likely to be seen and recognised by officers... Young men would benefit by developing 'smartness and cleanness, self-control and quietness, and respectful appreciation of superior merit and superior rank'.

From what he mentions concerning the rank of both types of territorial medical officer it can be deduced that Josiah had by 1910 been an officer of the Field Ambulance for several years. A regimental MO could not rise above the rank of Major, and if he were ambitious for promotion he would have been wise to have transferred to the Field Ambulance before being made Captain. Josiah had earlier served as a regimental officer and knew personally the deficiencies in the training offered, but now returned to that post with his regiment for part of the time spent at camp.

* 'A fortnight's mingled work and amusement, with travel, food and lodging paid, free medical attention and a daily allowance of between 1/- and 4/-.'

In the conclusion to his paper Josiah made several suggestions, the most important being that all volunteer medical officers should train with a Field Ambulance, and should all be encouraged to attend camp. He thought that the introduction of a brevet rank (whereby an officer was entitled to a rank above that for which he was paid) for men showing capability and special excellence would encourage keenness.

The officers who took part in the discussion following the delivery of Josiah's address largely concurred with his thoughts on the inadequacies of current training, but were themselves not necessarily willing to help. Major Waggett, for one, said 'We in the field ambulances have a very jolly time at present, and I hope you will not spoil it by adding on regimental work as well. There is only a fortnight to learn in, and it would only spoil our chance of becoming efficient in one direction if we were to attempt to train on another line at the same time'. Josiah gave these remarks short shrift - he was appealing for **training**, not just for a pleasant or merry time.

Colonel Harper, one of the senior officers present, remarked that meetings like that now in progress offered one opportunity for regimental officers to meet their brother officers, a chance they rarely had when serving at camp. Colonel James deplored the absence of a book detailing the regimental MO's duties: Josiah hoped he might be persuaded to compile one. In his final summing-up Josiah made a telling statement - when acting as a regimental medical officer he had always found the commanding officer to be 'kind and gentle to the MO, and willing to oblige him **in everything except in carrying out his recommendations**'. But he was confident that many medical men, once having trained with the Field Ambulance, might be persuaded to volunteer as regimental officers because they would then realise the breadth of opportunity offered by working with a battalion, and would themselves be appreciated as useful comrades.

A year later Josiah reiterated his views on the training of medical officers in a second paper, *The Scope of the Field Ambulance as a Training School* (RAMC Journal XXII, 685; 1914). Attendance at another camp at Maldon in 1913 had reinforced his belief that only in a Field Ambulance could a volunteer grasp all that was entailed in serving as a doctor with the Territorial Force. Josiah thought that when encamped, the field ambulance should supply an officer to each battalion so that these men could 'compare notes, learn experience, and gain the stimulus of competition by meeting constantly with fellow medical officers posted to other battalions, and fellow officers working in the field ambulance'.

His other main point was that stretcher bearers, men responsible for purification of water, and those charged with disposal of waste, should all be under the command of the field ambulance. Stretcher bearers, who normally served as bandsmen, were a particular thorn in Josiah's flesh, for they were responsible to the battalion commanding officer, not the regimental medical officer. King's Regulations stipulated only two per company, so that a regimental medical officer had only two men to train except at battalion drill. But then the OC wanted them in **his** ranks. Josiah likened the difficulty of 'capturing a reluctant bandsman for ambulance drill when his whole soul is yearning for undisturbed practice on the trombone' to catching a shadow.

Perhaps not everyone agreed with his priorities. At Maldon Josiah had arranged his aid posts, his dressing station, the lines of carriage to the nearest village and the nearest station, and had the assistance of a Red Cross detachment, but felt that 'the whole scheme lacked the pivotal regimental medical officers and regimental stretcher bearers, so that in real warfare there would have been a serious hiatus'. He was aggrieved that the general who reviewed the day's activities did not comment on this deficiency. (Regimental medical officers, generally busy GPs, were not necessarily all as keen on attending camp as Josiah himself.) Nevertheless Josiah's enthusiasm and practical suggestions no doubt contributed to his later promotion. Reginald Payne was a later member of a Territorial Unit, who wrote of his experiences in his autobiography *The Watershed*. While he could appreciate the necessity of the 'daily routine of drill or PT in the streets, trench-digging, lectures and demonstrations on machine-guns and hand-grenades, route marches and Saturday night visits to the YMCA' he found bayonet practice sickening. It is difficult to see how Josiah, who abhorred cruelty to animals, could have endured it.

When war broke out in 1914 Josiah, now with the rank of Lieutenant-Colonel, was instructed to form a second line of the 3rd East Anglian Field Ambulance RAMC. Of this period Josiah recounted that drafts of men were constantly being transferred from other divisions to his command for training, and for preparation for further service in the winning of the war. When he welcomed each new draft Josiah took pains to point out that each man brought with him a 'defaulter's sheet', or character credential, so that his past crimes accompanied him wherever he went. But now, he told them, 'you have come to a new world, and however badly you may have behaved in your past service, you start with me entirely afresh, with no black marks against you, but with the possibility of gaining fresh good marks every day. Now, then, is your opportunity to become great soldiers and, still more, great men'. Their previous records would be filed away in a sealed envelope without being read by Josiah himself, by any other officers or by the Sergeant Major. The company history of the 3rd East Anglian Field Ambulance records how some of his men regarded their commander:-

'He set about the task in such a way that it drew recruits from all the four corners of England. All sorts and conditions came in answer to his advertisements...finding a glorious muddle at first...' Headquarters was the Drill Hall at Walthamstow but once the skeleton of a unit had accumulated, there was a transfer to Burleigh Castle, Stamford, as "guests of the Marquis of Exeter". Who that was there will ever forget that arrival in the dark, and the Colonel's address impressing upon us that as guests of one so noble we must be on our best behaviour... They were beautiful stables, even if somewhat mouldy and musty from long disuse, but as dormitories - well, they left much to be desired, while as mess-rooms on cold wet December days they fully merited the curses showered upon them.

'It was a rude awakening from the dreams of many of us...It was there that we learned that a diet of apples, onions and cheese really did provide the necessary stamina to enable us to amble round country lanes and develop our leg muscles, or to do various company drills... Who remembers the Colonel taking the officers for a long double round the park as an aid to their digestions?

(Sometimes during Church Parade) 'it was so cold that the Colonel gave the order to mark time as we sang hymns... No-one was sorry when just after Christmas we received orders to move to Peterborough. We entered the town as a mob, but six months later left as a fairly well-organised unit, although as all NCOs were still "temporary, acting, without" there was not a lot of enthusiasm... How many will remember...the famous "Cabbage Patch", where on a diet of nuts and onions they learned to brush and scrub in order that they might become really efficient ward orderlies? To those possessed of a love of chance there was a source of constant enjoyment, for the odds were about even whether one found oneself billed in Orders as Colonel's batman or Sergeant-Major... "without", of course.

'About Easter 1915, after having speculated on how we should like being sent to nearly every spot on the globe, we finally prepared to go into camp at Thetford... As for most of us it was to be our first camp there was a good deal of excitement about. Very soon after our arrival Lt.Col Josiah Oldfield left us and his place was taken by Major Rudyard, who did not favour a "temporary, acting, without" establishment, and affairs soon became very much more settled.'

Reading between the lines it seems that the fruitarian diet was not universally popular, and that Dr Oldfield's organisational skills were not entirely in accord with those required by the army.

This was evidently not the only bone of contention. Josiah had recruited numerous Conscientious Objectors to his Field Ambulance, men who were willing to work as bearers or to carry out menial duties, but not to kill. When more and more fit men were being drafted to active units Josiah had much correspondence with the War Office, and 'I eventually got the men's claim recognised, namely, that they had enlisted relying on my word that they should not be called upon to fight. So to the end of the war they did fine service to their country and to humanity'. Some indeed were to win decorations.

Fellow vegetarians, however, did appreciate their commanding officer. Letters published in the *Vegetarian Messenger* in March 1915 from two men of the 3rd (Reserve) East Anglian Field Ambulance, 2nd Line, report that special Fruitarian food had been provided for them. One described how three months training in the unit had made him much fitter and stronger. The other wrote 'As this unit is going on foreign service under the command of Josiah Oldfield I think no vegetarian need hang back for fear of having to relax his principles should he join this unit'.

The same magazine printed an interview with Lieutenant-Colonel Oldfield himself the following month, and the relevant paragraph on Fruitarian diet is worth reproducing in full:-

'If a Fruitarian enlists', he answered, 'he must be prepared, like every good soldier, to suffer hardships. The rations of an army cannot be altered to suit an individual. So a man must take what he can get, and, if need be, live on bread and butter and potatoes, with a piece of cheese occasionally! He must be willing to work as hard and as keenly as his fellows, and not grumble. Before long he will find everybody willing to help him. His pay of 10/6d per week - with no expenses - permits him to supplement his rations with dried fruits, dates, and nuts and cheese; also fresh fruit occasionally, a bunch of watercress, or a tin of pine chunks. After a man has passed his examination in anatomy, physiology and First Aid bandaging and nursing, his pay is increased by 4d. per day. So soon as he has proved that he is not a faddist, but a keen soldier with a conscience, which will not allow him to eat meat, the Quartermaster will be found only too willing to put an egg on his plate when others are having bacon, and to see that butter, cheese, wholemeal bread, figs, apples,and such like find their way to him wherever possible'.

Whether all Quartermasters would be as accommodating is open to question. Another vegetarian writing of his five years spent in

France during the war years comments that he had not fared too badly. Wholemeal bread was what he missed most, but some army biscuits closely resembled it. Army bread tended to be at least a week old, and 'not infrequently slightly mouldy about the crust and cracks'. Bread or biscuit, margarine, sugar, cheese and jam were usually plentiful enough, dried fruit was occasionally supplied, but there never seemed to be enough potatoes or other vegetables. He was able to buy 'extras' from the canteen or from local civilians, and sometimes fruit was to be found in the gardens of otherwise devastated villages. But he was an officer, and acknowledges that the difficulties, had he been in the ranks, would have been much greater.

Josiah with Vegetarian Soldiers at Burleigh Castle

Perhaps it is relevant to quote here from *The Crown of Grapes*. This was available at 6d per copy, or 2/6d for six, in 1952, but it was probably written at about the time of the **first** World War, or even earlier.

'The armies that have carried the British flag to conquest and glory have been recruited from the yeoman and peasant class. This class, from poverty and stress of fortune, have for generations been chiefly Fruitarian in fact, and it is only during this generation that the advent of potted and foreign meat and the general rise of wages has enabled the wage-earning portion of the community to put into practice the false precepts that have been hammered into them, that it is beef that makes the man and game the gentleman. Further still, the pick of the army have always been the Scotch and Irish regiments, and no-one disputes that the dietary of the one has for many generations been drawn from the oat plant and of the other from the potato and the Indian corn and the buttermilk.'

As war broke out in 1914, Josiah had written two articles in the *Herald of the Golden Age*, the now quarterly magazine reflecting the views of many Fruitarians who sought a happier and more spiritual world. The first was headed 'The Lesson of War' and spoke of 'the spirit of fierce tigerism' disheartening the dreamers of beautiful dreams. Were there any lessons for those who believe in Peace? Josiah had two answers - the first his conviction that the surgeon had assumed the mantle formerly worn by the priest, in war proclaiming a higher ideal than patriotism; the second that endurance of the bitter agonies of war taught courage and self-sacrifice, schooling the soul and enabling it to reach a higher level.

Josiah's second article, published in the next issue of the *Herald*, was entitled 'Our Duty to the Coming Race'. Its message was simple: 'It is well for the bravest and best of our soldiers to marry before they go out to the battle... to leave behind children who will be doubly brave and trebly faithful to that dear Motherland for which their fathers died'.

It seems evident from the soldier's letter quoted earlier that Josiah was fully expecting to go abroad with his unit, prepared to serve under fire if necessary and to do what he could for sick and injured men regardless of race, religion, nation or colour. And did he practise his recommendation to leave behind children, though outside the bonds of marriage? Rumours about a 'tribe of little Oldfields' persisted during the twenties and beyond.. In fact he would officially have been too old for overseas service and would probably have been retained at the Unit's Headquarters Depot to recruit and train the third and fourth lines when the first and second went abroad.

Was this a source of disappointment - perhaps even leading to depression? Although still listed as an officer in 1916 he was eventually invalided out, with authority to retain his rank (as was usual for officers ranked Major or above). According to the 1926 edition of *Kelly's Directory* covering Doddington, Josiah had become a full Colonel, but this error was corrected in subsequent years.

A Field Hospital in England

He was awarded the Territorial Decoration (following twelve years of service, wartime years counting as two), and his *Who was Who?* entry records 'Mentioned in Dispatches' - but most commanding officers received at least the DSO. This suggests that his war service was relatively short, although for a period he was in command of a 200-bed clearing hospital in East Anglia. He says in one of his later books that he was in medical charge of an Irish Regiment on the East Coast in 1917. His daughter Josie, then an eleven-year old schoolgirl, wrote of visiting Lowestoft in January that year with a friend, playing on the beach in the morning, but staying 'with Daddy for the afternoon'. That evening, and on the following Sunday, she 'helped Daddy by tearing up a lot of old letters'. One envelope - without contents -

186

survived this exercise: it was addressed to Lt.Col. J.Oldfield at Oulton Broad, Lowestoft. Daddy was evidently still in England at the end of April 1917, when the diary entries cease.

Josiah was proud of his health and vigour, but he too was sometimes ill. He writes in *The Mystery of Birth* 'I have gone through several serious illnesses. I know the stark agony of the sharp steel cutting through sensitive tissue. I have endured the long sleepless nights wherein there was not a moment of peace; wherein even drowsing sleep only for a moment dulled the agony; where consciousness kept tearing its way through the exhaustion of unconsciousness into the vivid flames of an unquenchable hell...' It appears that mastoiditis was one such illness, and an operation for piles is also implied. He had been troubled by these even while still at Oxford: 'One summer when I was an undergrad (sic) I went for a week into the hayfield... Heat and unaccustomed exertion meant that I drank very much tea and lemonade... Before the week was over I was greatly troubled with discomfort at the anus...' The problem had recurred when the heat of the Indian plains had caused him to drink far more than usual. The curse of such a painful and miserable complaint meant that he could not sit, stand or lie, eat nor sleep, think, read or write. He described this attack as a long drawn-out ceaseless misery, one long intolerable agony. The problem usually subsided when he cut down severely on the liquid consumed, but this could not have effected a complete cure.

1st Eastern General Hospital

In *Get Well and Keep Well* Josiah writes 'there is no treatment so soothing for the acute pain of inflamed piles as to sit upon a chamber of very hot water and let the whole part be immersed'. The next paragraph describes how, while attached to the 1st Eastern General Hospital at Cambridge, he 'personally tested the effect of the perpetual hot bath into which wounded soldiers with painful septic wounds were placed and left day and night for days together. As an experience, I decided to spend the night in a bath. The Sister prepared for me a delightful little supper, which I ate while I was immersed...' This experiment no doubt added to Josiah's reputation as something of an eccentric.

It is not certain exactly when he left the army. In March 1918, when writing to the Editor of the journal of St Bartholomew's Hospital, he gave his address as 'Fort Pitt Hospital, Chatham', so perhaps it was then that he became a patient, recovering from a mastoid or other operation. He had not lost his sense of humour, however, for his letter reads:-

'When raising a Field Ambulance in 1914, one applicant wrote "Sir, I should like the honour of enlisting in your Ambulance. I want to join the RAMC. I am a butcher by trade, and if you accept me I could bring my tools with me and carry on." Whether he meant as a cook in the men's mess, or as a surgical assistant on the staff, or whether he thought we should work in Germany I never discovered.'

In *Eat and Keep Young* of 1928 he tells his readers 'When I was invalided out of the Army in 1918 I was supposed to have but a year longer to live... so I... worked and rested the livelong summer days in the open woods with the skin exposed to the sky light, and continued that summer habit all through the winter in the balmy air of Jamaica'. *The Times*, on Nov.18th 1920, reported that 'Dr Josiah Oldfield has left England for Jamaica where he will study the effects of some tropical fruits on constitution, digestion and endurance, and the effect of intense sunbaths and airbaths on certain forms of disease.'

188

Ward at 1st Eastern General Hospital

Fort Pitt Hospital at Chatham had originally been built at the beginning of the nineteenth century as a fort, part of the ring of defences protecting the Dockyard, but it had gradually been converted to a military hospital. During the Crimean War new wards were erected, Queen Victoria had visited the wounded there, and Florence Nightingale selected it as a temporary site for the first Army Medical School - the forerunner of the RAMC. In 1910 the central tower of the fort was demolished, providing space for a new wing. Construction of this was completed just before the war began, and it was probably here that Josiah was housed since it incorporated an area reserved for Officers (Ward 22 on the first floor), as well as a new operating theatre.

The kitchen too was new, with both closed coal ranges and gas cookers, and a number of 'large steam boilers, each holding 200 pints, for soups, meats and puddings'. Four meals were served daily, based on 200lb meat and 50 chickens, and, more to Josiah's taste, 200 lb of mixed vegetables and cabbage, and 200lb of potatoes (peeling these occupied four men for an hour and a half each morning). There is no mention of fruit... As well as housing 550 patients in 1915 the hospital employed a staff of about twenty medical officers, nearly fifty sisters and close to five hundred NCOs and orderlies.

According to a booklet *Comforts for the Wounded in our Hospitals* prepared by the staff at Fort Pitt 'The wounded invariably enter smiling... Comforts, manly sympathy and

189

entertainments keep them smiling.... Every day some form of entertainment is provided... Theatrical performances, variety entertainments, concerts vocal and instrumental... take place in the wards in turn...' Whether Josiah, with his inquiring mind and philosophical tastes, would have appreciated artistes from the Chatham Empire or Barnum's Palace of Varieties is questionable. Although there is no doubt that he liked to see pretty women about him he did not approve of cosmetics, which would have enhanced the charms of the female artistes on the hospital's movable stage.

Fort Pitt ceased to be a hospital in 1922, and is now a school. Many of the buildings remain in use, the 'rounded corners' in some rooms revealing their origin as wards where hygiene demanded the absence of dirt-traps.

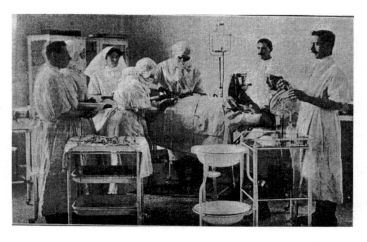

The Operating Theatre at Fort Pitt Hospital

Chapter 23

Margaret Hall, Tulse Hill and Lawn House, Broadstairs

It was mentioned earlier, when discussing staffing at Bromley, that Miss Sharpe was replaced as Matron there in about 1913. The reason for her temporary absence from that hospital is explained by the existence of yet another establishment set up by Josiah. This was at 71 Upper Tulse Hill, Streatham. Its exact history is unclear, for the premises are listed variously in the Post Office directories:-

1913	Henry Edmund
1915	No entry
1916	Lady Margaret Hospital, Miss L.E.Sharpe, Hon.Sec.
1917	Mrs Maude Daniel, Boarding House
1918-20	Lady Margaret Hospital, Miss L.E.Sharpe, Hon.Sec.
1921	No entry
1922	Miss Kate Birnstingl, Boarding House

The 1917 entry is puzzling, but perhaps Mrs Maude Daniel acted in the same capacity as Mrs McCowan had at Bromley, nominally in charge of the nursing home but subsidised by Josiah. Or it may simply be a mistake in the entry. Although Miss Sharpe is listed by the Post Office directories as the Secretary, brochures for the home at 71 Upper Tulse Hill required applications for places to be made to Miss Thomas.

These undated brochures, which style 71 Upper Tulse Hill as 'Margaret Hall Nursing Home', describe it as

'a beautiful house, fitted up and furnished with all the comforts and privacy of a private house, and with all the things that are needful for an up-to-date Nursing Home. It is on high land; very open; has large gardens, greenhouses, vinery, summer houses, etc.; electric light.

Patients can have absolute privacy and seclusion with a private room and a special nurse, and need not see anyone or be seen by anyone, or they may join in the general life of the Home and use

191

the drawing and dining rooms, and piano and the lovely garden, and may have friends to call in, or may have their friends put up in the Home, so as to be companions during the "cure", or the "operation", or the time of convalescence, whichever it may be.'

Other advantages of Margaret Hall were the convenient transport possibilities, for Brixton, Herne Hill and Tulse Hill stations all lay within a mile and a half, and trams and buses to Streatham and Norbury passed close by. Brockwell and Ruskin Parks, tennis clubs and swimming baths were also within easy reach. For all these conveniences the terms ranged from three to seven guineas a week for a private room, exclusive of fires in the bedroom, medical fees or the attentions of a special nurse. Occasionally a small room at two guineas was available, or the same amount secured a place within the 'open-air verandah'. Cheapest was a bed in a small ward at 30/- per week.

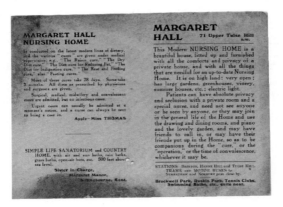

Brochure for the Margaret Hall Nursing Home

Most unusually for anything connected with Josiah, the word 'Fruitarian' does not appear. Instead the 'latest modern lines of dietary' were available, and 'cures' of various kinds, normally expected to take a month but sometimes considerably longer, were offered under medical supervision. As at Bromley no infectious cases could be admitted, but 'surgical, medical, midwifery and convalescent' patients were welcome, even at short notice (Telegrams 'Pitiful, London'). The earlier reference to patients who wished to maintain complete privacy makes one wonder whether Josiah also took in those with slight mental problems, as he was to do in later years at Margaret Manor. The latter receives a brief mention in the Margaret Hall brochures, being advertised as a 'simple life sanatorium and country home' offering air and sun baths, rain and grass baths.

By 1920 the charges for all forms of accommodation at Margaret Hall had risen, with the minimum cost of a private room now four guineas, and the home was described as 'the paying wards of the Lady Margaret Hospital, Bromley' on its stationery. Perhaps the price rises contributed to the home's demise, but there may have been other causes.

Although the wording of the brochures implies that the expected guests would be adults this was apparently not always the case. It seems that Margaret Hall was one of the places selected by a group of charitable organisations to send 'deserving cases', including children, for a week or two of rest and recuperation. Towards the end of 1918 a division based in Putney and Wandsworth which sought information by telephone about Margaret Hall from their main office was told that it was 'a Branch Home of the Lady Margaret Hospital' and advised to have nothing to do with it, perhaps because of the vegetarian food supplied, or possibly because there were rumours about Josiah's affairs. News of this advice prompted a letter in the home's defence from Countess Ferrers, who wrote 'I mentioned at some meeting that I used the above home from time to time .... our experience has been wholly satisfactory. We **only** use the various homes, Bromley, Sittingbourne, Tulse Hill as **guest homes**, never in any question of **health**. In sudden illness of mothers and other catastrophic happenings when the children are stranded we whisk the children away and they come back well - smiling and flourishing. Such parents as have seen Tulse Hill are most satisfied and serene. It is of course most blessed by near(by) Southern districts.' The Countess went on to counter complaints about the food: 'As to Vegetarianism - most of us are that perforce nowadays'.

Rather later, in 1932, the same source of allegations about Josiah and his hospitals has a brief note from B.E.Astbury saying 'Chief Inspector Grey, NSPCC, called re a complaint of a serious nature concerning a child at Margaret Manor. I told Inspector Grey what we knew of Dr Oldfield'. Whatever the complaint was, it was not upheld. There is nothing in the NSPCC Legal Archive concerning Margaret Manor or Josiah.

Some brochures for Josiah's hospitals at Bromley and Doddington also refer to a Convalescent Home at Broadstairs, named Lawn House. Eggs and milk were being sent there from Doddington in 1908. Reference to the 1901 Census show that it was adjacent to Harbour Street: the enumerator's listing being:-

6 Harbour St
13, 15, 17 Harbour St
11 Harbour St
Lawn House
7 Union Square
2 Harbour St

At that time it was recorded as 'Family House, family absent'. It was a contemporary of the Camberwell premises, for these and 'Lawn House, Broadstairs, (Dickens' old house, overlooks sea, Convalescence and Recuperation)' are both listed in a version from 1910-11. Dickens spent many holidays at the resort between 1836 and 1849, residing variously in lodgings at 31 High Street, 40 Albion Street, **Lawn House** in 1841, Chandos Place and Fort House. *Kelly's Directory* in its 1900 edition lists 'Lawn House', (then occupied by Frederick Boucher), in Fort Road adjacent to Flint House, which apparently stood at the junction with Harbour Street. Subsequent editions do not mention Lawn House, and Flint House too is missing until 1916, when it reappears in Harbour Street. There is no mention of a Convalescent Home in this area at any time between 1900 and 1920. Fort Road is quite short and overlooks the sea.

To confuse matters further, another leaflet featuring 'The Margaret Nursing Home, Bromley' and putting Margaret Manor at Otterden, presents also a 'Seaside Home for Visitors needing rest and change, with or without nursing. Special care of delicate children. Apply to Sister Frances, **St Edmund's,** Broadstairs.'

Dickens Corner, Broadstairs

This section had been crossed through in ink in the copy I saw. The reference to Otterden suggests that the leaflet may date back to the early years of the century, and again the 1901 Census provides the answer. Situated in Ramsgate Road, St Edmund's, like Lawn House, was in the parish of St Peter Intra, the two census entries being only ten records apart. It was a 'Nursing Home' whose superintendent was Miss Daisy Bedford, aged 28. She was assisted by a hospital nurse, Dora Curwen, and two servants, but only two patients were resident on census night, a 55-year old man and a girl aged eight. Another similar but rather larger establishment, Garrow Home, was almost next door, and there were numerous lodging-houses in the vicinity. St Edmund's

195

was in use in November 1906, as a letter from Gandhi to its Sister-in-charge testifies.   He wrote, mentioning his friendship with Josiah, requesting accommodation for 'a friend of mine, Mr Suleiman Manga, whose case in the opinion of Dr Oldfield calls for a change and rest for a week or two at your Convalescent Home'. This suggests that the home was not then actually owned or run by Josiah, although he may have maintained an interest.

Chapter 24

Doddington in the Aftermath of the First World War

Despite all its shortcomings the establishment at Doddington, like the Lady Margaret Hospital at Bromley, remained open throughout the First World War even though Josiah was otherwise occupied. Late in 1914 he had written that the 'Margaret Hall Soldiers' Hospital' and the 'Margaret Manor Convalescent Farm' were teaching wounded soldiers how to recover on a Fruitarian dietary, and were taking in soldiers' wives for confinement, and weakly babies and children to restore them to health and strength. It is not clear whether the 'Margaret Hall Soldiers' Hospital' referred to Bromley, Tulse Hill or Sittingbourne.

During the 1920s advertisements for the 'Lady Margaret Hospital and Sanatorium', Doddington, say that 'It is 500 feet above the sea: has sea air on three sides: is surrounded by pastures and woods and valleys in which primroses are often gathered even in December and January'. In the thirties these recommendations were extended: the sea itself was said to be within sight (it would have to be a clear day: the nearest coast is at least twelve miles away), and 'picnic meals are taken in the open all year round'. Today trees hide the sea views.

This particular brochure which paints an idealised portrait of what was offered at Margaret Manor was probably circulated as the establishment struggled to improve its image and clientele. There had been some worrying reports about the food and the accommodation, and perhaps there were other rumours as well. Before the war Mrs Sullivan had heard, via a cleaner at New Kent Road, that 'one of the nurses was the mother of Dr Oldfield's little daughter', and 'others' had questioned where Josiah slept when he visited. The Oast? The Lodge? Sister's Quarters? When Mrs Sullivan's hat was spoiled by a pail of slops, Sister Francesca had given her 2/6d as compensation, remarking as she did so that although it was from her own pocket 'I shall be able to make it up out of the children, when they come down, in some way or other'.

197

Doddington. Its Windmill is on the Horizon to the Left

Soon afterwards Hugh Fickling had been called in again, this time to inquire into the begging letters being sent out on behalf of a patient with neurasthenia who had been a resident at Doddington for eighteen months. His mother had been paying a guinea a week but now her savings were exhausted. Two likely charitable donors had each received identical letters, but in different handwritings, asking for support, and presumably had compared them and wondered what was going on. Apparently it was Josiah's suggestion (and very likely his words): the patient and his mother copied out the text, and Josiah despatched the letters. Appealing on behalf of deserving cases was common practice before the days of the National Health Service. But the *Charities Digest* in 1910 warned recipients of such missives that they often exaggerated facts and painted a false or fraudulent picture. 'The habit of replying to begging letters leads to the encouragement of this form of lying', it continued, emphasizing that facts should be ascertained and considered before money was given.

'Some Sick Babies being Mothered'

By 1920 Sister Ellen had replaced Sister Francesca. The *Daily News* published a photograph in June that year of four small children enjoying sunbaths, with an accompanying caption explaining how Dr Josiah Oldfield was 'taking to his open-air hospital at Margaret Manor, Sittingbourne, little weakly London children, and is effecting some wonderful cures by the aid of sun and fresh air'.

The magazine *Truth*, which had conducted a long-running campaign opposing Josiah and his hospital at Bromley, immediately pounced on this item, and sent a visitor (Unannounced? Incognito?) to see what conditions were like at Doddington. This person managed to see the ground floor of the oast house, and three wooden huts, each with four or five camp beds, in the grounds, though these were unoccupied. Apart from Josiah's daughter there were apparently only two children in residence, although up to fourteen had been staying earlier. No reference was made to food, or sanitation, and *Truth* had to be content with asking whether Josiah's work was truly philanthropic.

Josiah replied in a letter published in a subsequent edition of *Truth*, saying that he was not responsible for the newspaper report - he had asked them to postpone their visit since he himself had been away during the war years, and there had of course been general staff and labour difficulties. Before the war about sixty children had stayed each summer, and the holidays had recommenced in 1919. Financially the arrangements were 'generally self-supporting, but where there was a deficit it fell upon those of us who were responsible... no subscriptions were asked from others'. He invited *Truth*'s representative to record the progress being made in developing the hospital 'not as a building of bricks and mortar, needing costly fittings and demanding an ever present use of antiseptics, but as a village of healing, where sun and air and a natural fruitarian dietary may have scope, and where the great "medicatrix vis naturae" may have an opportunity of manifesting its potency'.

To which *Truth* added a postscript to the effect that "Medicatrix vis naturae" was certainly given free reign, for not much else was done, and the hospital might more correctly be described as a 'Fruitarian Boarding House'. It finished by reviving memories of the devastating report on the St Francis Hospital, and with a demand that accounts relating to the Lady Margaret Hospital at Bromley, now closed, be published.

The hospital at Doddington, having effectively replaced the Bromley premises, treated a very wide variety of patients. Some went purely to take advantage of the many special diet cures on offer - the range included 'fasting', 'dry diet', 'raisin', 'salad' and 'milk' cures. Air and sun baths were combined with these. Perhaps those taking advantage of such cures would today visit health farms, although whether climbing trees and sawing wood would appeal as much as the current use of a gym is a matter for speculation!

Medical, surgical and maternity cases were all welcome. The Lady Margaret Hospital's record for a safe outcome was on a par with that at Loughton. Josiah delivered 'hundreds of babies' there and did not lose one. He taught his pupil midwives never to give up hope of saving a baby; 'continuous hot baths, a warm down-feathered nest, a few occasional drops of sweet wine, alternated with drops of cream, and fresh warm milk mixed with honey will not infrequently reward the patient petitioners at Heaven's door' even with a seven-months child.

It seems highly probable that girls from well-connected families may have taken advantage of the isolation of Doddington if the babies they were expecting were illegitimate. Perhaps the initial consultation took place in Harley Street, and the confinement at Doddington. The patient's relatives could have announced that she was undergoing a 'cure'... Those with limited resources might have been tempted by an advertisement like that which appeared in *The Christian* in 1924, quoted in *Truth*:

'Accouchement. Quiet country place, from 30s. Special reduction for those coming sometime ahead and wishful to work. Book of advice free. Lady Margaret's, Doddington, Kent.'

This book was possibly one by 'Sister Margaret' entitled 'Advice to a Woman who is about to become a Mother', originally priced at a penny. Its main import was that confinement was safer and more convenient at a Nursing Home, where a nurse was always available to give advice or assistance, rather than at the patient's own home. A month's stay was suggested, a week preceding the expected date and three weeks after delivery. Details of Josiah's various establishments, and their charges, were given, together with his suggested diet which naturally excluded meat or any other animal products. A particularly pertinent sentence reads 'Where the Mother has no home to take the baby to, we can always recommend a trustworthy woman to take the baby, from about 7s.6d. to 21s. per week.' It is reported that a former incumbent at Doddington was sometimes asked by adults born at Margaret Manor to find their baptismal records, as their birth certificates were wanting in detail, or could not be traced.

Some cures at Doddington were spectacularly successful, as Josiah portrays:

'I once had a patient who came to me as one whose life story had ended. She went out rarely, and then only in a bathchair. She was very old but a very lovable woman. I took her under my care because she loved life and wanted to live. She was a simple and an obedient disciple. Within twelve months she was on horseback riding with me along the beauteous highland lanes of Kent. Twenty happy years passed in the comradeship of work for humanity... and then in a bleak spring the east wind seized upon a burdened chest and she lay upon a quiet bed of death'.

But in others the disease progressed despite Josiah's efforts. He describes a case of epilepsy:

'This lady, whom I will call Margaret, and who was in her thirties, was one of the most capable housekeepers I have ever met; a charming personality, a splendid cook, scrupulously clean and dainty in habits. An example of English womanhood at its best, she was kind-hearted, tender-hearted, loving, thoughtful. Then a fit. For days, or weeks, she became dirty, foul-mouthed, immodest, refusing to eat. Dangerous, violent, destructive - the two sides were complete strangers to one another. The interloper's gradual introduction eventually destroyed its host'.

'Epilepsy' here is possibly a euphemism for what is now regarded schizophrenia, in the early years of the last century as a form of lunacy, and in still earlier times as possession by devils.

Some memories of life at Margaret Manor in about 1920 were recorded in a letter from a Bromley resident, Mr F.Scott, in 1976. Having suffered some health problems he was sent, following an introduction via the then Headmaster of Bromley County School for Boys, Reginald Airey, to stay at Josiah's establishment at Doddington. His room was in the tower of the oast house, although occasionally he slept in one of the huts outside. There were very few other houses in the vicinity, but one was occupied by an elderly lady, probably the matron. It was here that work had begun on the extension which was ultimately to become the chapel. The remainder of his letter is worth quoting in full:-

'There was a lady in charge, called by us all "Sister", and it seemed that her job was to do everything. I had my meals in the same room as shepherd Lowther and two workmen engaged on building a small building not far away. They were engaged to save them from the workhouse, so it was said. Other "patients" or convalescents were there. A Colonel Roberts and a Miss Pearce dominated the scene and a few weeks later a Mr Clothier from the Prudential came, who was suffering from diabetes and hoped that diet would be of help. (I used to collect buttermilk for him from a farm not far away). He used to weigh himself at the windmill [now gone] regularly to check progress, and optimistically he was still engaged on selling policies to other visitors. Some came for week-ends. Round the grounds were scattered huts in which people slept. The colonel and Miss Pearce were good walkers and I recall her saying that she had walked to Sittingbourne. The diet was vegetarian. I mention these patients because it confirms that the place was a "convalescent" home.'

Some of the details Mr Scott mentions can be amplified by reference to Josiah's own writings. In *Fasting for Health and Life* (published 1924) he states 'When undertaking a "rest fast cure" it is well to have a small hut or an airy room, well-warmed and very quiet. A wooden house is warmer than a brick house: a panelled room better than a plastered. Good clean dry oat flytes make excellent bedding, for they are soft and warm, and no soreness results from long lying in one position'. Wheat chaff or beech leaves could also be used to fill palliasses.

The comment that "Sister" seemed to do everything accords with Josiah's philosophy, expounded in *Myrrh and Amaranth* in 1905, that at Doddington 'there are no servants, but doctors, nurses and patients alike take their share in the common work of the community, and hard work, well done, is the only badge of superior dignity... I have had to train many nurses and I have learned by experience that the daughter of a duchess will not scruple to turn up her dress and scrub a floor. The one who is taken from the servant class will often bring to me plausible excuses about her back being weak, but I smile within myself, and know that the real reason is that she will be afraid of being recognised as of the servant class if she does this sort of work. It requires a woman with breeding to scrub a floor and still retain the dignity of her high position. In the Lady Margaret Hospital the Senior Sister takes her turn at charring...' This sermon/essay ends with the words 'I bid you drudge no more. Consider the lilies of the field: they toil not - they transform the foul to fair in JOY'.

By 1922 women's place in the world had changed significantly. During the war many had experienced the world of work outside the home for the first time, and had found it more to their taste than housework. As men returned from the front to seek jobs, there was pressure on women to give up their paid employment if they did not need its financial rewards. Josiah had joined in correspondence to *The Times*, writing to oppose this view, but on the grounds that it 'idealised idleness'. He regarded the 'superficially accomplished women, with one eye on their work and the other on "a good time"' as those who overcrowded the labour market. Those women who found joy in working, whether as a doctor or a cook, a barrister or a housemaid, would always be needed. 'Work is a thing gladsome and comforting in itself, and so long as a woman is allowed freedom to develop in that form of work for which she is suited, it is better for her to work, and to work hard, at constructive work, than to fritter away her life in the toilsome labour of following fashions and playing the social games which happen to be in vogue when she is young'. This was the principle which he had instilled into his sixteen-year-old daughter, who apparently found relaxation from book-learning in 'fine stitchery and the physical recreation of scrubbing and cooking and gardening'. One wonders whether she agreed with her father, or whether she might have had different ideas derived from the girls she met at her boarding school.

The Chapel at Margaret Manor

Such enthusiastic, if unskilled, voluntary labour was extended to the construction of the chapel at Doddington. Josiah writes in his Preface to the same book 'We are trying to build a little chapel, and we want it to be as beautiful as a Hospital Chapel should be. We have no funds... We shall do much of the building and the decorating and the painting and the carpentering ourselves, so that we do not need much money... I hope this little book may bring a few shekels into the Treasury, and if it helps any in their time of suffering, maybe they will turn their faces towards our little sanctuary and offer some personal artistic assistance or send a thank-offering there...' The book itself, comprising two of Josiah's own lectures which he had written as ward sermons for Sunday evening services at the hospital, had been published at the request of his nursing staff.

The chapel was built next to what is now the Manor House. It was embellished with carvings carried out by an elderly Polish patient, Philip Yarnitz, and had stained glass windows, one of whose subjects was St Margaret, depicted allegorically. It seems likely that this window's design was similar to that used at Bromley. Only a photograph now remains. The caption beneath it reads

'The colourful stained glass window showing the Lady Margaret h o l d i n g t w o pomegranates, the fruit of the Tree of Life, the fruit of immortality, standing on the purple wings of a dragon to show the power of fruit over disease'. St Margaret of Antioch is commonly depicted with a dragon in church art.

The Chapel Window

The seating arrangements in the chapel were later described as 'unusual', and from a photograph it can be seen that seats resembling the stalls provided for clergy in a cathedral were

206

arranged lengthwise along the sides of the chapel. One Doddington resident remembers how she and her husband, who were passing through Greet, were pressed by the elderly Josiah to come in and see the building, which she described as 'a jungle', with its strange carvings and native ornaments. It made her feel uneasy.

One of the Carved Heads at the Entrance to the Chapel

'He was asked sometimes, said Dr Oldfield, why he had allowed devil's heads to be carved on the outside of the chapel. His answer was the significant one - they were "outside". And that represented a picture of the world.' This exchange appeared in a report on the dedication of gifts in about 1935. It has been said by others that one of the heads was intended as a portrait of Josiah himself. Though now decaying, the carved stone head at the right of the chapel door does bear at least some resemblance to the bearded doctor.

Chapter 25

Publicist and Pundit

Early in 1906 the *Herald of the Golden Age* reported that many of the illustrated newspapers had recently printed pictures of the Lady Margaret Hospital at Bromley. These included photographs of the staff, the wards, and 'dainty fruitarian meals', illustrations which were expected to 'familiarise the public with the healing efficacy of a hygienic diet in treating disease'. Josiah excelled in 'familiarising the public' with his ideas and ideals, using every method available. From the time he first came to London he had been writing pamphlets and magazine articles, lecturing, and composing letters to individuals and corporate bodies. Reference was made earlier to the unauthorised advertisements for his services as a lawyer, and to the misuse of photographs of patients while on the Executive Committee at St John's Hospital, but the reprimands he earned in these cases failed to stem his enthusiasm for publicity.

'The best way to advertise the cause (of fruitarianism) is to fill the world with daintily printed, capably written booklets' wrote Josiah in 1900, and he practised what he preached. He produced a steady stream of pamphlets, with titles such as *Shall we Vivisect?*, *The Evils of Butchery, How to Avoid Appendicitis* or *Diet in Relation to Cancer*. Their prices ranged from 1d. up to 1/- in the case of *Constipation - Causes and Cures*, and were frequently cheaper if purchased in quantity. There was a great appetite for reading material before the days of radio and television, but it did at first seem surprising that sales of his *1d Guide to Fruitarian Diet and Cookery* had reached 30,000 by 1903, the title going into a fifth edition three years later. Part of the answer lies in a small news item in a vegetarian magazine, announcing that copies had been presented by Mr George Cadbury and Mr W.H.Lever to every inhabitant of Bournville and Port Sunlight, and by Messrs. Nestlé and Idris to all their employees. These employers were philanthropists sympathetic to the cause of vegetarianism, and it was other men of similar disposition, like Arnold Hills and Henry Amos, who bore the printing costs.

The *Vegetarian Messenger* had remarked in 1898 that 'Josiah Oldfield seems to have succeeded to the position of Mr H.S.Salt as defender of Vegetarianism in the pages of the serious "Reviews".' He had found that an equally useful but simple and efficacious way of spreading its gospel and that of Humanitarianism was the insertion of 'little paragraphs or letters into the ordinary press'. Thus reports of Annual General Meetings, Bazaars, Opening Ceremonies, Christmas Festivities, as well as details of generous gifts or visits by celebrities could all provide the opportunity to advertise the different organisations of which he was an executive - the London Vegetarian Association, the hospitals at Bromley and Doddington, the Romilly Society... It is to be hoped that he was also a believer in the maxim that bad publicity is better than no publicity when faced with some unfavourable accounts of his homes in the press, especially *Truth*.

Certainly some appreciated his efforts in publicising the cause of Vegetarianism. This acrostic, addressed to Josiah as Editor of *The Vegetarian*, was composed by P.H.Echlin in 1895:-

J ustice demands that we should wish you well
O ur kindly editor, where'er you go.
S o much sage learning to your work we owe
I n 'Vegetarian' - may it ever sell!
A ll happiness attend you, still excel
H ourly in brightly uttering what you know.

O nly a few short days and 'ninety-five
L ives in the past; then let all strive to do
D eeds rivalling this year's, to keep alive
F ire of all fires, our Cause. Be firm, be true.
I f we should suffer, sense of being right
E ncouragement will give and ease the pain.
L ight, on the most obtuse and harden'd, light
D awns soon or late, and makes our deepest meaning plain.

A rather wider audience would probably have read of Josiah's main purpose in life in the *Daily Express* a few years later. In March 1906 this newspaper challenged him to conduct a series of experiments to see whether a meatless diet, with a cost not exceeding 4d. a day, really could keep a man fit and healthy. Four 'victims', three unemployed men from a Church Army Home, and one of its officials, were selected, and for three months they were fed exclusively on a Fruitarian diet of pulses like peas and lentils, fruit, cereals and similar items - no animal food. One was an elderly shoemaker, who lost his persistent cough, one a young clerk who had served in the army in South Africa, and one a middle-aged stonemason. All increased in health, muscle and weight, one gaining 3lb.2oz. as a result. Each reported that he had benefited by the change, and hoped now to be able to find work. The Church Army Lieutenant, returning to his duties 'thoroughly braced and ready for anything', anticipated that what he had learned during the experiment would serve him well in future social work. It appears that the four men also did without beer and tobacco for the three months, for the conclusions drawn noted that neither these nor flesh-food were necessary for man's well-being. If the English were properly educated in the use of correct foods like grains and vegetable fats rather than cheap meat they would be better nourished, and starvation and distress would be largely eliminated.

Josiah went on to contribute a series of articles to the *Express,* with the encompassing title 'How to Live Cheaply'. 'I do not believe in penury' he wrote; his aim was to teach how to live both cheaply and well. This item continued 'It has been my lot to live in the houses and accept the hospitality of three millionaires...'! But he pointed out that he had also endured conditions when life was one long ceaseless toil to get enough to satisfy the pangs of hunger, this presumably referring to his student days. No doubt he hoped that the paper's readers of all classes would therefore recognise his expertise.

Josiah had great skill with words, whether spoken or written. His generally flowery prose of the 1880s and 90s gradually became less ornate, although he was never at a loss for an erudite quotation. By 1929, as author of *Eat and be Happy*, he could recognise the deficiencies of his own early writing. 'I sometimes read the advice given in health papers by the Editor, and I say to myself "What piffle he is talking!" and then I realise that when I was the Editor of a food weekly, many years ago, I used to write that same sort of trash, and I honestly believed what I wrote'. It should be remembered that oratory in the Victorian age was valued: witness the reporting of lengthy parliamentary speeches in full, or the publication of volumes of sermons. Concentration spans today are not what they were.

Although not ordained Josiah had no hesitation in stepping into the pulpit, and in the chapels which formed an integral part of his hospitals he regularly gave short sermons. In a chapter headed 'A Little Sermon' in *Eat and be Happy* written in the 1920s he belittled his gift: 'I am always so afraid of getting into a pulpit and talking like a parson with ready glibness about problems that the thinkers and workers and experimenters of all the ages have failed to solve!'

It is frustrating not to know how successful he was as a barrister pleading his client's cause, nor how large were the audiences for his early talks. One early report on a lecture remarked that the subject was handled by Josiah in his usual forcible and convincing manner. When he officiated as Chairman at the Annual General Meeting of the Vegetarian Cycling Club he 'greatly amused friends by his humorous descriptions of his own experiences as a cyclist'. His subject matter varied, for as well as preaching the virtues of fruitarianism he spoke on penal reform and the abolition of capital punishment, on the evils of butchery and associated cruelty to animals, on anti-vaccination and anti-vivisection. A typical series of lectures given in 1912 gives some idea of how widely his ideas would range even when centred on a single subject - in this case 'Food'. The first, on October 9th, described what Food is, and what it does, then dealt with the effects of fasting and over-eating, mentioning the differences to be noted in childhood, youth and old age.

The series continued:-
Oct.23rd
　　How Food is used in the Body. The processes of Digestion,
　　　　　　Selection, Absorption, Excretion.
Oct.30th
　　The Values of Various Foods. Flesh foods, Animal secretions,
Animal products, Vegetable foods with Specimen balanced Dietaries.
Nov.13th
　　Food, and its Effect on the Birth-Rate. Economic and Physiologic.
　　　　　　Its stimulus towards Sterility or Fertility.
Nov.27th
Cooked versus Uncooked Foods. The effect of Scientific and Natural
　　　　　　Cooking, processes of Maturing.
Dec.11th
　　Some Theories on early Dietaries, and the Lines of Evolution.
　　　　Religious, Economic, Legislative, Experimental.

Earlier the same year at various venues he had spoken on 'Milk and Honey - Mystical and Practical'; 'The Secret of Youth'; 'Food of the Field of Ardath'; 'Diet Cures for Obesity' and 'Corn, Oil and Wine', and had delivered another series of talks all concerned with diet and its relation to afflictions such as rheumatism, appendicitis and dyspepsia. Obviously much of the content of his lectures would be repeated in others, although not necessarily framed in the same words. 'There should be a seven-day fast before elections' and 'The House of Commons is fed mostly on mutton chops, which may account for the sheep-like nature of MPs' are both examples of Josiah's headline-grabbing utterances, destined to be recorded and remembered by journalists and others who heard him speak.

By this date his eminence as an authority on Food Reform was recognised, for he was asked by the compilers of both the *Encyclopaedia Britannica* and *Chambers' Encyclopaedia* to contribute the definitive article on 'Vegetarianism'. The result, included in the celebrated eleventh edition of *Britannica* published in 1910-11, manages to promote Fruitarianism and the Order of the Golden Age, giving its address as Barcombe Hall, Paignton; the Vegetarian Federal Union - again with address - and

212

the magazines which he edited. The article defined the various diets adopted by vegetarians, and their reasons for adopting it, and listed some of their sporting achievements. But when discussing the different organisations and institutions where the vegetarian dietary had been adopted the Lady Margaret Hospital is not specified. Perhaps the encyclopaedia's editors drew the line here...

He was quick to reply to articles published in the press criticising any aspect of Vegetarianism. In 1912 Sir James Crichton Browne had expressed forthright views on the subject, especially its effect on impressionable young women who were dieting in an effort to lose weight. The *Daily Chronicle* and *Morning Leader* printed a lengthy answer from Josiah, pointing out that working-class women were already thin through want of nourishing food, while those of the upper classes were fine, muscular and handsome young women who had developed their healthy bodies by exercise (golf, hunting, fishing, walking, cycling, tennis...). To Sir James' contention that people should 'eat what they like' Josiah countered that they should consider what suffering had been involved in bringing meat to their table, and again cited the examples of armies that marched on corn.

P.G.Wodehouse satirised the vegetarian diet in *Something Fresh,* published in 1915, where his character 'Mr Peters' apologises to a friend for not entertaining him. "'I'd have asked you to lunch here", said Mr Peters, "but you know how it is with me: I promised the doctor I'd give those nuts and grasses of his a fair trial, and I can do it pretty well but only when I'm alone, not with someone else eating real food".

The general attitude towards Vegetarianism was, however, gradually changing, and by the 1920s vegetarians were no longer regarded as freaks. Whereas the emphasis at the turn of the century had been on humanitarianism and animal welfare, it was now a healthy lifestyle which attracted converts. Sunbaths and naturism were acceptable. 'Health Food' shops opened, selling dried fruits, all kinds of nuts and the alternatives to animal products which Josiah and others had recommended for so long. Raw foods became popular as the part played by vitamins was recognised. As early as 1910 King Edward VII, an unlikely supporter, had apparently given permission just before he died for his name to be placed on the programme of a fund-raising concert linked with the Order of the Golden Age.   This was firmly committed to Fruitarianism.

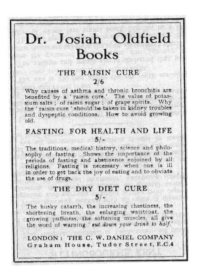

A Selection of Titles by Josiah Oldfield available in the 1920s

Josiah too had appreciated the altered climate of opinion, and the titles of the books and other works which flowed from Doddington during the 1920s and 30s reflect this - as do the advertisements for Lady Margaret Manor. *The Raisin Cure, The Dry Diet Cure, Get Well and Keep Well, Eat and Get Well, Eat and Keep Young, Eat and be Happy* are sample titles. His 'Best Food' series was a set of booklets delineating the benefits of foods such as apples, carrots, grapes and similar 'fruits of the earth', with recipes as used in 'England's only Fruitarian Hospital'.   At the same period perhaps the best-known proponent of Vegetarianism in North America, (Benjamin) Gayelord Hauser, was producing similar titles there. One of his best-selling books was called *Eat and Grow Beautiful,* whose message was that radiant life-giving foods would build vital healthy bodies. From Josiah in 1935 came *The Beauty Aspect of Health and Living* and *Eat and be Beautiful,* preaching the same message. Mainstream publishers were now prepared to publish such books.

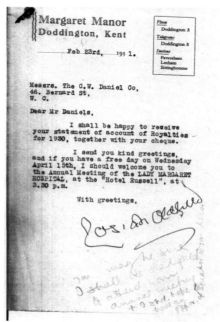

Josiah's Request for a Royalties Statement

It is fascinating to trace the course of the relationship between Josiah and one of his publishers over a decade, for it indicates a gradual change from the 'between friends' approach of the earlier years to a rather more distant 'business terms' attitude ten years later. C.W.Daniel specialised in books on diet, health food and alternative therapies and philosophies, so *The Raisin Cure* and *The Dry Diet Cure,* published in 1923 and 1925, fitted well into his list. Correspondence between Josiah and Daniel in 1928 included commiseration from Josiah on the publisher's recent 'loss and nervous shock', friendly agreement on how difficult it was to persuade booksellers to stock their titles, and news of Josiah's plans to produce two new books that year. In May Josiah congratulated Daniel on finding new premises in Bloomsbury, writing 'You will be quite a close neighbour to us when we open our Outpatient department off Red Lion Square' and offering its basement as storage space.

By September 1929, however, Daniel was regretting that Josiah's *Eat and be Happy* had been 'siezed (sic) upon' by an American firm, and that Methuen were to bring out *Get Well and Keep Well* in competition with the very similar *Eat and Get Well* at a lower price and on more favourable terms than Daniel could offer. A few months after this it was just a postcard from Josiah's secretary, Miss Garrett, which asked for copies of some of his best-selling titles to be delivered to Red Lion Square, but in 1931 Josiah resumed the correspondence, accompanying his request for a statement and royalties cheque with a personal invitation to the Annual General Meeting of the Lady Margaret Hospital in April.

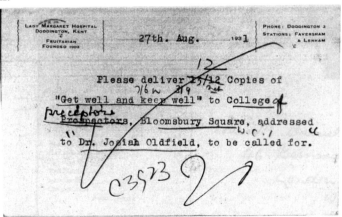

By 1931 Josiah has Plans for a Clinic in Bloomsbury
The friendship did not preclude some hard bargaining

216

between the two. When a new edition of *Fasting for Health and Life* with a print-run of 1000 copies was planned in 1932 Daniel's initial terms were that Josiah should contribute £60 towards the cost and then receive 1/8d per copy sold. He might buy copies at 1/4d each, royalty-free, but not, as Josiah hoped, at 1/-. The publisher insisted that the title remain unchanged despite revision, but it it is not clear which man won the battle of whether the book should be divided into two sections ('History and Philosophy' and 'Practice'). Josiah then demanded clarification of the expression 'lowest trade terms' before signing any agreement... A rather formal note from his secretary (now Evelyn Clare) informed the publisher that Josiah would call on the firm the next week, presumably to signify his acceptance, 'unless prevented by any professional engagement'.

This frostiness did not last, for in February 1934 Josiah wrote from Jamaica to say that he would willingly contribute to a new magazine which was about to be launched by C.W.Daniel. He was glad to hear of the venture, for he himself had considered a similar plan, and this would save him the trouble.

Correspondence continued until 1936. August 1935 brought an application from the 'Women's Christian Temperance Union of South Africa' for permission to translate *The Raisin Cure* into Afrikaans without charge. Their request was granted on condition that Josiah should receive 3d per copy sold (on which C.W.Daniel wanted 10% commission). The final letters in this archive material concern the supply on a sale or return basis of books for a stall at a 'Health, Beauty and Humanity Market' to be held at the Central Hall, Westminster in December 1936. This event was actually organised by Josiah and had mixed success, though one stall-holder took £10.7s.3d. and another nearly as much. Those less fortunate at least gained valuable publicity.

As recorded earlier, Josiah's fame was now such that his travels might be reported in *The Times*, notice of his departure for Jamaica in November 1920 being a case in point. Short accounts of his doings also appeared at intervals in the *New York Times* between 1913 and 1931. The first of these, headed 'Feeding the Army', referred to a lecture on dietetics given by Josiah in

London, and was picked up because of 'Secretary Garrison's decision to eliminate chocolate as a U.S. Army ration'. Josiah had said 'Give me an army corps for twelve months and I will solve some of the world's most important problems of dietetics. What a waste that soldiers in times of peace should be kept pipe-claying belts when they might be used for valuable scientific experiments...' He went on to say that Caesar's army was fed on grain - the men mutinied when they were given mutton. Food has three aspects, sustenance, sufficiency for extra output, and pleasure. Grain supplies the first, oil the second and wine the third, he continued. The accounts of men under Josiah's command shortly after this lecture was delivered make no mention of this third constituent. He was not the first Englishman to question the traditional diet of his country's troops, for in 1683, while on a visit to Tangier, Samuel Pepys had noted the 'superiority of the diet of the Turkish Navy, almost meatless and rich in water, oil, olives and rice, over the beef-and-beer obsessed English'.

The British Broadcasting Corporation was set up in the early nineteen-twenties by a consortium of leading radio manufacturers, and its first transmission took place in November 1922. BBC Archives reveal that Josiah was one of the pioneers of broadcasting, for as early as July 1923, less than a year after the 'wireless' had begun its output, he gave a lecture entitled 'Fruit and a Long Life'. This led to a further series of talks in 1925, commencing in June with 'Secret of the Summer Salad', and ending in December with 'Foods that Keep us Warm'. Unfortunately there is no longer any record of what he said on these occasions.

As has already become clear, Josiah's literary efforts were not confined to books and pamphlets. Throughout his long life he was an inveterate letter-writer, suiting his style to the perceived audience. The begging letters to illustrious VIPs seeking donations may not all have been devised by Josiah, but undoubtedly he would have influenced their composition even where he was not the author. His booklet *The Diet of the World's Workers*, dating from about 1920, tells how he wrote to the

218

Embassies of many countries to find out 'from those best qualified to answer, what was the general dietary of their peoples'. Amongst those who responded to his request were the Legations of Czechoslovakia, Chile, Germany, Finland, Norway, Roumania, Serbia, Spain, Sweden, Persia, Japan and the Netherlands. The answers from these countries all largely supported Josiah's view that it was not the hunters but the 'garden men - the men who produce the world's wealth and who live on the bounteous gifts of Mother Earth - (who) are the makers of history and the builders of the Empire'. This seems rather a sweeping assertion regarding the countries of the Empire, none of whose Embassy views are quoted. Perhaps not everyone was prepared to answer unsolicited mail, or perhaps their answers did not fit...

The same source reveals that Josiah communicated with well-known figures: Col.T.E.Lawrence was courteous in replying that the Arab troops employed by him during the desert campaign in Palestine lived mainly on unleavened bread. This was supplemented with sugar, some coffee and tea and rice, and sheep or camel meat two or three times a month. It is possible that the two men may have met and talked.

There has been a suggestion that George Bernard Shaw modelled one of the characters in *A Doctor's Dilemma* on Josiah. It might have been expected that Shaw, famous as Vegetarian as well as playwright, would have been the recipient of letters from Josiah, but if so, few are preserved. An undated example in the British Library, probably from 1937, seeks Shaw's interest in the Community at Doddington, but suggests that the men were merely acquaintances rather than friends. Shaw did acknowledge Josiah's work when replying to Symon Gould of the American Vegetarian Party in 1945, writing 'Please stop telling the blazing lie that vegetarians are free from disease. Ask Josiah Oldfield (if you have not heard of younger authorities) whether he can cure rheumatism, or arthritis, or cancer.' Josiah had never promised to cure such diseases, but showed that the Fruitarian diet could alleviate their effects or prevent their development. No doubt many other important figures would have disregarded his communications, or they might have been weeded out by efficient secretaries. Correspondence between Josiah and Sir Samuel Hoare on the subject of the death penalty continued intermittently between 1947 and 1951, and this **does** survive. The Editor of *The Times,* Geoffrey Dawson, heard from Josiah when he retired: he must have encountered a large number of Oldfield missives, though what proportion were published cannot be known. Of those that were, not all were printed in the later editions of that day's paper. Regional newspapers and specialised journals, such as the *Western Mail* or *The Motor-Trailer* also received letters from Josiah. The subjects varied wildly - allotments, exercises for women, smoking, children's homes, Good Friday observance, whether patriotism is affected when people choose to live abroad - all could be made the pivot to which the advantages of Fruitarianism would be attached. Many examination candidates are familiar with the technique of mugging up on a couple of topics and then tweaking the set questions to accommodate their special subject!

When necessary Josiah could convey the essence of his message in very few words, as in some of the advertisements for his hospitals placed in small magazines. He had mastered the art of 'keying' these advertisements to trace which brought the most favourable responses, usually by adjusting the address to which they should be sent. Thus the Doddington establishment could be contacted postally through a wide selection of addresses which included

> Margaret Manor, Doddington, Sittingbourne
> Greetynge Cottage, Margaret Manor, Doddington, Kent
> The Warden, Margaret Manor, Sittingbourne
> Lady Margaret Hospital, Sittingbourne, Kent
> Matron, Margaret Cottage, Doddington, Kent
> Lady Margaret's, Doddington, Kent

Even *Truth* had to acknowledge his business acumen in so doing.

Chapter 26

Truth's continuing Vendetta against Josiah

The magazine *Truth* had been founded in 1877 as a journal of Liberal principles in which, according to the Press Directory of 1903, 'the latest news of London and Paris is told in a series of articles on current topics. The "Entre Nous" are made a special feature'. Stage and financial news featured strongly in earlier editions. By 1903, however, its original Editor Labouchère had been replaced, and the content was changing. (Labouchère retired to Florence soon afterwards, his own share-rigging deals having been exposed in *The Critic*.) The *Press Directory's* entry for 1920 reads: 'Principles - Liberal. *Truth* has always been famous for its fearless and valuable exposure of frauds'. Its fame was sufficient for Dorothy L.Sayers to feature it in *Clouds of Witness*, published in 1926. Her character Sir Impey Biggs is delayed since he is 'engaged in Quangle & Hamper v. "*Truth*"'. Told that Sir Impey is defending *Truth* against 'people who profess to cure fifty-nine different diseases with the same pill', Lord Peter Wimsey retorts "Astonishin' position for a lawyer, what?", perhaps implying that the magazine was not the usual reading of the upper classes.

Josiah and his enterprises were favourite targets. That Josiah's 'fruitarian boarding house' remained popular despite malicious rumours and complaints from some quarters is evidenced by the construction of the chapel by willing volunteers, and by the regular gifts received. After seventy or eighty years there is no-one alive today to testify to the efficacy of his 'cures', whereas written criticisms are kept on file. It is well-known that satisfied customers rarely bother to put their thoughts on paper - it is the dis-satisfied who broadcast their grievances.

Truth ran another article about what it regarded as Josiah's shortcomings in March 1924, referring to him as 'an old humbug'. By now it had obtained a copy of the report and accounts of the Lady Margaret Hospital for the period 1921-23.

This report made it clear that the work formerly carried out at Bromley was now based at Doddington, although the new hospital had only been fully operational since January 1923. *Truth* therefore concentrated its criticisms on the financial transactions for just the few weeks of early 1923, regarding the £11.12s.0d. spent on 'postage, stationery etc. in connection with appeals' as excessive, especially when compared with expenditure of only four guineas on medical fees. Traditional hospitals would, of course, have spent far more on doctors and medicines. The appeals had brought in £76.0s.0d., bringing the total subscribed since the closure of the Bromley hospital to nearly £190.0s.0d. *Truth* continues its article:-

'He remained at the end of March with £316.16s.6d. in hand - and is still asking for more. It looks as if he considers it more blessed to receive than to give, which is hardly the accepted idea of charity. It is probable that the place itself belongs to Oldfield, and the "private cost" of keeping impecunious patients removed from Bromley in 1920 may possibly have been his own. But the material fact is that he has been taking in paying patients at Doddington for years past; and though the charges are low, they are more than enough to cover the scanty, cheap, and nasty rations which seem to be the essentials in Oldfield's idea of a nature cure'.

So the free treatment of poor patients is glossed over, and the 'cheap and nasty rations' emphasized. Would the excessive charges at some more comfortable, tasteful establishments purporting to cure rich but indolent ladies have provided better value for money in the eyes of *Truth*? It next condemns the medical staff, mainly because of the matron's age (nearly eighty). After a paragraph wondering why Josiah advertised nationally if the original stated purpose of the hospital was to take the sick poor out of London, the article concluded by questioning whether any of the numerous titled patrons listed in the report had ever visited Doddington to see for themselves what conditions were like.

Nearly two years later, in December 1925, *Truth* returned to the attack when 'Scrutator' wrote a three-column article about Doddington which was headed 'An Obnoxious Nursing Home'. It began by quoting three recent advertisements:-

EPILEPTICS - One or two suitable cases received for dietetic treatment - Lady Margaret Hospital, Sittingbourne, Kent.
FRUITARIAN DIETARY - Cases of delicate digestion, nervous and weakly cases, received from 3 guineas - Matron, Margaret Cottage, Doddington, Kent.
ACCOUCHEMENT - Quiet country home; advice booklet free; from 3 guineas; may stay unlimited time - Lady Margaret's, Doddington, Kent.

Even these were criticised, firstly by their mere appearance in an authoritative paper like *The Times* rather than in parish or similar magazines; secondly because of the differing addresses (which Scrutator admitted was probably to show which wording brought the best response); and lastly because 'Sittingbourne' gave little idea of the isolation of Lady Margaret Manor.

Earlier concerns such as the Matron's age, the inadequacy of the food, the draughty accommodation and poor sanitary arrangements ('what you would expect to find provided in labourers' cottages in a rural district'), were once more raised. One particular patient, presumably the lady named Margaret whom Josiah regarded as epileptic, caused consternation when glimpsed naked during one of her disturbed periods by a gentleman who 'after having gone to the place for dietetic treatment left generally dissatisfied'. The final theme discussed was the financial arrangement at Doddington - was it truly a charity run by voluntary subscriptions, or was Josiah making large profits for himself by overcharging for the facilities provided?

It is apparent from the article that 'Scrutator' had not himself taken the trouble to visit Doddington - all his information was second-hand. The overall impression given is of envy of Josiah's success and the generally favourable publicity he received in the press.

The old accusations were reiterated in 1926, when *Truth* tried again to discredit Josiah, entitling its sneer 'Oldfield as a Charitymonger'. This time it reproduced a different appeal, a specimen illustrating another of Josiah's beliefs, describing it as 'the sort of gammon on which this queer example of philanthropy is run' -

'Dear Madam,
What more delightful remembrance of the birth of a child than the planting of a fruit tree!
Every father and mother looks upon the new-born baby and wonders and wonders and hopes and prays that the little one will grow up strong and well, and will be a source of sweetness and comfort and blessing in the many years of the future...
What a joy to a boy or girl to come down to this Hospital and to see and to gather fruit from the laden boughs of the tree that was planted in grateful thankfulness for the touch of baby fingers.
And if, perchance, the baby should be garnered into the garden of God, what a sweet memory of its coming...
A young apple, a plum or a pear tree will be planted in memory of a baby born, or of a friend beloved, in the new orchard of the Lady Margaret Hospital. A label will be attached to it with the memorial name inscribed; the name will be printed in the report, and at any time a welcome will be given for the tree to be visited by the donor, or a sample of the fruit will be sent on request...'

A large proportion of his patients were maternity cases, and could confidently be expected to respond to the appeal.

Truth's campaign was picked up by the magazine *John Bull*. It too in 1926 criticized Josiah's habit of writing letters to the press in which he purported to give free advice to the suffering public, but which in fact put him in touch with many charitable people, thus gaining free advertisements.

But apart from the flowery prose (*Truth* failed to denigrate the literary style) is Josiah's appeal so different from today's requests for subscriptions which entitle a family to have the name of a loved one written in a Book of Remembrance kept in a glass case, or to pay for the floodlighting of the church tower for a

224

week? His idea seems eminently practical: 'Tree-planting' is listed as one of his recreations in *Who was Who* and was a key tenet of the Fruitarian Society.

Map showing Location of Lady Margaret Manor

Doddington lies about 5 miles south east of Sittingbourne; Josiah's establishment at Greet (marked with a triangular Youth Hostel symbol) a further 2 miles south west of Doddington. The dotted line through Charing and Hollingbourne traces the Pilgrims Way.

Chapter 27

Events and Eccentricities at Doddington

As the new decade began, Josiah must have felt that all his work was prospering. He was a successful author and lecturer, and in 1931 he could afford to tell his publisher that he did not want to be associated with 'unqualified' authors when they placed their advertisements. Many wealthy and well-connected supporters, including a Maharajah, were patrons of the Lady Margaret Hospital at Doddington. The Chapel there was nearing completion, and there were plans to open an out-patient clinic in London.

Josiah's Sister Ellen

His sister Ellen had come to live in Doddington itself, only a mile and a half from Margaret Manor, while his daughter Josie, a medical student, shared his aims. Both Josie and Ellen were on the Council of the Hospital. Josiah often discussed matters with Josie: his book *Eat Nature's Food and Live Long* was dedicated to 'my daughter Josie, with whom I have worked out many problems of life'.

In 1931 Josiah was responsible for arranging a lunch for his friend Gandhi, now as the Mahatma famed for his campaign of civil disobedience which had finally led to recognition of the Indian Congress Party, and acknowledgment that Indian independence was a just cause. The lunch took place at the Grosvenor House Hotel in London's Park Lane: tickets cost 5/6d.

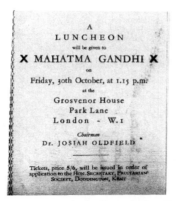

Announcement of a Lunch for Gandhi

Gandhi was in England to represent India at the Round Table conference. He stayed at Kingsley Hall, an East End Settlement House, rather than at a hotel, and treated all those he met, from the King and the Archbishop of Canterbury to the children playing in the East End streets, with the same courtesy.

Although he spent time in both Oxford and Cambridge, and visited Lloyd George at his farm in Surrey, it is unlikely that he came to Doddington.

Josiah and his Daughter Josie with Gandhi in 1931

The tranquillity of that village was rarely disturbed, but one area was sometimes the scene for unseemly behaviour. Just opposite

227

the Post Office were some fine walnut trees, some of whose fruit fell into the cherry orchard adjoining Miss Ellen Oldfield's garden. The village boys coveted the nuts, so would climb in to collect them. If Miss Ellen saw them, she would run from her house, Newlyn, through the garden gate in an (always unsuccessful - she was in her seventies) attempt to catch them. One boy was usually posted as look-out, warning his friends with the cry of 'Here comes Cinders' or 'It's Cinderella', sometimes if she **was** in sight, sometimes if she wasn't. On such occasions he could harvest all the fallen fruit for himself.

Miss Ellen's Home, 'Newlyn', at Doddington

Miss Ellen was described by her friend Lucy Norrington as 'a dear old soul and a regular church-goer'. Perhaps it was she who was influential in encouraging her brother and some of his staff and guests to attend Doddington Church once a month. Josiah felt that this encouraged the Margaret Manor community to integrate with the parish, and considered the Vicar, the Rev.John Hobbins, to be a spiritual father to them all.

Newlyn was the venue for an annual sale of work in aid of the Lady Margaret Hospital, and for a brief period it was advertised as a 'Fruitarian Guesthouse'. There is a reference to the opening of a 'simple guesthouse' at Doddington in 1931. Miss Ellen, though, was not a member of the committee (Treasurer Miss Garrett, Secretary Evelyn Clare) which arranged a flower show in the village in 1932, at which the Mayoress of Faversham distributed the prizes. Although the event was a success, it made a profit for the Hospital of only £4.3s.7d, owing to heavy initial outgoings. At Margaret Manor lavender was being grown on a large scale at the time, and its sales helped to support the work there.

Miss Norrington was a long-term resident of Doddington, and had observed the Hospital from its foundation. Apologising for missing its Annual Meeting in London in 1934 she wrote, possibly with tongue in cheek, 'I have watched its progress with interest. A good work is going on efficiently and unostentatiously, and I am convinced that all who come under its influence, whether patient or visitor, must benefit by the regimen of Fruitarian Dietary advocated there'. Miss Norrington lived until 1970, reaching the age of 92, and recorded her memories of Margaret Manor. It is the services she remembered best:

'The little choir of girls wore white caps with M.M. (Margaret Manor) on the front, and at every service recited the words of Psalm 133:
"Behold how good and joyful a thing it is, brethren, to dwell together in unity.
It is like the precious ointment upon the head, that ran down unto the beard, even unto Aaron's beard, and went down to the skirts of his clothing.
It is like the dew of Hermon which fell upon the hill of Sion.
For there the Lord promised His blessing, and life for evermore."
Then the Doctor would appear in his academic robes and read from the first chapter of Genesis the text which ruled the lives of the Community, "And God said, Behold I have given you every herb bearing seed, which is upon the face of all the earth, and every tree, in the which is the fruit of a tree yielding seed; to you it shall be for meat."
'Each year Hemlock Sunday was observed, commemorating

229

the life and death of Socrates. He often had a special speaker and one particular year invited a Greek official from London. There were many hemlock plants in the garden. A long procession walked round the garden singing "Onward, Christian soldiers". There was no musical instrument. The Doctor liked everything natural. Harvest Festivals were great occasions; he often asked me to sing a verse or two of a hymn, and I always complied if I might pitch the tune myself, otherwise it might go sky-high [so] that no-one could reach - rather amusing.'

Miss Norrington noted that although Josiah was regarded as somewhat eccentric, he was also very hospitable, and gave parties at his home. These parties continued for many years, but some found his habit of inviting female guests to sit on his knee as they sang or recited unnerving. Since he was quite short it must have been uncomfortable in more ways than one.

A somewhat confusing advertisement from about 1935 in *Honey for Health* reads

'St Francis and Lady Margaret Fruitarian Hospital, Doddington
Please send Donations or come in for Treatment.
Volunteers welcomed with Free Board:
Domestic, Secretarial, Garden, Giving Nature Treatments.
Margaret Cottage Home Guest House - from 2 guineas.
Opening for Apiary, Poultry, Geese, Goats, Milk, Market Gardening,
Jams, Bottled Fruits, Mail Order, Secretarial Training, Weaving.
Apply Hon.Sec.
Boarding School, Co-Educational. Apply Head Mistress, Margaret
Manor.'

Even for Josiah the last item sounds unlikely, unless his guests at the time included some teachers. Admittedly he had, some fifty years earlier, spent a short time as an assistant master at a boys' boarding school, and had no doubt tutored his own daughter more recently. There were, however, attempts to broaden the appeal of stays at Margaret Manor during the thirties by offering 'weekend schools'. The fee of 15/6 included simple board residence, admission to all lectures, and transport by special car to and from the nearest station.

Josiah in his Cottage, Little Greetynge

According to *A History of Margaret Manor*, a pamphlet produced by the Stansfield Association in 1960, when Josiah first came to Doddington he had occupied the house known as 'Little Greeting'. In November 1933 this was destroyed by fire, together with all his collection of dietetic books. The *East Kent Gazette* reported the occasion:-

'Disastrous Fire at Doddington'

The rest house used by pilgrims of olden times, known as 'Lyttle Greetynge' at Doddington, the residence of Dr Josiah Oldfield of the Lady Margaret Fruitarian Hospital, was completely destroyed by fire on Saturday.

'The fire broke out in the upper part of the house, which was largely constructed of timber. Dr Oldfield and the staff at first attempted to deal with it themselves, but the task was

231

very soon beyond them, and the Faversham Fire Brigade was called.

Little Greetynge, destroyed by fire in 1933

Owing to the age of the house and its construction the flames rapidly made headway, and when the firemen arrived, after an eight or nine mile journey from Faversham, all the upper part of the house was in flames. Moreover the water supply immediately to hand was limited and difficult of access, for although the Mid-Kent Company's main passes by there is no hydrant.

Eventually the Brigade made use of a wash-out on the main some distance away, necessitating the use of 22 lengths of hose.

In the meantime as much of the contents of the ground floor as was possible was salvaged, but the whole structure was practically destroyed, and Dr Oldfield lost much that was valuable.

Happily the hospital itself and other buildings were not immediately adjacent to the house and so there was little danger of the fire spreading. The loss is reported to be considerable. The origin of the fire is a mystery.'

There is no mention of the event in the Lady Margaret Annual

Report for 1934.

The Monks Hut

Nothing daunted, at the age of 72 Josiah proceeded to convert a hut formerly used as a woodshed to living accommodation. He built a bathroom at one end, with a small hole leading from the living room, through which he would double up to reach his bath. This was his test for rheumatism, for as long as he was able to crawl through this hole, so was his body free from the dreaded disease. Rainwater was collected for baths, and afterwards it served to irrigate the adjoining garden, for 'Men should gather all the resources that nature provides to bring their lives to fruition'. By living here he was able to practise what he had advocated when explaining how to live cheaply in 1907 - 'Better to have a tiny house and live a good deal out of it than a large and spend all your time within'.

This hut was to become known as 'The Monks Hut', since it was supposed to have been used by Friars en route from Faversham to the Bishop's Palace at Charing, but the claim is somewhat dubious. There is no trace of any building on the site on the 1737 map of ' Grith Farm' and its environs. It is possible that pilgrims and others did stay at 'Great Grit(h)' in the fourteenth century, and there is said to have been a small shrine on the corner of the lane just past Little Greeting. Certainly in the sixteenth century the road from Faversham to Lenham, passing close to Doddington, was an important route. Symondson's 1596 map of Kent shows it as similar in status to the road between Rochester

233

and Faversham (the present A2). What became known as the 'Pilgrims' Way', in reality an ancient trackway that probably existed before the coming of Christianity, lay along the southern escarpment of the North Downs, but Greet was two miles or so to its north.

Generous donors had continued to offer gifts to beautify the chapel, and at a service of dedication there, also in the mid-thirties, offerings comprised a St Francis stained glass window and a sanctuary lamp, presented by Dr T.G.Vawdrey; two crucifixes, one from Oberammergau; a tapestry depicting St Margaret, an etching of the chapel and a copy of Holman Hunt's 'Light of the World'; a chair 'handsomely carved by Mr P.Yarnitz, helped by Mr P.Bartlett'; a lectern, and a bell. At this service, which was performed by Archdeacon J.F.Ozanne* from the Seychelles, 'Dr Oldfield, with his mass of silver hair, and wearing his scarlet robe, made a very striking figure'.

In his address Josiah emphasised the spirit in which the gifts were given. Whereas some 'worshipped God by taxation' (via dances, whist drives and other pleasures which were taxed), of the chapel it could be said that 'there was nothing there but what had been laboriously, and therefore cheerfully, given by those who spared a little time for it while staying there.' He mentioned that all the wood used had been grown, cut down and fashioned at the Manor. Two sisters had made the mortar for the basis of the chancel. The St Francis window was the work of a lady who was a devoted friend. He concluded by hoping that the chapel might be a 'sanctuary of peace to those who wanted comfort of body or soul'. Another gift had been a slate slab engraved by Eric Gill. Scouts who camped in the valley each year helped with construction, and were responsible for laying the last section of mosaic in the chancel in early Autumn 1935.

*James Ozanne had originally been ordained as a priest in the Roman Catholic Church, but had become an Anglican in 1914. He served in the war, then became Rector of a parish in Guernsey before being made Sub-Dean of St James's Cathedral in Mauritius. He later became an RAF Chaplain.

The balance sheet for 1932 values the chapel as part of the assets of the hospital, noting the 'expenditure to date' as £130.10.5d, a figure which is reproduced every year until 1937, when the chapel disappears from the accounts.

Miss Norrington's memories are corroborated by a report of the Hemlock Sunday service 'of somewhat unique character' in the *East Kent Gazette* for July 27th 1935, when a large congregation of patients, nurses and friends from near and far completely filled the church. This was described as 'beautiful in its quaint originality, a point which never fails to call forth expressions of surprise and admiration from all who visit for the first time and hear its history'. On this occasion there were seven little girls in the choir, and the service began with an introit, 'I will arise and go to my Father'.

After the usual recitation of the verse from Genesis and Psalm 133, hymns and scripture readings followed. The readers, all visitors at the hospital, were Mr H.E.Nobbs, Major C.A.Williams, Mr Hudson and Dr Trevor Powell (who also sang solo verses). Josiah himself preached, pointing out how Socrates was fearless in speaking out for his beliefs. After the blessing the whole company 'marched to the garden where some fine specimens of hemlock seven or eight feet high grew. Dr Oldfield explained that these were given to him by the Head of St John's College, Oxford, where he graduated. After examining the plants and taking away many a leaf as a memento the company dispersed'.

Josiah liked to attend the Oxford Encaenia (the conferring of Honorary Degrees) each June when the University's dons gather in their full robes. He met many of his contacts there, but the two whose personalities most impressed him were General Booth and Mark Twain, both of whom lived on the 'kindly fruits of the earth'.

Perhaps it was Socrates' example in standing up for his beliefs that inspired Henry Brown Amos. The same local paper in November 1935 reported that Henry Amos, 66, of Margaret Manor, was fined ten pounds for damaging a window at Exeter Cathedral by poking his umbrella through it during Evening Service on November 3rd. This window, a memorial to the late

**Oxford University Robes,
Doctor of Civil Law**

Earl Fortescue, offended Henry Amos because it glorified stag-hunting. In his defence Amos, who was editor of the journal of the League for the Abolition of Cruel Sports, said that he had spent 47 years of his life trying to stamp out such practices. He would have met Josiah through the VFU, for he had been Provincial Secretary of the Lincolnshire branch. A contributor to the *Vegetarian Yearbook* in 1896, he had produced his own annual from 1905, and published a book of recipes in 1916.

Henry Amos was one of the many whose contribution of £1.0s.0d was recorded in the annual report for 1933. Amongst other supporters at this period were Boots Chemists (a guinea), the Marmite Food Company (two guineas) and numerous Rotary Clubs and branches of the Women's Institute. These societies had generally given their guinea or so following a lecture by Josiah. Although most of his talks seem to have been given within striking distance of London, at venues such as Staines, Finchley and Southend, he was staying at a Country Club in Llandrindod Wells in September 1931, perhaps because of a speaking engagement in the vicinity.

There were persistent rumours in the village about Josiah and the community at Doddington: that his chapel choir was a 'row of little Oldfields'; that 'if the nurses weren't pregnant when they came to Margaret Manor, they soon became so'; that the members of the brigade who attended the fire in 1933 were implored by some of the nurses to take them away. There could be many reasons for this latter request: young girls might have found the fruitarian diet restrictive, the isolation of the hospital overwhelming and the work they were asked to perform rather different from the 'nursing' they had anticipated.

Tea for the Children in 1932

The 'case of the pregnant nurses' is also susceptible to other interpretations. Perhaps some girls, with fewer financial resources than the society women previously mentioned, may also have found the rural surroundings of Doddington a convenient refuge from disapproving families. Since Josiah employed some 'nurses' with few, if any, formal qualifications, they could have worked for the hospital in order to cover the cost of their confinement and care.

There is a further possibility. Josiah encouraged those in search of health and glowing beauty to enjoy the benefits of cold baths followed by a brisk rub-down. At Doddington the cold-water treatment could take the form of rolling naked in the dew, a sight which encouraged local youths to investigate. The village policeman was sometimes called out to eject such unwanted visitors - but did the young men always content themselves with watching? Even in winter, when there might be frost or snow on the ground, Josiah insisted on the early morning open-air bath.

237

Dew baths in her 'wild garden' at Garsington Manor near Oxford were favoured by Lady Ottoline Morell, the society hostess who entertained the Literati of the day, including the Bloomsbury set. A similar free outlook was shared, to some extent, by many at this period. During the 1930s both men and women were enjoying cycling, rambling and similar open-air pursuits, clothes having become far less restrictive since girls had discarded tight corsets, dragging skirts and flannel underwear.

Displays involving large numbers of nubile young girls performing exercises with hoops and other apparatus were popular: we have probably all seen films made in pre-war Germany of such events. Josiah speaks proudly of his daughter's abilities: 'My daughter is a doctor (she had qualified in 1933, not long before those words were written), and I always challenge her to a contest in tree-climbing when she comes home and we are wandering together in our beech-woods'. Presumably some had criticized such activities on the part of a young lady, for Josiah dismisses those employing the terms 'hoyden' or 'tomboy' as having a warped mentality.

Josiah with Josie

He had much to say on the subject of clothing for women. 'Wear but few clothes so that sun and air can caress your skin' was one injunction. He thought it wrong that 'prostitutes and wantons' wore bright and attractive colours, while saintly women chose poor and ugly garments. 'Religion should teach us to have a beautiful soul, and so to care for and cherish and train the body....that we help to produce on earth the honest glory of Heaven. The better the girl, the more beautifully should she be turned out'. He did not favour bobbed hair.

238

Josiah's views on a woman's role in 1922 have been quoted earlier. A decade later, probably with a more fashionable and sophisticated readership in view, he suggested that a woman should also stimulate her mind: 'Grow plants of scent or beauty, take clay and model it, or wood and carve it, do stitchery, tapestry, become an artistic chef, learn your songs of gladness...' This is a quotation from *The Beauty Aspect of Health and Living*, published in 1935, of which the main themes are:-

To retain beauty, remain young. Think young.
The spiritual moulds the material; thought transforms matter.
Take the greatest care to dress attractively and suitably: taste and delicacy are of more value than cost.
Diet is crucial, and in youth should be based on bread, cheese, fruit and salads.

He had advice on improving pimply or coarse skin: milk, groats and honey three or more times a day, this diet to be accompanied by vigorous bodily exercise such as 'sawing, digging, dancing, skipping, walking, trotting, scrubbing floors or laundering'. Smoking and tea-drinking were to be condemned. Josiah suggested aids to hide deformity, or skilled surgery to correct it, but also recommended the employment of 'thought forces'. This teaching echoed Coué's earlier prescription of the regular recital of the mantra 'Every day, in every way, I become better and better'. Sidney Beard too thought it 'helpful to make mental affirmations - especially during trying conditions', some examples being 'I am Spirit - perfect, holy, harmonious', or 'The abundant Christ-life, strength and health, are being built up within me!'

Chapter 28

Josiah's Travels

Travel was something which Josiah obviously enjoyed. That he was familiar with several modern languages as well as those employed during his theological studies is evident from the frequent quotations from French and German authors in *The Penalty of Death*. As a young man he had been to France - writing in *The Vegetarian* in 1893 he recalled days 'when we used to ramble over the wilds of Fenouillet on the Mediterranean shore in search of wild asparagus...' (A search on current maps for this area has found only Fenouillet north of Toulouse, hardly the Mediterranean shore.) The memories were still strong fifty years later, for in *The Mystery of Marriage* he wrote 'I well remember my first all night journey when as a youth, growing into a man, I sat upright in a hard wooden third-class carriage through the long hours between Paris and Marseilles...'

There were other visits to France. The large horse chestnut tree close to Ellen's Oast at Doddington was grown from a conker Josiah said he had picked up from the grave of Marie Antoinette (of whom according to Roy Ashby he was a great admirer) in Paris in about 1900. Josiah refers in *The Penalty of Death* to an 'annual continental holiday of spiritual physicians' which he presumably attended. The Riviera was, however, the area he preferred, and there are frequent references to his times there in his letters and books. Perhaps at first he stayed as a guest in the type of Vegetarian establishment which was advertised by its proprietors, Mr and Miss Lalla, in the *Herald of the Golden Age* in 1910:

'In the sunny south of France - Beautiful Winter residence - Magnificent situation in up-country amidst pine forests. Pure air laden with ozone - sun and steam baths. Terms 4/- to 6/- daily.'

By 1914 his travels had taken him to Northern Africa. He wrote to the Editor of *The Times* on March 24th of that year from

Hammam-Meskoutine, in Algeria, his subject an apparently as yet unconsidered aspect of patriotism. 'In conversation with hundreds of English men and women whom one meets on the Riviera and in Algiers and Tunisia' he wrote, 'I am struck with the important fact that the difficulties of domestic house-keeping in England loom largely among the reasons that have induced them to adopt a more or less gipsy life abroad. A very large percentage, having given up the large house that they inherited, have taken a small place as a pied à terre which they occupy for a few months of each year and which they shut up for the greater part of the year while they are travelling. The simplicity of life which is covered by a weekly cheque with no responsibility whatsoever is very attractive to a growing class of people who find that keeping house in a fixed home in England is one long wearisome worry with a kaleidoscopic succession of servants. It is well that we should face changing social conditions and understand their causes, especially in cases where the changes will tend to affect the patriotism and the home life of the race.'

This letter illustrates the fact that Josiah by now was mixing with the respectable upper classes - forgotten, at least temporarily, were the days of stone-breaking or boot-cleaning to earn a shilling or two. (Some of today's VIPs find it just as expedient either to forget or recall student life, working behind a bar or clearing tables for a pittance, as circumstances demand.) No doubt he too found it something of a relief to leave the responsibilities of his hospitals completely in the hands of others for a while.

He did not confine his activities abroad to talking to fellow countrymen, however, but spent his time in observing the customs, and particularly the diet, of the native population. After he returned to England from India in 1901 Josiah concluded 'I felt that I had not travelled from Harley St to India without adding considerably to my stock of knowledge of preventive medicine.' His natural curiosity and desire to understand must surely sometimes have led to misunderstandings in certain countries. In *The Mystery of Marriage*, before describing his idea of perfect womanhood, he mentions 'my own observation in lands where women live behind the veil...'. Discretion was not a trait usually associated with Josiah.

When he visited Kairouan in Tunisia, a desert city formerly forbidden to non-Mohammedans, he 'had the privilege of being present in the black tent' where he watched the dervishes roused to religious frenzy apparently piercing their bodies with knives and skewers without feeling any pain. Josiah sought to explain what he had observed: he thought that perhaps their cheeks and tongues had been pierced long before, so that the insertion of foreign bodies was akin to women putting in earrings. What he found more mysterious was the effect on the whole of those present of the sound and the motion, for he himself felt the urge to join in the frenzied dance and howl with the rest of the audience. Others have described the 'strong sense of spiritual intoxication' experienced at similar ceremonies, watching spinning Sufi dervishes with one arm extended to heaven and the other to the ground in order to receive Allah's grace and extend it to mankind.

Josiah's scepticism in the face of such scenes came into play in India also. During a tour ('while a guest of one of the Rajahs') his quarters one night were in a 'devil's temple', and the local villagers sought to impress their visitor with a performance by the resident fakir. He 'bashed himself with iron chains, ate glass, howled and contorted himself, and in the end mouthed large quantities of red powder which they assured me was virulent poison'. Whereupon Josiah produced from his waistcoat pocket a pill which he told them was powerful enough to kill three men within three minutes of being taken, and challenged the fakir to swallow it. The offer was refused, the villagers remarking only "Ah, Sahib, you know too much". A pleasant evening's chat followed. Describing these experiences later Josiah concluded that 'jugglers and jongleurs have amazed the world since the earliest time and every religion has utilised psychological phenomena to gain power for their priests'.

The foods eaten by the indigenous populations of the many places he visited were always of paramount interest to Josiah. One factor that he noticed while in the Mediterranean area was the universal use of olive oil in the preparation and serving of

242

food. Here too he 'was very much struck ... in the South of France, that boiled potatoes were shown on the menu as **English** potatoes - the only way we know.' As well as enlivening potatoes olive oil could replace butter at breakfast - dry toast might be dipped in it. And it had another, non-culinary, function, for rubbing it into the hands prevented chapping.

One winter during the nineteen-twenties Josiah had been 'watching sturdy Ligurian peasants carry sacks of grain up the long hill roads, and great logs of firewood timber down, hour after hour, always cheery, always willing, breathing deeply and soundly and with clean strong healthy teeth, perspiring steadily'. This was despite the fact that their principal, or perhaps their only, daily meal was based on vegetables, macaroni, beans, salads, onions, Indian corn meal, oil and a little cheese and milk. The arrays of olive oil and pasta on British supermarket shelves today, therefore, perhaps owe something to Josiah and his fellow-thinkers who sought to promote the availability of such foods in more northerly climes. In the early years of the twentieth century Josiah had found it necessary to explain what macaroni was. And little had changed fifty years later when Richard Dimbleby had many television viewers fooled on April 1st as he described the Italian spaghetti harvest...

Later, as his fame grew, Josiah spent more time abroad: in 1926 he talks of lecturing in 'the salon of one of the hotels on the Riviera where I happened to be spending the winter', and it is possible that he actually owned a residence in France for a time - in *Healing and the Conquest of Pain*, (written 1944) he speaks of 'my country-house door on the Riviera...'. His travels had also encompassed other parts of Europe. In an article written in the same year he recalled his experiences 'in the hospitals of Spain and Italy where pre-scorbutics were treated with rough red claret drinks, and in France and Switzerland where tisanes were the agencies invoked.'

But by 1949 he was giving his address as 'The Monks Hut, Doddington - except when wintering in Jamaica'. Having visited the colony on many occasions he already had friends there. One was the politician Norman Manley, himself a scholar, lawyer and athlete, who as leader of the People's National Party (and later Prime Minister) was a passionate advocate of universal suffrage.

One of the Fyffe's Line Vessels

When sailing to the West Indies Josiah preferred to travel by banana boat. He would not have lacked acceptable company, for Elders and Fyffes, well-known importers of the fruit, regularly advertised passages on their ships to those wishing to winter in the Bahamas or in the British West Indies. The boats carried about twenty passengers, all of whom dined with the Captain and had their own saloons and decks. There were weekly sailings to Jamaica, and on at least one occasion, during the winter of 1936-7, Josiah earned a fee of £1.0.0 for giving a lecture aboard the SS *Carare*. Josiah is said to have brought back bananas to the children at Doddington, the first they had seen.

One of his activities in Jamaica was studying the health of the children in different environments, and he speaks of examining the mouths of hundreds of children in rural areas and in the capital, Kingston. Here white bread and sweets in the diet were leading to dental caries. In contrast the children on the sugar plantations, whose food was mainly fruit and vegetables, and who cleaned their teeth as they chewed the fibrous cane, had healthy mouths.

His always-receptive mind also recorded other aspects of the way of life on the island. From his earliest days as a student of Theology beliefs and practices of other cultures had been one of his major interests, and presumably these would have provided a fruitful area for discussion with his brother William and others. In *Fasting for Health & Life* (1924), for instance, he describes how 'Today in Jamaica they don't sleep under a cotton-tree, for here, they believe, ghosts hold carnival during the hours of darkness...' His friend Sidney Beard believed sleep provided an opportunity for communication, maintaining that the words 'He giveth his beloved sleep' were more correctly rendered as 'He giveth **to** his beloved **during** sleep', and that in that time some were permitted to enter a higher plane of consciousness from which they returned both refreshed and enlightened. Repetition of maxims such as 'God's abundant Life and Knowledge are available for me!' could help to achieve such a state.

Josiah had a rather different view on what might happen during sleep, comparing the dreams experienced then with 'day-dreaming', where imagination supersedes reality to some extent, but during which we are still aware of the physical world around us. Despite the persistence of belief in the power of dreams like those experienced by Pharaoh and interpreted by Joseph, Josiah himself did not think that 'the Creator of the Cosmic system ever uses a night dream (as opposed to a day meditation and a scientific search into the arcana of theology) to convey planned directions to individuals or nations.' Josiah tended to agree with primitive peoples who regarded sleep, in which they might perhaps be able to fly, to become all-conquering heroes, or to live a completely different life, as a state of temporary death. Some awoke and related their experiences to relations and friends: others remained permanently in that dream world, leaving a lifeless body behind. Eventually, Josiah was to write, all will 'associate the dream state with supreme happiness and contentment and safety'. The fear of death which has dogged man from primeval times will be overcome, and sleep and death will be regarded as 'twin brothers in all their beauty and attractiveness'.

Josiah, as a member of the Overseas Club, would there have encountered others with equally enquiring dispositions with whom he could discuss his theories. His own circle of friends already included many well-travelled men, such as James Ozanne, who had held clerical appontments in Mauritius and the Seychelles, and Francis Langford-James, whose ministry had taken him to France and to South Africa.

As Josiah's obituary in *The Times* would record, 'He became so taken up with the peculiar problems of the West Indies that he applied for and was admitted to the Jamaican Bar'. His name remained on the Law List as a Member of the Jamaican Bar from 1935 to 1949.

There is also some evidence, in the form of a number of unused postcard views of these countries, that he visited both Barbados and the Bahamas. The cards, together with various leaflets concerned with the Lady Margaret Hospitals at Bromley and Doddington, and a few other odds and ends, were found when alterations were being carried out at Josiah's former home at Margaret Manor. They date from before the fire, but were almost lost when the builders discarded them as rubbish. If they **do** represent souvenirs of Josiah's travels, then Perth and Albany in Western Australia might be added, and even Chile. There are several copies of a postcard showing a single-storey hospital at Creswick, Dr Abramovski's institution north of Melbourne in south-eastern Australia.

Josiah's paper *Starch as a Food in Nature* is listed as an excerpt from the transactions of the Congress of Vegetarian Federal Unions in Chicago in 1893, but it was not delivered in person. The delegates from England on that occasion were W.E.Axon, Rev. James Clark and Ernest C.Clark: Josiah's paper was just one of forty given.

Did he later visit the United States? The answer is almost certainly yes. He was a member of the English-Speaking Union, whose links are mainly with that country, although no details of his period of connection with the ESU remain. The society aimed to promote good understanding between the people of the United States and the British Commonwealth. Josiah certainly

246

shared its vision of a better world, for it had been founded on the belief that 'the peace of the world and the progress of mankind can be largely helped by the unity in purpose of the English-speaking democracies'.

How far east did he travel? The only reference I have found is in a wide-sweeping paragraph where Josiah describes how 'It has been my **duty** [my emphasis] in life to spend hours and days in asylums and workhouses, in hospitals and infirmaries, in homes for the dying and homes for incurables, in the lazar houses of the east and the sanatoria of the west, in palaces of splendour and hovels of squalor, in the society of princes and millionaires, and in the comradeship of paupers and scalawags'. Some of these visits, surely, must have been more than a duty? But the words were written in 1929, so perhaps it was in later years that duty receded and pleasure played a larger part.

Chapter 29

The Red Lion Square Project

Reference has been made (in his correspondence with the publisher C.A.Daniel) to the acquisition by Josiah of premises in Red Lion Square, London. This square, lying between Theobalds Road and High Holborn, was originally laid out in 1684, and even today retains some of its central grass and trees. No.17, on the southern side, was once the home of D.G.Rossetti, and later of William Morris and Sir Edward Burne-Jones, but by the 1930s it had been divided up, providing offices for a solicitor, for the Fellowship of Reconciliation and for the University Examination Postal Institution. The same fate had overtaken most of the original houses, including Nos.18 and 19. Contemporary street directories confirm what can be seen in a photograph (taken, probably, in the early twenties), that the next building was No.20, on the opposite side of Red Lion Passage, housing a law stationer's business, Lloyd & Co.

Red Lion Passage

From 1934-39 Nos. 18 and 19 are listed as the premises of 'International Sponge Importers', but not until 1935 is there a record of No.19A. At first its name is given as the Lady Margaret Fruitarian Hospital, with a change in 1938 to St Francis Hospital.

Inspection of the relevant large-scale Ordnance Survey map

248

dated 1938 agrees with the other information, so presumably Josiah's clinic was to occupy part of No.19.

The annual reports of the Lady Margaret Hospital are dominated during the early 1930s by the proposed out-patient department of the hospital which it was intended to open in Holborn. In 1933, when explaining the previous year's balance sheet to those attending the Annual General Meeting, Josiah stressed that the purchase of freehold premises in the Square had proved a satisfactory investment, the rents paid by tenants being sufficient to pay off the loans raised earlier. It was evidently taking longer than expected to open the department, for a letter quoted in the same report from a Miss Jameson regrets that 'the splendid venture, the Outpatient Clinic in Red Lion Square, is not yet in working order owing to lack of funds'. She herself was unable to be one of the ten friends sought by Josiah to give twenty pounds each.

When the report for 1933 was published, it was confidently headed 'The Lady Margaret Fruitarian Hospital, 19A Red Lion Square and Doddington, Kent'. A summer opening in 1934 was predicted, and an appeal was made for volunteers of all kinds to help with 'cleaning, painting, carpentering, sweeping, decorating, book-keeping, general service, giving helpful talks to individual patients, &c.' A particularly keen enthusiast was Miss Dorothy Marshall of Bristol, who had already volunteered to come and live in London to organize the out-patient clinic. She would welcome all who would help her to make it a 'centre of attraction to those who needed more faith, more hope, and more wisdom in the ways of living, so that they might attain to higher and sounder health and well-being'. Hundreds would, she hoped, learn there of the right food, clothes and habits of living and looking upon life.

Though somewhat delayed, the Outpatient Clinic was formally opened on the 21st November 1934 by Lady Smith-Dodsworth, and it was probably on this occasion that it was given the name of St Francis' Hospital, honouring the saint who loved animals. When she reported on its activities the following April, Miss Marshall spoke of gifts including pictures and bandages, and of payments for window-cleaning and the cost of a telephone - but did not mention patients. Josiah, in his address, emphasized that it was intended as a **diagnostic** centre: treatment was more appropriately carried out in the country at Doddington. Much of the hospital report for 1935 was concerned with the recent change in status of the Battersea Anti-Vivisection Hospital, which had been forced to give up its ideals and principles in the process of transformation to a modern scientific hospital.

There was a further appeal for voluntary help in 1936, and a year later it is evident that the clinic in London was not a success. Dorothy Marshall had resigned as Honorary Secretary, as had Treasurer Hugh Marshall on the grounds of old age and failing health. (Were they father and daughter?) Josiah spoke of slow progress, pointing out that there was no attempt to measure the work numerically, a statement he was to reiterate a few months later when he explained that the aim had always been to attract the more difficult cases, patients who had not been helped by orthodox treatment.

Although the secretarial and financial positions remained unfilled Josiah's outlook in April 1939 was positive. 'The work in London has steadily progressed, and now that the whole premises are taken over it is hoped that ere long the upper portion, which is now sub-let, may be utilised for fitting up necessary treatment rooms and installing all the latest methods by which cases of illness can be wisely diagnosed and efficiently treated'. This, of course, was linked with further appeals for help, financial or otherwise. The name of St Francis had disappeared from the cover of the report: perhaps there were still unfortunate memories of Josiah's previous hospital of the same name in the New Kent Road.

By this date there were other factors impeding progress. An apology for absence from the AGM written by a Miss Stephenson hoped that 'you will have a good meeting, and that by the time it comes (19th April 1939 was the date arranged) Hitler will have come to his senses. He is certainly a good advertisement for the energy-producing attributes of reformed diet. As for the humanising influence of the same, the less said, the better...'

Hitler, however, pursued his aims, and the Lady Margaret Fruitarian Hospital report for 1940 begins by relating the reduction in the clinic's work to the blackout and transport difficulties now that the country was at war. Many prospective patients had moved away from the town, which had one advantage as far as Fruitarians were concerned - it sent people back to the soil, the source of health, wealth and fertility. Despite all this, a doctor had attended once every week without fail, Josiah usually seeing outpatients each Wednesday morning, while Dr Olaf Gleeson attended in the afternoon. Although Red Lion Square had frequently suffered from enemy attacks, so far St Francis' had lost not even a chip of paint, and its staff appreciated the blessings which had kept them safe.

Red Lion Square in 1946 - No. 19 has disappeared.

Alas, Josiah was premature in his thanksgiving, for between the preparation of the report (which would have been presented in mid-April 1941) and its printing, the building was totally destroyed. The last page of the booklet reads

'This page was reserved for the Audited Balance Sheet but owing to the destruction of Offices and Books the Balance Sheet cannot be prepared at present. A typescript copy will be available for every subscriber to see a little later on. It is with the greatest regret that we have to announce the complete annihilation and total destruction of the St Francis Clinic in Red Lion Square. Special donations are invited towards its rebuilding in due course, in a far more glorious building'.

Photographs taken during the war reveal the damage to Red Lion Square, with No.17 the last house left standing at the south-eastern corner. Nos.18,19,20,21 and 22, and the whole of Red Lion Passage, had disappeared. It was probably the raid of 17th April 1941 which was responsible - there were many casualties in the Holborn area on that night. Only a week later, on 23rd April, a resident of Margaret Manor named William Leach was killed by enemy action in Red Lion Street nearby.

Chapter 30

The Declining Appeal of Doddington in the Later 1930s

The story of the new clinic, at least until 1940, perhaps mirrors what was happening to the Lady Margaret Hospital as a whole. One problem was the recruitment and retention of trustworthy staff. Josiah wrote that 'the classes who formerly took up housekeeping and home-making duties with eager zest are now being attracted into other channels'. Four voluntary workers needed to be on duty every day at the hospital, helping with administration and treating the patients. There were vacancies for 'cleaners, washers-up, keepers of books, receptionists, attendants, visitors, collectors, teachers, lecturers, administrators, masseuses, hostesses, organisers, typists, sewers, craftsmen and women - people already skilled and people who will humbly learn how to become useful. All who want to help (by some personal self-sacrifice) either sick men or suffering animals are invited to offer their services in London or at Doddington.' By now there was no 'free board' available: instead comfortable accommodation at moderate terms could be arranged at the guest house, where those in search of increased vitality and renewed health were invited to spend a few weeks, observing the work of a 'community for healing'.

It had become increasingly difficult to attract nurses to Doddington, a place where there were no excitements or amusements, particularly in winter, and in consequence there had been no proper nursing care available since 1932. The elderly Miss Garrett was, by 1934, both Acting Matron and Honorary Secretary, and in 1936 two long-serving members of staff, Miss M.Paul and Miss M.Hunt, left to open their own seaside home.

Josiah was gradually coming to realise that the rural life at Margaret Manor, where all cooking and heating was via wood cut down, sawn and split on the premises, where waste water was simply thrown on the nearest patch of earth, and daily work was disguised as a 'daily interest', was no longer universally acceptable. The 1937 report spoke of the hope to instal a hot water system to provide hot baths, and indoor sanitation: septic tanks would be placed in the fields. The following year the report appealed for gifts of beds and mattresses - presumably straw palliasses were another source of complaints by guests. Josiah continued to maintain, however, that 'central heating is always associated with a close atmosphere and lack of sufficient fresh air', recommending instead the regime of open grates, log fires, and open windows practised at Doddington.

By the winters of the late thirties, though, Josiah himself was usually more comfortable in the warmer climate of Jamaica. The 1933 annual report explained that arrangements were being made by which 'elderly or weakly persons of limited means can escape the cold winds by spending their winters in the West Indies', and this offer was accepted by at least one gentleman, for at the Annual General Meeting the following year he spoke of the benefits he had derived from such a stay.

Josiah's annual absence was another factor contributing to the general decline in the fortunes of the Lady Margaret Hospital, where the inhabitants now were mostly old and depressed. In the latter years of the thirties the patients treated were those with digestive, pulmonary or nervous disorders, rheumatism, wasting or obesity, skin troubles, insomnia and 'loss of hope in life'. It was emphasized that 'cases **must** be mentally able to understand, and physically able, to look after themselves sufficiently that they need neither external restriction, nor what is commonly called "nursing"'. By the end of the decade the hospital had become largely a place where 'a certain number of pathetic cases of refugees not wanted by anybody' could find a resting place and a peaceful home. It was on these grounds that Josiah had appealed to George Bernard Shaw (and no doubt to many others), writing:

'I noted with pleasure the report of your birthday a little while ago.
May I assume that since you have attained to the age laid down by the psalmist as the age of wisdom and benevolence,

254

that you would be interested in poorer men and women who, through the stress of economic conditions, and who having attained the age when the labour market no longer requires them, have to do the best they can in a somewhat unsympathetic world.

For many years I have faced the problem of men who are met wherever they go asking for work, with the reply that they are 'too old'.

You and I well know that the physical powers may have become less flexible, and the vital energy behind the muscles somewhat reduced in intensity, and the breathing apparatus is beginning to be unable to stand up to exhaustive strain, but none the less the brain power, the will to live, the interest in life, the stored-up experience, and the consciousness of creative capacity, all remain and ask for an outlet.

The pressure of life is to make such men either become despondent and lose the joy of living, or to drift into public houses, or to become satisfied with the lazy life of an animal, or to become a burden upon their relatives and friends.

Even when having attained the age of the old age pension, it is not very much of a life to sit in one room, to walk about the streets, and to draw 10/- a week for food and lodging.'

Elderly men resting

Josiah then drew Shaw's attention to the life offered to such cases at Doddington, referring him to articles printed in *Reynolds News* and the *Weekly Illustrated*.

255

He continued 'It would be well if this scheme, which has proved itself by experience, could have a wider scope and greater development. For myself, I have gladly carried out my share of it, and [for] up to a dozen men I have been only too pleased to have had the opportunity of devoting time and capital to carrying it out.

Now that it has proved itself, I shall be glad to have the interest of others to form a board to raise a fund for opening further centres elsewhere or developing this one in Kent.'

The *Weekly Illustrated* article cited portrays Josiah in the smock which was then his favoured clothing, and has photographs of the old men at their various occupations - hoeing, bricklaying, milking, carpentry, and resting outside the small huts in which they lived. Its report begins

'What are old men to do? Retire into idleness or cling on to jobs that younger men might have? At Doddington, in Kent, old men have transformed a derelict estate into a happy, thriving, and almost self-supporting community. They have done it for pleasure, not for pay.'

Josiah and some of his 'Refugees' at Work

It is a sign of the time at which this was published that emphasis is placed on the fact that no-one was put out of work and that there was no conflict with trade union principles. The labour the men offered was largely unpaid (board and lodging and pocket money only were provided) and the work would

256

otherwise not have been carried out.

Josiah was at pains in ending his letter to point out that he merely sought Shaw's opinion and interest, not a monetary contribution. Nevertheless he no doubt had hopes... It seems that the articles, and a Pathé newsreel also made in 1935 with the Doddington colony as its subject, led to a considerable increase in the amount donated by well-wishers.

Philip Yarnitz

Shaw's response to this appeal is not recorded. He may well have been regularly invited to attend the Lady Margaret Annual General Meeting, for it seems that Josiah freely distributed such invitations.

Those proffering their apologies in 1938 (no fewer than 69, of whom ten enclosed a cheque) included Sir Hamilton Harty, Beverly Nichols, Sybil Thorndike and Ellen Wilkinson. Yvonne Arnaud and Vernon Bartlett were approached in 1940, the latter being asked by Josiah to use his influence with the BBC to persuade people to forgo imported meat in favour of foods where energy was concentrated - oils and legumes. Perhaps Shaw was asked to do something similar, for that sage wrote back 'I'm too old (he was three months short of 85) and the Public knows all about my Vegetarianism and is tired of it. As most Vegetarians,

257

like bulls, rhinoceroses and enraged sheep, are extremely ferocious, they should be popular in wartime. I have always warmly appreciated your heroic activities in the Vegetarian Cause'.

It is instructive to compare the total amount shown on the balance sheet each year for printing, stationery, advertising, postage and similar expenses (A) with the sum designated as 'Maintenance (Doddington)' (B). This latter appears to be the **only** expenditure devoted to the hospital, covering everything from food to fencing.

All figures are to the nearest pound:

Year	1932	1933	1934	1935	1936	1937	1938	1939
A	156	162	164	151	224	221	245	207
B	172	194	145	112	167	184	166	183

Admittedly a large proportion of the food consumed would have been grown at the farm, but dried fruit, lentils and similar pulses would have to have been bought, as well as soap and oil for both cooking and lighting. Although curtains and rugs were probably deemed unnecessary, linen or towels wear out and need replacing. All labour was voluntary, so there was nothing allowed for wages, but fabric maintenance surely demanded the occasional new roof slate or pot of paint. This neglect of his property in the late thirties, followed by six years of war, meant that the buildings were in a very poor state when they were eventually sold following Josiah's death. Equally interesting are the amounts subscribed (D) and donated (E) over the same period. The outpatient department income is shown separately (F), and clearly demonstrates the London clinic's failing fortunes.

Year	1932	1933	1934	1935	1936	1937	1938	1939
D	144	111	152	118	217	153	182	128
E	251	158	71	306	166	169	172	233
F	67	161	272	40	69	31	1	0
Total	**462**	**430**	**495**	**464**	**452**	**353**	**355**	**361**

Members of the governing committee each gave £1 per week, a

sum which in 1938 had been unchanged for thirty years, and which does not appear to be shown in the accounts. This might explain the low figure shown for 'Maintenance' at Doddington.

Sometimes there were windfalls in the form of legacies, with a particularly welcome amount of £2000 in 1936. When announcing its receipt Josiah declared it to be 'the first instalment towards the £5000 needed for the purchase of suitable premises and alteration and fitting up, so as to make a small but complete Hospital of Nature Cure Healing'. Perhaps this confirms his appreciation of how unsuitable the current buildings at Margaret Manor were for treating discerning patients. There were still at least some women who were glad to come, for in the same year's report there is mention of the good maternity record being maintained, with no deaths and no sepsis. One mother wrote expressing her 'good will and good wishes to the author of *I want a Happy Baby*. This was possibly an updated version of *Advice to a Woman who is about to become a Mother*, by 'Sister Margaret' which was sent to enquirers in the Bromley days.

In 1934 Josiah had bemoaned the fact that although no fewer than six Governors had died, including the generous Lady Earnshaw Cooper, none had included the hospital in their wills. The deaths of many of his former patrons and friends during the decade meant a diminution in annual subscriptions and donations, and Josiah, as always, had some original ideas as to how to increase funds. In the 1936 Report he suggested that friends, on receiving their bank statement, might ask their bank managers to 'send the odd shillings and pence quarterly to the Lady Margaret Hospital account at the Midland Bank, Sittingbourne'. All gifts were faithfully listed at the end of each annual report, even gifts of used stamps and silver paper being acknowledged. In 1939 he was forced to announce, for the first time in the history of the hospital, a deficit on the balance sheet: expenditure had exceeded income by £7.1s.2d. His recommendation that year was that supporters should give 15/- Savings Certificates.

In spite of the signs of failure Josiah remained optimistic, his

259

address at the 1940 Annual General Meeting being entitled 'Blockaded but Unbroken'. As usual the hospital's friends met at the Russell Hotel in London, which apparently waived its charge for hire of the room by Josiah. The Right Reverend Bishop James proposed a vote of thanks to the hotel before all adjourned to the lounge there for a 'Conversazione, introductions and questions'. At these April meetings it was Josiah's daughter Josie whose role it was to read the annual report for the previous year.

Josiah aged about 80

Chapter 31

Josiah's contribution to the War Effort 1940-45

Josiah had been well aware of the worsening situation in Europe as the 1930s drew to a close, and war seemed inevitable. In a letter to his old Medical School journal he set out once again the principle by which he had served in the First War, that compassion crosses the boundaries of language, creed or uniform. 'I felt it a great privilege to be able to explain that by joining my command (the men) would have perfect freedom to heal and care for a German, Austrian or Turk... and it was of entire unimportance to them to what nationality a wounded or sick man belonged'. He addressed members of the RAMC as 'representing the Spirit of Compassionate Healing, the spiritual transformation of the arrival of the future...'

The Buildings at Margaret Manor seen from the Chapel Roof

261

A picture of the farm at Doddington as it was at the beginning of the forties can be gleaned from the National Farm Survey of 1940-43, whose records are stored at the Public Record Office. When war broke out in September 1939 there was an immediate realisation that food production would need to be increased, and therefore every holding of more than five acres was assessed. Each farmer had to fill in forms providing information about his acreage, his crops, stock, resources and manpower available. This was in June 1941. In addition every farm was visited by a member of the District Committee, which was made up of experienced practical farmers. This gentleman would record the area on the appropriate ordnance survey map, and interview the farmer concerned.

Josiah's forms, addressed to 'Lt.Col.J.Oldfield, Margaret Manor', are filed under reference MAF32/1022 158/12. They show that Josiah's land supported a small herd of cows, 23 in all, and a flock of 39 sheep. A single sow was kept for breeding, and half a dozen hens completed the farm stock. Much of the land was permanent grazing, but mangolds and turnips were grown for fodder, together with two acres of potatoes and smaller areas of other vegetables and soft fruit. At the time of the survey crops in hand included six tons of hay and a quarter-acre of strawberries. The labour available, according to Form C47, consisted of four males, all over 21, of whom only one was full-time. He was noted as 'family'. There was no tractor: a small petrol engine and a 3kW electric motor were the only mechanical aids. The latter provided light and power for household use only. Piped water **was** available.

The Farm Survey Form B adds details of the condition of the farmhouse (good), its buildings and fences (fair). The soil was of medium quality, its drainage good, but the land was infested with rabbits, moles, rooks and pigeons. Form B was completed in December 1942 by the District Committee Inspector, who also had to give his view of the state of the farm and the quality of its management. Lady Margaret Manor was graded 'B', the reason for such an assessment being given as 'old age', with 'owner not seriously interested in farming' under 'personal failings'.

The inspector added that most of the holding was let to neighbouring farmers, Josiah using only a few small fields for his own stock. Mr Sage of Temple Farm rented some fields; a Mr Thompson, described as a café proprietor, had occupied 30 acres of the Margaret Manor land for six months, but in this case form B noted that his was 'poor land, very badly farmed'. On it he kept poultry and three cows, presumably to supply eggs and milk for his café.

What of the Hospital? Josiah still took in a few patients, notably pregnant girls or young women. It frequently happened that under wartime conditions, when an air raid might curtail their life, or a lover or fiancé might not return from the front, that a couple would make the most of the time they had together, often with unfortunate consequences for the girl left behind. Two London nurses found themselves in this position in 1940, and were taken in without question at Margaret Manor. Their babies were born there, with the assistance of the village midwife, and were subsequently adopted. One of those babies later was to find and speak to her birth mother, who had nothing but good words for Josiah - 'A very kind man'.

Apparently Josiah's position on vaccination remained unchanged. One of those babies born at the Manor in 1940 retains the 'Notice of Requirement of Vaccination' supplied by the Registrar requesting Dr Porter, the Public Vaccinator, to call at Margaret Manor to vaccinate Isobel Mary Henderson. The space for Doctor Porter's signature remains blank, so presumably he was not welcomed at that address. [Isobel's name was changed when she was subsequently adopted.]

Farming and treatment of just a few patients evidently did not satisfy Josiah's need to keep busy. In 1944, while engaged in writing a substantial book, he intimated that he had volunteered for a large Midlands mental hospital, but whether his services were accepted is not known for certain (he would have been over eighty at the time). It seems that he did spend at least part of the war years living in a large hospital where there were long-term patients, but the clues to which are scanty. From *The Mystery of Death* we learn that its site was less than ten acres, and that its 'heavy' buildings were connected by long tree-shaded corridors. In all there were some 2000 patients and staff. Approximately thirty deaths occurred each month, and while Josiah was there about six hundred died. This would mean that he was employed there for perhaps eighteen months.

Josiah also volunteered his services in another direction at this period, for he wrote to the BBC offering to speak on a variety of subjects including the declining birthrate, Gandhi, and work for the elderly. His offers were not taken up.

It was as a result of the war, in particular the destruction of a particular house in Brixton by a land mine, that Ellen's Oast, formerly the larger part of the hospital at Margaret Manor, took on a new role.

Roy Ashby and his partner Jim Babbington were co-founders of the Stansfield Association, which took in boys orphaned by the blitz, or from unsuitable homes, or who had perhaps been referred by the courts.

Roy Ashby and Jim Babbington

When their London refuge was destroyed they had found temporary headquarters on a farm near Reading, with a chance for the boys to cultivate 15 acres of market garden. Realising that such an environment was ideal Roy and Jim placed a single advertisement in *The Times* seeking similar more permanent accommodation. They received just one reply - from Doddington. Agreement was reached, and the Stansfield Association rented the former oasthouse (Ellen's Court) and its surrounding land as a home for boys from London's East End.

In his account of the Association, *Never a Dull Moment*, Roy Ashby describes the estate in 1949. At this time Josiah appears to have used both the Monks Hut, whose snug interior Ashby says was filled with carvings and treasures from all parts of the world, and also 'Greetynge Lodge' on the opposite side of the road. Ashby writes:

'Learnt, perhaps, while he was a Lieutenant-Colonel in the '14-18 War, everything had to be done at the double to satisfy the Doctor's activity, and one knew immediately when he was home, as the traffic across the road between Greetynge Lodge and Monks Hut was continuous. Secretaries could be seen with skirts lifted to their knees, haring across the road with their sheaves of paper, as if their very survival depended on it... And yet, oddly enough, in advertising for a new secretary, he would add "in a quiet Private Country Hospital - would suit a cripple"'

In fact Josiah's desire for speed dates back to his student days, for he writes in *Get Well and Keep Well* (1926) 'when I was an Undergrad(sic) at Oxford I made the trot my habitual pace, and I found it quite as easy as walking'.

Greetynge Lodge was used by Josiah's private patients. Most of these were exploring the fruitarian and other diets, but there were also some mentally disturbed patients. Roy Ashby continues:

'And so, added to his dietetic guests at Greetynge Lodge, there were scattered round Margaret Manor quite a number of these mild cases, many of whom on first acquaintance you would not think had anything missing. And the Doctor made a practice of never telling anybody which was which, and that added considerably to the whimsical appeal of the place... A most charming, educated and cultured gentleman gave me my first real initiation. He asked for the loan of a comfortable bed, which I was delighted to oblige him with.

During an air raid he worked it out that bomb blast might kill him, but not if he was lower. So he sawed off the legs...'

Peter Jones, a Doddington resident, wrote later of Josiah's patients that 'He also took men into this Hospital that were backward or slightly mental; these men all came from wealthy families who were prepared to pay Dr Oldfield very well to keep them at his hospital, to keep them from being a social burden on their families'. Some of the patients would walk down from Margaret Manor to Doddington itself, sometimes even to Sittingbourne or Faversham.

Most of the occupants of Margaret Manor, however, were female. When a barn in a field close to Ellen's Oast caught fire, they did their best to help, bringing cups or jugs of water and 'tiptoeing back to refill them'... It is difficult to visualise the same ladies chopping or sawing wood each morning after their bath in the dew, as they were required to do before breakfast was served. Some were epileptic, and wore tea-cosies on their heads to protect them if they fell while suffering a seizure.

Roy Ashby also quotes Josiah as saying 'If you ever have a loved one, never let them go into a Mental Home', citing his 'life-time connection' as a Medical Officer in such homes. It is not clear whether this means that Josiah **had** been formally attached to some large public institution(s) in this capacity, or whether his experience was largely confined to the patients whom he treated in his own hospitals. In *Get Well and Keep Well*, published in the mid 1920s, he refers to the Hanwell Asylum (Middlesex's first County Asylum) where he had observed the preparation of gruel in the kitchens. One of his many early publications was entitled *Diet in Relation to Insanity*.

Chapter 32

The Postwar Years

By 1945 Josiah was over eighty, but despite his failings as a farmer, as vigorous as ever. Although now enjoying the warmer climate of Jamaica during the winter months he was still, as Roy Ashby writes, displaying 'the vitality of a boy. Even at that age I have heard his challenge to climb any tree on the estate to prove his agility, subtlety of limb and freedom from pain in any joint, which would still the laugh from any of those who can't at half the age.'

The Interior of the Chapel

The buildings put up at Doddington, however, were not in such good shape. Mr Ashby gives an idea of how some of those erected a generation earlier had fared. Speaking of the 'Arch of Peace', he says 'Like many of the structures put up with too much amateur enthusiasm and not enough expert advice, it lacked the necessary foundations, and although the inscription above invited you to enter beneath with Peace in your Soul, its positively dangerous lean downwards struck fear into most stout hearts, and soon none would venture through.'

The Chapel, attached to Greetynge Lodge, also had its

problems, although these were not confined to the construction. The stalls there had been designed so that occupants were not disturbed by their neighbours, although a few benches were also provided. But tranquillity was not always maintained. While the Stansfield boys, most of whom had rarely been inside a church, were living at Ellen's Court, they enjoyed the services held there, for 'anything could happen - and frequently did'. Jumping on loose floorboards could rock the pillars, palm fronds used for decoration were equally handy for tickling an unsupecting neighbour, a flying cat might suddenly land on the preacher's shoulders...

The Stansfield boys were able to perform similar work to that which Josiah had recommended, and performed, working on the farm of which the Monks Hut had once formed part, to raise useful crops. These boys were 'other people's difficult children - youngsters alleged to be out-of-hand, delinquents, probation boys with long Borstal sentences suspended for a last try, chaps out of mental homes with those flat dark minds, fellows who have thrown half a dozen violent fits in a day...' The rehabilitation of such boys would have been a project which appealed to Josiah's humanitarian feelings.

He himself must have appeared equally strange to them. Wearing a singlet and khaki shorts, from which protruded spindly white legs, he was remarkably spry on his feet.

....'spindly white legs'

Young trespassers discovered this to their cost when caught scrumping fruit (which no-one was bothering to harvest) in his orchard. Two brothers from the village, who were aged about six and ten at the time, had collected a basketful of apples when Josiah found them. He took the basket, and made them follow him to his study, a small room with many books, scented by wood smoke from a fire burning there despite the heat of the day. He stood them in front of his desk and lectured them at great length, quoting from the Bible. The six-year old was reduced to tears when told that as a thief he was doomed to hell: Joseph, the elder, was not so easily intimidated. A week later they were sent by their mother to retrieve the basket. They were admitted by a 'little grey lady, then, as always, sad, as they all were'. The fruit was still in its basket, untouched and beginning to rot. Joseph bravely persisted in his request until eventually, when faced with another lecture, he seized the basket, tipped out the fruit, and the two made their escape.

The boys and their parents were familiar with several of the residents of Margaret Manor - usually about half a dozen. One patient was an elderly gentleman who invariably wore a thick black overcoat and a woolly hat drawn down over his forehead whatever the weather. He walked always in the same position, one hand on his breast, the other as though protecting a tail. Another, who was known as 'David', appeared to do much of the hard work, especially collecting firewood. When passing the brothers' bungalow he would look longingly into the kitchen, and was often given a thick hunk of bread, butter and jam, for which he was most grateful.

Harvest was still celebrated in the chapel each year, and most of the local residents were invited. The two boys and their parents attended on one occasion, curious to see for themselves what such a service entailed. The chapel, which was only 12-14' wide, appeared crowded. Joseph found the service boring, remembering only the excruciating singing of traditional hymns like 'We plough the fields and scatter'. Josiah's daughter Josie, who was regarded as a very pleasant lady, was probably present, although her visits were infrequent.

Josiah did have other visitors. The names of George Bernard Shaw and Rabindranath Tagore (who died in 1941) as well as that of Gandhi have been mentioned by latter-day residents, but usually it is a case of 'My mother told me she thought she once saw...' Some local people had a chance to meet him in different circumstances, and what they observed of his habits only added to his reputation for eccentricity. The builders carrying out some essential repairs at the Manor, which had been afflicted by woodworm, were somewhat taken aback when he insisted on remaining in bed, dictating to the faithful Miss Oliver a letter to *The Times*, while they removed the ceiling above him. Ignoring the noise, dust and even danger he invited them to carry on with their job while he did the same. The same workmen on another occasion (they were running a waste pipe from his bath to the garden) noted that his breakfast that day consisted of a quarter of a raw savoy cabbage. Josiah, though, always paid their bills on time.

Ken Parfitt

Ken Parfitt, first Warden of the Youth Hostel into which Ellen's Oast had been transformed in 1947, was another who observed the privations of Josiah's 'guests'. The structures in which some of them were housed were in a state of squalor, for Josiah in his later years neglected the upkeep of his property.

While he was wintering in Jamaica Miss Oliver ('his secretary for countless years') was nominally in charge. She was a dear lady, but had no idea how to care for the men during the bitterly cold Kent winters. Ken, young and inexperienced, supplemented their disciplined vegetarian diet with large saucepans of soup - made from meat broth! He had seen for himself the meagre salads, so insubstantial that a draught might have blown them away, which Miss Oliver (though officially 'Secretary' of the hospital) helped to prepare for them.

She herself was not averse to a kipper, as Ken discovered when he called at her home one evening, her secret revealed by the pungent smell and fishy tail just visible protruding from a hastily covered plate. Miss Oliver at the time lived in a little room at one end of a nearby farmhouse, but when Josiah died he left her a small strip of land. Here she installed a gypsy caravan which became her home until she moved to sheltered accommodation some ten years later. Miss Oliver was a woman of great tact, and never referred to Josiah's affairs. She herself is thought to have borne him a daughter who was fostered out, but never mentioned. It was probably because of this that she adopted the courtesy title of **Mrs** Oliver.

Although apparently oblivious to the hardships suffered by the elderly folk in his own establishment, Josiah maintained his interest in other aspects of humanitarianism. In December 1947 a talk by Sir Samuel Hoare on the subject of capital punishment had been broadcast in which he pointed out that many murders were unpremeditated, committed in moments of passion or by the insane, so that the death penalty could not act as a deterrent in such cases. In others life imprisonment would be just as effective. 'I am not prepared to abandon the hope of reforming the murderer', he said, arguing that the Abolition of Capital Punishment should feature in the Criminal Justice Bill just introduced by Chuter Ede.

Such sentiments accorded with Josiah's thinking, and in April 1948 he wrote to Sir Samuel (now Lord Templewood) from Jamaica:-

'Dear Lord Templewood,

I read with much interest the report in *The Times* of your Plea that there is no longer any place in the Penal Code for capital punishment.

I venture to suggest to you that if ever you have a spare hour you might glance through one or two of the chapters in my book entitled *The Penalty of Death*. I wrote this book when I was taking my DCL degree at Oxford. Bell & Co published it and copies can be found in most libraries.

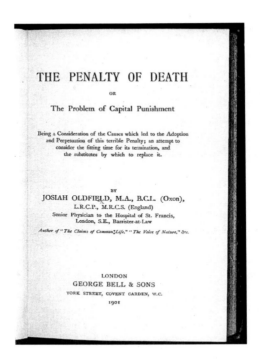

Title Page of *The Penalty of Death*

'If you have the wish to write a little prelude I think it would be well worth while to issue a leaflet containing some of the salient points in support of the claim that "humans do not come into this world to be sent out again". Boys and girls of all sorts, good and bad, are sent to school for education. The best schools turn out the best scholars. Any school which has to expel its pupils is stamped thereby as being an incompetent spiritual power. In the same way we are shirking our life duty towards those poor individuals who come here for help, by despatching them out of the world instead of attaching each one to some spiritual teacher or yogi or leader for conversion to higher principles of living.

272

I send your Lordship kindest greetings and good wishes.

Josiah Oldfield.

It is possible that Lord Templewood had met Josiah, or at least knew of him as a committed Fruitarian, for a note from Victor Gollancz to Curtis Brown written in 1951 reads 'I have an idea that Templewood is a vegetarian'. There is, however, no copy of a reply to Josiah's letter among the Templewood Papers. When Sir Samuel, who was later to become known as the architect of the 1948 Criminal Justice Act, gave evidence to the Royal Commission on Capital Punishment he stated:-

'Capital punishment is objectionable because, contrary to the modern developments of penal reform, it abandons the possibility of reforming the murderer; secondly, being irrevocable, it gives no opportunity for reversing a wrong sentence; thirdly, it places a hateful duty on all who take part in an execution; and fourthly, it lowers the moral standard of the whole community'.

Josiah immediately sent a lengthy further communication to Lord Templewood, this time enclosing a copy of his book rather than recommending use of a library, but reiterating the points made in his previous letter. Josiah's handwriting was by now somewhat wavery and difficult to interpret, perhaps not surprising at the age of 87. This may explain some obvious errors in the typing: ('Directorate' rather than 'Doctorate' when Josiah mentions his degree in Civil Law; 'excuse' rather than 'execute' when he referred to homicidal maniacs as being the only class of murderer for whom no reform might be possible) and it may also be responsible for the obscurity in meaning of some paragraphs. The concluding lines emphasise Josiah's personal idea of treating murderers:-

'I always feel that the church of every country should be responsible for its murderers and to every bishop for

273

example or priest or monastery a murderer should be assigned until he is cured. Just as the medical profession of today never put (a) leper to death but doctors still spend lives in solving the problems of obscure diseases - so professors of religion should spend their time in solving the problems of spiritual diseases'.

Lord Templewood thanked Josiah for his 'very valuable book' on 2nd January 1951, promising to send a copy of his expanded comments on the evidence he had given to the Royal Commission at a later date. This prompted a swift reply, dated 4th January, in which Josiah looked forward to seeing 'a matter of scientific value which may possibly startle your colleagues' brought to the fore. Less rambling than his last letter, it designated murder a 'manifestation of Spiritual Disease' to be treated by an ecclesiastical authority, a practice first 'begun in Paris by Les Frères Chrètiens, only wanting to be brought scientifically up to date'. This reference to the work of the Christian Brothers recalls his early acquaintance with their history, of which he had written in *The Vegetarian*.

A note amongst Lord Templewood's papers records that a copy of *The Shadow of the Gallows*, published by Victor Gollancz, was sent to Josiah on its publication day, 16th April 1951. He found it illuminating, opening up 'vistas of thought from many sources and cogent arguments founded upon the instinct in Human Nature, the power of habit, the compulsion of the Evil mind, the influence of Religion, and the problems connected with the Evolution of the Human Race from Cruelty to Kindness, from Enmity to Amity, from Brute Covetousness to Brotherly Amity, and the extension of the Divine to the ter(r)estrial habits of Humanity'.

It is noteworthy that this series of letters was headed by Josiah's address in Harley Street.

Despite the appearance of Lord Templewood's book, which apparently sold well but produced little profit in the form of royalties for the Howard League, there was no immediate change in the law regarding capital punishment. Not until 1964 was a sufficient majority (355-170) obtained on a free vote in the Commons for legislation to proceed without fear of reversal in the Lords, so Josiah did not live to see his hope of an end to the death penalty fulfilled.

Aerial View of Lady Margaret Manor

Trees (top right) hide the site of Little Greetynge. The remains of the Chapel form part of the large house close by. Ellen's Oast is bottom left and the Monks Hut lies about halfway between them.

275

Chapter 33

An 'Arbitrarily Eclectic Brand of Theology'

When Josiah wrote his article on Vegetarianism for the *Encyclopaedia Britannica* in 1910 he included a section naming those religions which recognised the practice, amongst them 'Seventh Day Adventists, Bible Christians; worshippers of Vishnu, the Swami Narang and Vishnoi sects; the Salvation Army, Tolstoyans, Doukhobors; some Roman Catholic orders such as the Trappists; and Hindus, for example the Dadupanthi Sadus.' This list give some idea of the breadth of his studies as a younger man, and no doubt his thirst for knowledge extended this during the next forty years. Elements of many of their tenets would contribute to his own beliefs.

Josiah now had time to consider the experience gained throughout his eventful lifetime, considerations culminating in four books which sum up his philosophy. *Healing and the Conquest of Pain* was published in 1944, *The Mystery of Birth* in 1948, *The Mystery of Marriage* in 1949 and *The Mystery of Death* two years later.

Perhaps even Josiah was feeling an occasional twinge when he wrote 'We know that the spirit powers can entirely annihilate pain, and that it is therefore in the spirit field that man must explore for the final conquest. The very first step in the pathway is the entire destruction of selfness or selfishness. It was want of cleanliness... which led to destroying waves of plagues and poxes. It is the want of spiritual cleanliness - the disobedience to those divine laws by which the Cosmos is governed - the neglect of those beatitudes which bring painlessness and peace - the continuance of those ways which will always give pain and death their ultimate foothold [which hold man back] - and therefore it is spiritual perfection and divine goodness in the human souls which will make this world into the joyous anteroom of heaven'.

How was this Gnosis, secret spiritual knowledge, to be achieved? It would only be through avoidance of all contact with death and corruption. 'This is forgotten by a material age which

276

thinks that by processes of pasteurisation stale milk may be made fresh, diseased cattle turned into human food, blood and bones may be added to the purest of nature's soups in order to "enrich" them'. Instead man should confine himself to 'foods and fruits of the earthly paradises - the bloodless feast - the blood of the red grape and the body of golden corn - the daily communion feast upon which angels and men alike may feed together. To a select few, who are willing initiates, will Gnosis, added to Euphoria, offer a life of continuous health and happy freedom from pain.'

The celebration of this New Covenant, whereby Christ was made the final and fulfilling sacrifice for sin, had been the subject of an early Good Friday sermon by Josiah, reprinted for readers of *The Vegetarian*. No longer did God demand the killing of animals; Man too should dispense with the unnecessary slaughter of beasts. 'Love your enemy' should replace 'An eye for an eye' as the basis of human behaviour. The jealous, vindictive God of the Old Testament, still invoked by many priests, was entirely rejected by Josiah. His God was one of infinite protective tenderness, of beauty and loving care.

Preaching on the same subject on another occasion Josiah referred to the Eucharist as a feast of cereals and fruits, bread and wine, as a reminder that blood-letting and slaughter were transient but that self-sacrifice and mercy were permanent. These sermons, dating from about 1900, were composed when Josiah truly believed that mankind, and ultimately animals too, would be transformed by universal vegetarianism.

Josiah's last book, *The Mystery of Death*, was published in 1951, and had a wide circulation. It is one of the few titles sometimes to be found on the shelves of second-hand bookshops - most of his other works have disappeared into limbo. The following review appeared in the *Hibbert Journal* in 1952 (Vol.50 p 306):

'Dr Josiah Oldfield, who is a distinguished and benevolent doctor and an ardent vegetarian, for whom the slaughter of animals is a grave sin, sets forth his philosophy of life in 'The Mystery of Death'. He is chiefly anxious to allay the fear of death which besets so many. He has witnessed hundreds of death-beds, happy and unhappy. Dr.Oldfield has no use for the popular theology of heaven and hell, or for the belief in an angry and avenging Creator. He believes in reincarnation. We pass, he is assured, from life to life. His theology seems to be rather arbitrarily eclectic, and he makes no attempt to prove his dogma of reincarnation. Still, the serene faith in the "Father-Motherhood of God" which he voices at the end of his book will command respect even from those who cannot share it.'

Rejecting the popular view, Josiah saw Heaven as peace and loving-kindness, and Hell as discord, hate and violence. He recognised 'Devil men and women [who] are only happy in destroying, Angel men and women [who] find their highest joys in creating', and he had rather more to say about the evil force 'always at work to drag back the spiritually evolved human into that pit from which he has been dug'. In a discussion of one of his patients diagnosed as epileptic he speaks of her apparent possession by a devil, pointing out that some forms of epilepsy 'offer wider fields for exploration and spiritually-minded research'. The same patient today would probably be described as schizophrenic.

For Josiah there was apparently no clash between his beliefs and his scientific training. 'All science must be religious and all religion scientific' he had declared in 1924. He considered that revealing the proper position of life in the Cosmos was a primary, even sacred, duty of the Scientist. 'In doing so he will place man in his true position of contact with the Divine creator'. I have found no direct reference in his writings to Darwin, or to the debate on Man's origins which must still have been discussed during the years when he was a Theology student. He referred (in an article on Dietary in the *New Century Review* in October 1902) to a fossil trilobite found in Cambrian rocks having 'an organization almost as complex in nerve and muscle as his descendant lobster and crab of today'. But in his frequent use of the word 'pneuma' - breath - he seems to have favoured the Biblical view. Perhaps the saying 'Some call it Evolution, others call it God' is apposite. His version of the origin of life was given in *The Mystery of Birth* in 1949:

'God took of the dust... breathed into it life... Creation sang a birth song. Listen lowly and deeply and silently enough and you will hear the cosmic chords'. Half a century earlier he had written 'For me long days of thousand, thousand years the great Creator toiled and drudged... whose majesty of [a] million years of toil as shown in flower and fruit and sparkling dewdrops... and in the wonder of the karyokinetic mystery, is treated by the race of pygmy men as so much commonplace'.

(The word karyokinetic preceded the use of 'mitotic' when describing the processes within the nuclei of living cells during division.)

For Josiah the mystery of birth lay in 'the chaining of energy to matter', and in the book to which he gave that title he has much more to say on the subject. He suggests that - possibly - the 'ether' is filled with millions of 'spirit men' beyond the ken of our physical senses, one of which forms a 'symbiotic entity' with an ovum when it is sufficiently developed eventually to produce a human child. This is couched in somewhat obscure terms:

'A human conception is the moment when that materialistic permutation of vibrational plasm which constitutes the formation of a new living organism is of such a suitable and harmonious vibrational complexity that the pre-existing Spiritual entity can so enmesh its spiritual vibrations harmoniously with the material physical vibrations of the living organisms, that there comes into existence an "incarnation of the spiritual"'.

The later book contains similar passages, and it was presumably to these that the *Hibbert Journal* reviewer alluded when speaking of Josiah's belief in reincarnation, spirit men being the souls of those who, in human terms, had perhaps already died.

His views may sound unscientific, but perhaps before disregarding entirely Josiah's talk of 'cosmic vibrations' we should be aware that atomic vibrations lie at the heart of all matter.

279

Chapter 34

Celebrated Author

The success of *The Mystery of Death* was probably the main reason for Josiah's invitation to one of Christina Foyle's 'Literary Lunches' in June 1951. At this he professed not to remember his age, and did not correct those who believed him to be well over ninety, or even 103 years old! This last figure was provided by the reporter Rosalie Shann, who interviewed some of the guests, asking them 'What makes you look twice at a woman?' Describing Josiah as 'that sprightly white-bearded old gentleman, physician and philosopher', she recorded his reply: 'I always look twice if she's got pretty eyes. Eyes always speak the truth. And smiling eyes... Ah, my dear young lady, a smiling woman is like the rising sun...'

The *Daily Graphic*'s report of the occasion devotes more space to Josiah's words than to those of the speaker, while his photograph takes precedence over those of fellow-guests Dean Inge and George Robey, equally vigorous 'grand old men'.

Josiah at a Lunch in 1951

The speaker was Benjamin Gayelord Hauser, whose theme was

'Live longer, look younger', and the three guests exemplified the truth of his doctrine. Josiah commented later that even if presented with all the healthful ingredients recommended by Mr Hauser, 'that prize saboteur, the English cook, would in half an hour make the whole blooming lot taste like spring greens'.

Josiah is quoted at length:-

'It depends on men and women themselves whether they shall be old or young. An old man is a calamity. An old woman is a crime. If you want to live in happiness and health adopt a fruitarian diet. Don't adopt the bad habits of old age - smoking and tea-drinking.' He was particularly critical of women, stating that 'the chief part of a woman's work is to be beautiful, but how few of them there are... And when they try to be beautiful by using lipstick they should be treated as Jezebels - thrown out of the window.'

He also disapproved of their diet, saying that they ate meat and drank too much, scornfully adding 'Whoever would want to kiss a girl after she has just had a mouthful of rabbit?' He once again proffered his view that 'old women wear too many clothes. Each year after a woman is thirty she adds a pound to her clothing'. Perhaps it is not surprising that he was a controversial figure.

Statements such as 'Meat is the cause of revolutions' or 'All ugly women should be drowned' would catch the ear of any reporters listening, and lead to another paragraph in the papers. Similar pungent remarks were to be quoted in his obituary only two years later. Those who received such memorable answers to their questions never forgot the occasion. Ken Parfitt still recalls, more than sixty years after he asked Josiah the secret of long life, how the old man simply 'looked at me for a moment - then pointed to his mouth: "What goes in here!" he said.'

Did the publicity following his appearance in London stimulate his ambitions? In spite of his age Josiah's optimistic view of the future persisted, for at the annual meeting of the Lady Margaret Hospital held at the Savoy Hotel in July he outlined plans for its re-creation. Completely new wards might be erected at Lady Margaret Manor, leaving the existing buildings for staff accommodation. Alternatively other suitable premises for the hospital could be sought elsewhere. Ellen's Oast had by now taken on another role, having been converted from a boys' home to a youth hostel.

Ellen's Oast, converted to a Youth Hostel

Josiah was almost ninety years old when there was a health scare in Kent. A young visitor staying at the youth hostel in Dover had become ill, the local doctor diagnosed rabies, and wardens of other hostels in Kent, Surrey and Sussex were asked to detain any folk coming from Dover. Ken Parfitt was in charge of the hostel at Doddington at the time, and had nine such young people staying. As a precaution he set up tents for them in the Valley of the Pilgrims, and notified the Medical Officer of Health. Ken writes 'When villagers from Doddington found out the situation they came to the Youth Hostel, demanding that the youngsters be sent away. I felt it wrong to pass on the problem to others, so consulted Josiah. After I had explained the problem he just put his hand on my shoulder and said just this (and it has stayed with me and guided me all my life) "When you **know** you are in the right, **stand alone** - others are waiting to join you". Such wisdom!'

It may have been the publicity (and possibly the financial rewards) afforded by the success of *The Mystery of Death* that prompted the production of further Fruitarian brochures and advertisements. A new appeal to every young man and woman to plant a tree in the Autumn of 1951 (Festival of Britain Year) pointed out that **every** Festival Year baby should be commemorated in this way, as should the death of a friend.

Interior of the Youth Hostel

This might be in an individual's garden, or in the 'Garden of Birth' or 'Garden of Remembrance' at Doddington, where trees could be purchased at a cost of 10/-.

A separate booklet preached the advantages of a stay at 'Greetynge Cottage, Margaret Manor'. Visitors were invited to come for a 'very simple cottage rest - sea air and fruitarian cookery'. Old well-loved clothes were advised, together with a sunbathing rug, sheets and towels. 'Learn a lesson in gardening, cooking and in domestic home-making. Do not come and find fault. We are the apostles of the simple life. Go out and cut and gather wood and make roaring fires. Dig in the garden, saw or read, or play in the common room, sing or paint, or lay mosaic or

283

carve in the chapel, but do not come to be entertained'. For such delights visitors might be charged up to five guineas a week for a ground floor room with fireplace, although simpler accommodation, sharing a hut or a cubicle, could be had for 30/-.

The note that no outside entertainment was to be expected perhaps followed a series of rejections from local players - a terse note in the Committee minutes of Maidstone Choral Union in October 1949 records 'A letter was read from the Lady Margaret Fruitarian Hospital, Doddington, asking if the Society would give a free entertainment at the Hospital. This was not considered possible.'

Those unwise enough to try a visit to Greetynge Lodge at this date might have found comfort in another of Josiah's aphorisms: 'There is no reason medically why a man should not get roaring drunk once a month', he had declared in later life. But he himself, while not a teetotaller, was abstemious. A small glass of good wine was one of the few features he had been able to appreciate while taking his Dinners as a fledgling barrister, describing it as 'poetry for the soul'. He had found 'the aroma and bouquet of a '24 port reminiscent of merry girls singing in a sun-kissed vineyard and whispering to each other love stories of clove-scented Araby'... More prosaically, when commanding a Field Ambulance during the First World War Josiah ensured that the Officers' Mess was always well-supplied with liquor, but made it clear that it was never to be pressed upon visitors: they were to help themselves if thirsty. In several of his books he pointed out that drinking was often simply a habit. Perhaps he also warned his visitors of this, thereby deterring them! His criticism that drinking was often a habit rather than a true need for liquid applied as much to a woman's cup of tea as to a man's glass of beer.

Josiah's thoughts on tea and coffee were not always consistent, for in some of his writings he recommended that in hot weather alcohol (and pulses) should be avoided, and hot weak tea drunk instead. Early morning tea for women, though, was definitely unsuitable. 'No woman should begin her day with a cup of tea. It is a habit which superficially trained nurses especially indulge in, and this class of nurse usually makes a very neurotic wife'. Black coffee was merely a stimulant, although a small quantity was permissible if diluted with boiling milk. Even this was not ideal, for if the cells of the body were 'overworked' by the stimulus of 'extreme chills or the very hot, such as a cup of hot coffee after a meal' they tended to 'slack'. This advice was proffered in *Rheumatism, its Causes and Cure.* Nurses on night duty might be allowed a couple of tablespoons of black coffee with a dessertspoonful of cream rather than repeated cups of tea to postpone sleepiness. His particular aversion to tea was shared by others who had witnessed its frequent adulteration in Victorian times, when tea was considerably more expensive than alcohol.

A mug of old ale, mulled with honey, was Josiah's favoured treatment for a chill by the time that he himself had reached what others would regard as old age. For all his older patients whose 'assimilation power' had been reduced he suggested a wineglass of bran tea, with a teaspoon of honey and a slight bittering of hops each morning. Their evening benediction should consist of a tablespoon of good red wine mixed with a dessertspoon of honey and enough boiling water to fill a claret glass. His recipe was published in the St Bartholomew's Hospital Journal in 1944, when he was just over eighty, as part of a short paper on the importance of vitamins, and headed 'Trifles in Food'.

In another pamphlet, *Honey for Health*, apparently reprinted at this period, in which he extols the benefits of honey Josiah also appears to accept that Vegetarianism is not for everyone. In a throwaway paragraph he suggests that if a man's appetite is tempted by 'the memory of flesh food of younger days ' he should 'humour himself with pottage made from wild grouse or mountain venison' but never touch the slaughtered flesh of stall-fed beasts, or pigs in any form. He recommends, though, that after the age of fifty meat in the diet should be replaced by a jar of honey three weeks out of four. People could then decide from their own experience in which weeks they felt stronger and full of activity

What was Josiah's attitude to smoking? His views seem to have changed with advancing age. He certainly did not approve of young women indulging in the habit, and it seems too that when he had carried out his experiment in conjunction with the *Daily Express* in 1906, the men practising a Fruitarian diet were not expected to smoke or drink alcohol. He adopted a condemnatory tone in 1928 when composing *Eat and Keep Young*, for there he wrote 'Beware of the man who ruins his artistic sense of taste by smoking innumerable cigarettes'. A few years earlier he had declared the idea that tobacco smoking destroyed germs to be a fallacy: the reverse was in fact the case. (*Rheumatism, its Causes and Cure*).

But in 1947, just after learning details of the budget in which the price of a packet of cigarettes was raised from 2/4d to 3/4d, Josiah had been prompted to send off a letter to *The Times*. The printed extract, published on 28th April, reads

8 Harley St.

Sir

Mr Dalton will have done a great service to England if he teaches us all to smoke once more. Smoking is a delightful addition to the joys of living. The two wars have vulgarized smoking into a habit which gives neither pleasure nor poetry to living.

Reading this evokes mixed feelings. It implies that Josiah himself was not averse to tobacco, but that he thought cigarettes slightly 'common'- he was something of a snob. Perhaps he indulged in the occasional pipe in the same way that he enjoyed his evening half-glass of superior wine. In photographs his generous white beard appears to have remained unstained to the end of his life.

It was just two years before he died that Josiah wrote 'It is through self-control that man's greatness develops... Where are those dreaming aspirants? Have they set themselves free from such bounds as constant smoking, over tea-drinking, wasting precious hours each day in trivial talk and gossip?' His views on smoking may have been affected by the knowledge that his beloved daughter Josie indulged in the habit. Not long before her death from cancer, when emphysema and coughing fits frequently incapacitated her, she remarked to Ken Parfitt 'You and I know my father would have been **so angry** to find me smoking so much'. She was also prepared to eat meat when dining with friends who were not vegetarians, another fact of which her father was happily unaware.

Entrance to the former hospital at Doddington in 2002

Chapter 35

The Final Years

Readers of the *Herald of the Golden Age* had usually found within its pages an address from Sidney Beard, their Founder and President, or another member of the Order of the Golden Age. Josiah's contributions were sometimes based on quotations from the Apocryphal books of Esdras. One example used some verses from chapter 9 of the second book:- 'Go into a field of flowers where no house is builded and eat only the flowers of the field. Taste no flesh, drink no wine, but eat flowers only, and pray unto the Highest continually, then I will come and talk with thee'. So I went my way into the field which is called Ardath, like as he commanded me, and there I sat amongst the flowers, and did eat of the herbs of the field, and the meat of the same satisfied me... and I opened my mouth and began to talk before the Most High.'

Such communication with the great Creator was dependent on periods of silence, so that a certain amount of time each day ought to be devoted to quiet thought. Josiah practised this throughout his life, writing in 1951 'Listen for one full hour without speaking and without allowing your lower self to intrude even a thought. Silence. A waiting void. A bride's chamber. Nothingness. At the end of the hour, start a song in your heart. Tip your tongue with a benediction (a "Good Morning") and your lips with a smile. Carry this out to the end of the day. Tomorrow begin the same exercise again. Ere long a message will come into your hour of silence and it will tell you what the angels wish for you to do'. (But the ability to concentrate solely on listening, and to ignore hunger or other pains, was reserved for only a select band: as Josiah put it 'How few men can talk philosophy when the dinner-gong is a quarter of an hour late').

His daily silent vigil might be equated with the hour of prayer practised by other, perhaps more orthodox, Christians. Josiah, though, saw alternative opportunities for spiritual exercise. In 1943, with the World War engaging the thoughts and activities of so many, the Bishop of Birmingham was one who pleaded that Good Friday might be observed as a Day of Prayer, with a cessation from labour in factories even where this was regarded as 'essential war-work'. Josiah had been quick to respond, pointing out in a letter to *The Times* that 'Laborare est orare'. ('To work is to pray')

Josiah's regime of fruitarian diet, fresh air and vigorous exercise for both body and mind, preceded by a daily hour of quiet contemplation, clearly contributed to his long life, and he outlived many of his contemporaries. Arnold Hills had died in 1927, Sidney Beard, perhaps for many years his closest male friend, in 1938, and Gandhi in 1948. Josiah himself would not, as he had undoubtedly hoped, become a centenarian, for he died peacefully after a short illness on 2nd February 1953, his daughter Josie and Ken Parfitt beside him. The official phrases 'mitral incompetency' and 'aortic stenosis' of the death certificate describe what might previously have been called simply 'old age': he was certainly free of cancer, gout, stomach troubles or any other of the debilitating diseases which he would have attributed to the consumption of meat.

He had held firm views on the treatment of the dying, writing in 1924 'The shortening of the lives of weakly and febrile patients by frequently dosing them with food as well as medicine is a matter of the greatest seriousness'. He hoped that when his time came, he would be able to depart quietly and restfully, with only such drinks of water or fruit juice as he might crave for, and that he might be spared the 'nauseating weariness of a stomach filled with decaying milk foods or decomposing broths'. He was equally clear about where he wished to be buried - at Doddington, in the hillside overlooking the 'Valley of the Pilgrims', an area known to local children before Josiah acquired the Greet Estate as 'Clifford's Mountains', after the farmer who had previously occupied the farm.

A fervent believer in fruit tree planting to the last, Josiah wished his grave to be surrounded by four examples, a walnut, a Charles Ross apple, a Victoria plum and a William pear. Even the funeral feast was prescribed: it was to consist of fruits, nuts, fruit cake, fresh milk, cream, cheese, honey and wines.

Doddington Church in 1900

But in fact Josiah was to be buried in the Churchyard at Doddington, where the church has the unusual dedication to 'The Beheading of St.John the Baptist'. The funeral report in the *East Kent Gazette* records that Canon W.A.R.Ball officiated at the service, which was attended by a large congregation, Dr Josie Oldfield being the chief mourner. (The obituary in the same paper remarks that 'Dr Oldfield leaves **a** daughter', implying that she was his only living relative, although in fact his wife Gertrude and twin daughters all survived him). The organist played Handel's 'Largo' and 'Peace, the night has come', and the hymn 'Praise my soul' was sung in church. "The Doctor's favourite hymn was read at the graveside" concludes the report, but does not say what this was. Perhaps it was that which he had composed for use at Bromley. As they left the churchyard one of the mourners looked heavenwards and asked, with a sad smile, 'I wonder what he's up to **now**?'

Today the grave is marked by a plain stone, on which is inscribed:

JOSIAH
OLDFIELD
BORN FEBRUARY
28TH 1863
DIED FEBRUARY
2ND 1953
When death draws nigh
I'll bid Good-Bye
To all I fear
There is no fear
For God is here.
J.O.

There are no fruit trees, but Josiah's last resting-place has towering limes to east and west, and is shaded by the trees of Doddington Place on the north side.

Josiah's will was short and to the point. On a single sheet of paper headed 'Doddington, Kent', and in his own handwriting, it reads:-

'This is the last will and testament of me Josiah Oldfield made the fifth day of June one thousand nine hundred and thirty three. I give and bequeathe to my daughter Josie Magdalen Oldfield MRCS LRCP all my real and personal property of every sort of which I may die possessed.
Signed by the testator in the presence of two witnesses who in his presence and in the presence of each other appended their signatures'

Josiah Oldfield.

The witnesses, whose addresses are given in both cases as Margaret Manor, Doddington, were K.G.F.Garrett, Hon. Sec. of ???? and Evelyn Clare. In the margin of the document are the signatures of Josie M.Oldfield as Administratix and Charles H. Puisent(?), Commissioner for Oaths. The date of the will is significant, for it was in 1933 that his daughter Josie qualified as a doctor.

What were Josiah's beliefs on death and resurrection? His book *The Mystery of Death* discusses the fear of death at length, attributing it in part to a dread, inherited from primitive ancestors, of the darkness where danger may wait. But to a greater extent Josiah blames the teaching of priests of all kinds, for every religion has its own set of 'divine laws', and those who break them are apparently condemned to suffer. In different ages and areas the Furies, witch-doctors, and Catholic priests who sold indulgences to those in fear of Hell have been just some of the many authorities which, by threatening punishment for those who 'sinned', have exercised control over the spiritual lives of the people.

When speaking of the death of his much-loved brother, Josiah's feelings were mixed: sorrowful because he would miss William's comradeship and wise words, but glad too. 'I was sure that somehow, somewhere, my brother was now deep in sleep awaiting the time when he would start a new life as someone's beloved baby - longed for, welcomed, cherished, comforted, cared for'. Josiah himself was unafraid. He did not believe that ritual incantations could affect a soul's fate: would a loving God reject an infant simply because it had not been baptized? Josiah rather foresaw a future world where through 'freedom of thought, by progressive research into the essence of the divine... man shall take all the existing "divine laws" claimed by every religion, and find the answer by solving the common denominator of them all'.

Though not using the term 'Resurrection' Josiah believed that some form of reincarnation would occur after the death of the body. It was obvious to him as a scientist that the particles of which any corporeal body was composed would eventually be dispersed, to become part of some new organism (and he professed himself happy to consume fruit grown above a grave). He also queried the form which a resurrected body might take - would it be the elderly grandparent recalled by a child, the virile young husband, or the tiny baby remembered by its mother? Dismissing the idea of an eternity spent playing a harp and singing

292

Hallelujah, to Josiah it seemed logical to propose an alternative form of 'life after death'. This he summarised as follows:-

'All life is in a constant state of change.
Every life is destined to become higher, cleaner and purer.
Every life, therefore, passes through many schools of training,
teaching and purifying.
Between each stage there is a period of rest and assimilation.
During each such period of rest the "memory" of the "past"
is blotted out, but the "effect" of the "past" is perpetuated in the
formation of the new characteristics that have become moulded into
the altered character.'

Josiah's Grave

Such 'blotting out' of all previous memory would deny the recognition of loved ones in that new world. Josiah concluded that each of us has already had many different conscious 'lives', separated by periods of oblivion. We should prepare for our next awakening. 'If we have learned to be supremely unselfish, always seeking for and finding good in life; always striving earnestly to make everybody round us happy; never satisfied unless we have every day the consciousness when we go to sleep that we have not said nor thought one unkind, ungenerous or uncharitable word or imagining; that we have definitely helped each day and every day somebody to be happier in mind or body; that we have definitely reduced the sum of the world's agony and

293

pain and suffering, human and animal; that we have lifted up our eyes to God and to heaven in all that we have spoken or done - then indeed we shall have the full assurance that we shall meet just such honest, kindly, loving people as ourselves, waiting to welcome us into their midst on the other side'.

Is Josiah's vision so very different from that of that Anglican priest who became a Roman Catholic, Cardinal John Newman, whose *Dream of Gerontius* portrays the passage of a soul from death to purgatory, there to await the moment of perfection and one-ness with the divine? At the end of Newman's poem, after Gerontius has had a momentary glimpse of God, come the words

'Take me away
That sooner I may rise
May rise and go above
And see Him in the truth of everlasting day'.

It is from Ken Parfitt that we learn that when writing little notes to friends, Josiah would often close with the words 'Great Joy'. They seem to summarise both the ebullience he displayed throughout his life, and to anticipate his vision of the future.

The Chapel (centre) and adjoining Pumphouse (right) after Josiah's Death

Chapter 36

Josiah's Contentious Views

Josiah recognized that the deep study of physiology and anatomy, coupled with clinical experience, must be the foundation of any doctor's training, but his belief that diet was at the root of man's state of health coloured the whole of his career as a physician. He saw that many illnesses were interlinked, with a single cause giving rise to symptoms in different parts of the body. He fervently believed that any patient's condition would be improved by giving up flesh foods - 'by patient perseverance in eating suitable foods, and living under suitable conditions, a man may be transformed within seven years from disease to health, from invalidism to positive vitality, from a sufferer in pain to a hymner of gladness, from a mournful trudging in the valley of sorrows to a light-stepped marching along the heights of joyousness.' Life and vitality would be prolonged in those conforming to a Fruitarian regime.

When embarking on his medical career Josiah was fortunate to have as friends wealthy men like Arnold Hills and Sidney Beard, who shared his idealism and enabled him to put his ideas into practice. He must have had a silver tongue, and what today might be called charisma, to attract such patrons. In later years he looked back on the assurance, even arrogance, of the young Josiah with a critical eye, writing 'I talked as if diet reformers and nature curers were wiser and more successful than physicians and surgeons... I laid it down that all a sick man had to do was to fast and then change his diet, to rub himself and take deep breathing, to do some exercises, physical and mental, and perhaps drink some herb-tea, or use emetics or enemata or baths, and his sickness would fall from him like the white scales from the skin of Naaman'. This was the time when he and others believed that even cancer might be cured by diet and without recourse to surgery. The Oriolet Hospital was founded with this in mind. A century later an edition of the BBC Food Programme (Nov.4th 2001) was devoted to 'Diet and Cancer' although there was no mention of Josiah or other pioneers. The discussion spoke of on-going controlled scientific investigations of the plant substances (phyto-oestrogens, present in high-fibre foods such as strawberries, lentils and soya-bean products) which appear to prevent some types of cancer. There was evidence to suggest that animal fats may contribute to the development of some cases of breast cancer in obese post-menopausal women. All those appearing on the programme agreed that a diet high in fruit and vegetables was a sensible option. Although there were **individuals** who had apparently been **cured** by such a diet, no controlled trials had been held comparable to those which had preceded chemotherapy or radiotherapy.

Dr. Robert Bell

Dr Robert Bell was one of the fiercest proponents of the belief in diet to fight cancer, publishing under the imprint of the Order of the Golden Age numerous books and pamphlets on the subject, including *The Prevention and Treatment of Cancer, Cancer and its Remedy* and *The Futility of Operations in Cancer.*

A further title, however, did accept that other treatment might be necessary: *The Cancer Scourge and How to Destroy It* proved 'the curability of cancer and ... efficacy of treatment by Fruitarian diet and Radium'. In 1912 Dr Bell won a libel case against the British Medical Association, which had called him a quack because of his views on cancer.

It is unlikely that Josiah ever used radiotherapy in his treatment of cancer patients, and by 1935 he was less keen to carry out operations than he had been while at Bromley. His advice to a woman who found a lump in her breast at that date was to 'let it alone and forget it. If it reminds you again by any shooting or other pain that it is still there, avoid any young surgeon whose zeal for operations may not yet have become tempered by experience and wisdom, but consult a wise and experienced physician, and carry out his advice, and all will be well with you'. (*The Beauty Aspect of Health and Living*).   This seems a somewhat cavalier attitude, although it should be borne in mind that many breast lumps are benign.   Even today opinion as to whether an operation should be performed is not unanimous where mammography finds evidence of early cancerous signs in older women.

In many fields Josiah held 'advanced' views, and perhaps that which most shocked and outraged the communities where he lived was his attitude to sex and marriage. His philosophy concerning the latter is outlined in *The Mystery of Marriage,* published in 1949. He believed that marriage was not a matter of ceremonial, but lay in 'the harmonious blending of two spirit harmonies into a full complemented unity' leading to a 'fellowship of work, food, mutual help and reliance and of sex functions'. From this it followed that human marriage was a human contract, so that when the conditions involved in it were not carried out this human contract came to an end. But a sacramental marriage, where two harmonious halves had been bound together by God, could never be dissolved because there was now only one whole being. It was only God who could so select and so join, and 'what God hath joined no man CAN (not MAY) put asunder...' Such sacramental marriages were pre-determined and pre-existing, independent of any religion. There could be no death, no widowhood in a union completed by God, for sacraments are not bounded by Time or Space.

Unfortunately for Josiah, it appears that his marriage to Gertrude may not have been of this kind. There are several bleak passages in *The Mystery of Birth* which suggest this. At the beginning of the book, written late in life, he refers to 'Those who win in the marriage market and who learn through freer trust, and greater confidence, each in the other, and each through the other, attracting a larger and larger circle of love and affection'. If a later passage is written from personal experience, he was not a winner. It reads 'Social laws should be so framed as to penalise Money, as compared with Health, in a bride.... Many a modern bride... is hiding a heart of bitterness and a spirit as cruel as Hell. Such women can never know the joys of the bridal ecstasy, nor the entrancing thrill of Motherhood - even though they may own a dozen as their offspring. A man full of fire himself may find, too late, that his lifemate is a sexual iceberg. Respect and affection must always and always be the prelude to the entry into the Garden of Sex'.

On other pages he deplores that there is no escape from the marriage contract, the Law being more highly regarded than the Spirit. He rejects the general attitude, asking 'will the freedom from traditional religious and social opinion work to create social unrest and moral laxity? I think not.' Josiah apparently practised what he preached, for the daughter of whom he was so proud, Josie Magdalen, was conceived in 1905 or 1906, and there is no official record of the birth of a child with surname Oldfield called by those names. Her death certificate gives only 'about 1906, England' as her date and place of birth. Even her name is in doubt, for a newspaper in June 1913 reported that Miss **Joice** Magdalen Oldfield presented a purse. Josie was apparently told that her mother was 'of the aristocracy, Lady.... ' Given the number of such supporters Josiah attracted, her identity must remain a mystery.

According to Ken Parfitt the combination of powerful personality and entrancing blue eyes made Josiah irresistible to women. He writes 'Over many years folk who knew Josiah called over to Ellen's Court to visit their hospital ward, both ex-nurses and patients. Now and then men and women appeared... I'd see their blue eyes - and **know** they were Oldfield's offspring'.

In the early pages of *The Mystery of Marriage* Josiah surveys marriage customs and rituals in different parts of the world, drawing on his own experiences while travelling as well as on his reading, and then compares the giving of a woman in marriage with both slavery and sacrifice. Both Josiah and Sidney

Beard thought that because 'fear, hatred and deceit reproduce their kind', the offspring of an unhappy marriage would be less fortunate than those whose 'cells born in the atmosphere of Euphoria start life with gay gladness and hasten to their new work with eager zest and power, and go on building up a more glorious body and one fuller of grace and harmony'. In plainer terms, children growing up where the relationship between parents is absent or unhappy tend to do less well, both materially and mentally, than those from a stable home. Josiah's daughter, Josie, was one of those exceptions that prove the rule. From the diary she kept as a schoolgirl the affection between father and daughter is clear, and there is no hint that the absence of a mother held her back in any way. Those who knew her speak of her delightful sense of humour.

Other areas where Josiah's views are contentious lie within the field of eugenics, a term first coined in England in 1883 by Francis Galton, whose vision of improving the quality of the human race through breeding complemented the desire of idealists like Josiah and other members of the Order of the Golden Age to attain a better society. An editorial in the *Herald of the Golden Age* in 1891 suggested that flesh-eating tended towards race degradation, pointing out that the largely vegetarian Chinese and Indian races were multiplying whereas Red Indians and Eskimos, whose diet contained more meat, were dying out. By 1911 a more forthright view was expressed: 'Eugenics is the key to the problem of physical degeneracy. The diseased, criminally profligate, imbecile or hopelessly unfit for parenthood should not be allowed to propagate'. Similar statements appeared the following year. Whether these are the words of Josiah, of Sidney Beard, or of both, is not clear.

Miscegenation too, according to Josiah writing in 1944, was to be discouraged. He regarded cultured white men as racially superior. 'Even the crossing of a negro with a white woman is fraught with many curious genetic problems which entail retrogressive results and rarely if ever produce any evolutionary progressive prizes. A black man may be a better man than you, therefore honour and respect him, share the world with him, but don't give your daughter in marriage to him, for their children's sake'.

In the same volume, *Healing and the Conquest of Pain*, Josiah discussed what should happen to idiots and imbeciles (then defined as those with an IQ of under 20 and under 50 respectively) who were incapable of managing their own affairs. He considered that the lives of fine young men and women were being vainly wasted in cleaning, feeding and dressing 'these animal men and women'. Medical skill and public money were being diverted from aspiring intelligent children who could more usefully benefit from it. His answer was that idiots, at least, (the mentally ill were a different category, for they might recover their sanity) should be put painlessly to death, answering those who would condemn this idea by stating that the severely mentally sub-normal did not possess a soul - they were merely animals. He was by no means alone in his view, but did not, like some, advocate the use of a lethal chamber. D.H.Lawrence* was one who did, with a dream in 1908 of removing from the streets the sick, the halt and the maimed and placing them in a lethal chamber 'as big as the Crystal Palace, with a military band playing softly and a cinematograph working brightly' where they would end their lives to the strains of the Hallelujah Chorus.

Josiah was familiar with the concept of a lethal chamber, for he had reviewed the possibility of its use when attempting to limit the suffering of animals awaiting slaughter at abattoirs. He had found that idea, compared with electrocution or the guillotine, to be equally obnoxious. He himself had been forced to shoot a pet on one occasion, a cat which had been badly burned. Although firmly opposed to the death penalty, in a chapter entitled 'A Gentler Death' in his DCL thesis he had advocated the use of a

---

*This sweeping statement came in correspondence about the case of Daisy Lord, sentenced to death for murdering her illegitimate child. Lawrence was perhaps out of humour when he wrote it: in the same letter he described Stockport and Manchester as 'vile, hateful, tangled, filthy places both, seething with strangers' and was scarcely more complimentary about London.

lethal injection instead of hanging condemned men, and recalled the execution of Socrates by the administration of hemlock (though death would scarcely have been painless in such a case).

There were many who thought that the 'unfit' should not be allowed to marry, or should be sterilised to prevent them producing children who might be equally handicapped: in America by the 1930s more than forty states insisted on sterilisation of the insane and the feeble-minded. I have found only a single possible reference to this practice in Josiah's works, in the *Herald of the Golden Age* of 1912. This proclaims 'When we have consolidated our ideas, the following will all be considered immoral:- All parentage without love; all irresponsible parentage; **all parentage of unmature or degenerate persons**; all violence or seduction'. There is no explanation of how these concepts were to be attained. Others went further, arguing that idiots, morons and the similarly afflicted should not be allowed to live, a practice vigorously enforced in Hitler's Germany. Here compulsory abortion for those women with a hereditary disease was introduced in 1935, 'mercy-killing' (a euphemism for mass murder) of those whose condition fell short of the Aryan ideal in 1939.

Josiah **may** have been thinking along similar lines when he wrote 'We must not waste time in patching up old broken-down scraps from the dustheap of life but must concentrate all our Science upon the Fountainhead of Power and Creative Energy', but this quotation more probably refers to the continuing, sometimes invasive, treatment of patients with chronic illnesses.

When Josiah was writing during the Second World War, although it was probably realised that in Hitler's Germany the 'unfit' were being quietly removed, news of the mass extermination of the Jews had not reached the world outside. Josiah did praise Hitler on one occasion, commending his purchase of Manchuria's soya bean harvest as 'the most sustaining food in the world' which the German people might eat on the meatless days which had been decreed by their Fuhrer, himself a

301

vegetarian.

Less than ten years later Josiah seems to have had something of a change of heart - perhaps after learning of Nazi excesses - for in 1951 he was to write 'We should never be depressed by the births of the unfit... Like Job, may I bless God if he does me the honour of entrusting to me an idiot child'. What he did continue to advocate was the practice of euthanasia. By the middle of the twentieth century he felt that the general view in the medical profession was that a doctor, 'after consultation with his colleagues, upon the earnest and urgent request of his patient and approval of the patient's friends and relatives, has the right, and the duty, if his conscience permits, to administer such drugs and treatments as will terminate the patient's sensation, [and] consciousness, and in due course, shorten his life.' Certainly Josiah himself was prepared to assist in such cases, referring in *The Mystery of Death* to 'my old friend Margaret who relied on me during the last days of a pathetic illness, and who bade me a loving farewell as the hand-maiden of Death handed to her the last poppy-draught'. Morphine was one drug whose benefits he did appreciate, as the 'gift of a beneficent Creator who sends his skilled physician to deaden the agony with a few minims'. Perhaps he too had been glad of its power when a patient in hospital.

Josiah had no qualms in hastening the death of his own brother William, who died aged 77 from prostate cancer. This event he introduces in *The Mystery of Death* with the words 'Modern churches can whisper in the dungeon of loneliness or on the rack of pain "I will give you the cup of Lethe and the gentle hand's grasp into the realms of peace. Go, put forth your hands into the hands of God". It was in such a religious spirit as this that I dealt with my own beloved brother.' William and Josiah had always been close. It was his brother whom Josiah, when they were still young men, had asked to examine what proved to be the first onset of piles. In 1929 it was to William that he dedicated *Eat and be Happy*, with the words 'To my brother, the Rev.Dr.W.J.Oldfield, who taught me that the highway to happiness passes through the rocky defile of self-conquest'.

302

On the question of abortion Josiah made his opinion plain. Although he was often approached by women asking his help in terminating a pregnancy, whether because the child would have been illegitimate or simply one mouth too many for the family to afford, he denied their request. 'As a doctor I can see that an abortion **may** mean the turning of a helpless little spirit, longing for love, out again into the blackness. I for one will have no more part or share in putting an end to a pregnancy once a conception is accomplished.' This was in spite of his knowledge of what might subsequently happen to such babies, for while still living in Shropshire he learned of one mother who had overlain three illegitimate children in succession.

At Doddington he was able to offer an alternative by arranging for an unobtrusive birth followed by adoption. There was no formal need for paperwork until 1927. Rumours of proscribed operations and 'bodies down the well' cannot be substantiated, and no hint of malpractice of this kind reached the files of the Charity Commissioners nor the pages of *Truth*.

Josiah was equally dogmatic where birth-control was concerned. In *The Mystery of Marriage* of 1949 he forecast 'woe to a race which worships Sex and despises Maternity. Today the Priests of the Temple of Science have been seduced: contraceptives are being sold and advertised from their portals. Abortion operation rites are performed within their secret chambers'. He was acquainted with Marie Stopes, and theirs was evidently an amicable relationship, in spite of their differing views. In a letter to Josiah in February 1949 requesting reference to scientific papers for a statement he had made regarding the length of pregnancy in Hottentots, she writes 'It is so long since we met, but I hope you have not forgotten me. I am glad to see... that you look well able to face another twenty years of hard work'. Unfortunately he was unable to trace the required information immediately, but in his by now shaky handwriting he told her that he would keep the matter in mind.

In contrast to the main body of public opinion before the days of the pill Josiah promoted the rights of the unmarried mother. 'Give [a woman] sexual freedom, social freedom, economical

303

freedom, so that she may without any grave responsibility, and without any social ostracism, choose to become a mother to an unknown, unborn little visitor from the realm of the pre-borns, if she wills'. He anticipated that the State would provide for these mothers and their children, and hoped that they would be 'free from the sneers of the world of women who pay greater regard to a marriage ceremony' than to the call of the 'indwelling spirit'. (Army 'wives' had been recognised by the Government, if not by priests, for many years.) To Josiah Motherhood, not Marriage, was all-important.

Josiah was, however, ahead of his time in stressing that God the Father was also God the Mother. In the preface to *Myrrh and Amaranth* he explains his perception: '"Grant, beautiful Mother of Heaven..."   Some readers of my proofs bid me cut this 'Romanist' sentence. Surely anyone who will take the trouble to read these pages would not imagine that I called the earthly human mother of the body of Jesus by the sublime spiritual title of 'Mother of Heaven'. My only wonder is that people go on ascribing the purely masculine name to the great Creator, where the feminine element is essential to our concept of the infinite tenderness and love of God. It is astounding that women, who are clamouring for their rights in everything else, are forgetful of the greatest of their rights - the right to claim that all the good things exclusive to their sex must also be found in God, and that therefore **Motherhood** is as essential as **Fatherhood** to the divine fount of all that is Holy'. Josiah and his circle thought the Roman church superstitious, particularly in their veneration of the Virgin Mary. Sidney Beard had not been a believer in the Virgin Birth, and considered Mary to be the 'symbol of the human mind or soul, which, being overshadowed by the power of the Highest... experiences conception and brings forth a Christ...' But Josiah regarded the story of Joseph and Mary sharing the stable with cattle as rather more than a fable. He was not, like Beard, a member of the Society for Psychical Research, nor was he a Spiritualist, but he had his own strong ideas about what happened after death.

Chapter 37

Postscript

Little remains of the chapel at Margaret Manor today. After Josiah's death his daughter Josie sold Greetynge Lodge to the former village policeman, Mr Wall, who made extensive alterations. The building erected so lovingly was now unsafe and had to be largely dismantled, but part was incorporated into the house, now renamed. Further deterioration of the whole structure occurred as its occupants grew older, and only when the current owners took over were the last remnants - the entrance and some of the ornamented or inscribed stones - saved for posterity. But the remaining brick-arched porch, lacking keystones, has an ominous bulge...

The remains of the Chapel now form part of a House

Beside the house stands the former pump-house, roofless but still containing a couple of galvanized tanks. The windows with their gothic arches and the panels of flints set into the brickwork

Construction of a Chimney

give some idea of how the chapel once looked, while the way in which the walls are constructed reveals why it lacked stability! No scaffolding was deemed necessary when the chimney of the pumphouse was built in the 1930s. There was formerly an arch separating the chapel from the pumphouse, with the legend 'With hope renewed this portal pass' in gothic script above it.

This arch has disappeared, but another, attached to Ellen's Court, remains in place. Josiah's initials appear at each side. He favoured gothic rather than round arches, since they 'pointed to Heaven'.
The same style was employed for a small house close to the Oast which had been the home of a Jamaican nurse who was employed by Josiah.

Remains of the Pumphouse

This too had to be rebuilt a few years later. Another hut, probably that once occupied by the epileptic and mentally disturbed patient called 'Margaret', was deliberately burned

306

down.

Relics of different periods of Josiah's career were found at the Manor or in its outbuildings after his death. Brochures, pamphlets and stationery dating from many different periods were found in an attic. There were souvenirs of his time with the Territorial Army, for after his death six portable stoves in excellent condition were found in a shed at Doddington. Another yielded a case of surgical equipment, including a patent push-button blood-letting device. His medical instruments, including a complete set of dental equipment, and an operating table (with tank beneath it) would be sold for five pounds.

The Monks Hut (now renamed) Today

Following Josiah's death and the conversion of Ellen's Oast to a Youth Hostel the Stansfield Association initially advertised both the Monks Hut which he had occupied, and the Hermitage, another small bungalow, as holiday accommodation. The Hermitage, which had formerly housed up to six elderly men, was set in a peaceful walled garden. It now had just one large room and could sleep two. Josiah's wooden cottage, in addition to the main room with a cosy bunk in one corner, offered a small bedroom and a bathroom with choice of mains or rain water. Its sunken garden was described as 'Olde World', charming and unique. Both properties were all-electric, but the brochure implies that occupiers would need to make use of the Youth Hostel's facilities.

After serving as a Youth Hostel for over thirty years, Ellen's Oast became a Field Study Centre. It is now owned by a Housing Association.

Josiah's Entrance to the Monks Hut

When, about thirty-five years later, the Monks Hut was offered for sale at auction there was a guide price of £40,000, despite the fact that its total area was only 368 square feet, that the bathroom doubled as a kitchen, and that the front door was only four feet high. Its sale attracted press attention, for Josiah's reputation as a 'ladies' man' has endured rather longer than familiarity with his Fruitarian philosophy, both in Doddington and beyond.

308

Josiah's Books and Pamphlets

Even this lengthy list is probably incomplete Some titles are short pamphlets, merely reprints of articles published in *The Herald of the Golden Age* and elsewhere, others are far more substantial. I have endeavoured to trace copies of all, but this has not always been possible, (though serendipity has found some). The dates may not always be those of initial publication.

1890	Longevity
1892	The Cost of Living
	The Influenza
	The Ideal Diet in Relation to Real Life
1893	On Starch as a Food in Nature
	Best Way to Begin Vegetarianism
	Best Penny Cookery
	Tuberculosis: Flesh-eating a Cause of Consumption
1894	A Groaning Creation
1895	The Evils of Butchery (A Groaning Creation)
1897	The Voice of Nature, or What Man Should Eat
1898	Are Animals Immortal?
1899	Claims of Common Life
	Essays of the Golden Age, comprising
	Aristophagy
	Our Christian Leaders
	The Festival of Peace
	Tiger or Angel, a Tale of Shame
	Shall we Vivisect?
	Cruelties of the Flesh Traffic (4th Edn.1922)
	Rheumatism and Diet
	Constipation: Causes and Cures
	Indigestion: Causes and Cures
	How to Avoid Appendicitis
1900	Diet in Relation to Insanity
	Indigestion and How to Avoid and Cure It
	Diet in Relation to Cancer
1901	The Penalty of Death (DCL Thesis)
1903	A Tale of Shame
	Diet of the Human Race
	Penny Guide to Fruitarian Diet and Cookery (3rd edn.)

1905	Myrrh and Amaranth
1907	How to Live Cheaply (Introduction only)
	Hanging for Murder
1909	Food and Feeding in Schools
	Diet in Relation to Appendicitis
	Modern Cookery
	Rheumatism: its Causes and Cure
1920?	The Diet for Cultured People
1923	'Best Food' Series, including
	Carrots and Complexion
	Milk and Growth
	Nuts for Strength
	Porridge and Brain
	Salads as Blood-Purifiers
	Fruit and Long Life
1923	The Raisin Cure
1924	Fasting for Health and life
1925	The Dry Diet Cure
1926	Get Well and Keep Well
1927	Eat and Get Well
1928	Eat and Keep Young
	Eat and Keep Well
1929	Eat and Be Happy
	Eat and Keep Happy
1930	Apples and Health
1934	Eat and be Beautiful
1935	Beauty Aspects of Health and Living
1944	Healing and the Conquest of Pain
1949	Mystery of Birth
1950	Mystery of Marriage
1951	Mystery of Death
1952	Crown of Grapes (Eat Right and Live Long)
1952	Popular Guide to Fruitarian Diet and Cookery

(The 1952 reprint of this title brought its total sales toward 165,000)

Acknowledgements

First and foremost I would like to thank all those inhabitants of Doddington, past and present, who have shared with me their memories of Josiah and the hospital at Margaret Manor. Some have lent or given me books, photographs and reports; some have pointed me towards new sources of information, others have welcomed me to their homes and gardens to see where Josiah spent so much of his long life. Among them are Babs and Sandy Angus, Rachel Burcombe, Mrs Mary Chastney, Alan Houlgraves, Audrey Hunt, Mrs Hilda King, Hans Meyer, Ken Parfitt, Mrs Phoebe Pitts, Mrs Stella Smith, Mrs Margaret Westwood, Mr & Mrs John Wildash, Mrs Irene Wyver, and staff at Mortimer Homes Ltd. And I should also mention the friendly elderly lady at Condover who still remembered members of the Oldfield family attending church there.

I am grateful too to the many individuals, librarians and archivists who have unearthed for me copies of works by Josiah Oldfield or material referring to him or his relatives. They include David Ainsworth (Wandsworth Library), Simon Bailey (Oxford University Archives), Mr R.L.Barrett-Cross (RAMC Historical Society), Linda Beecham (British Medical Association Library), Frances Bellis (Lincoln's Inn Library), Joan Bennett (City of Wakefield Metropolitan District Library), Maria Calzado (General Dental Council), Margaret Davies (St Catherine's College, Oxford), Robin Darwall-Smith (University College, Oxford), Sally Gilbert and Marion Rea (St Bartholomew's Hospital Archives), Chris Olivant (The Vegetarian Society), Richard H.Perks (Anglia Ruskin University), Dr.Chris Pond (Loughton and District Historical Society), Mark Pool (Torquay Central Library), Mark Priddy (St John's College, Oxford), Margaret E.Rayner (St Hilda's College, Oxford), Elizabeth Silverthorne (Bromley Library), Barbara M. Tearle (Bodleian Law Library), Kristiaan Tuppen (Broadstairs Library), and Jeff Walden (BBC Written Archives).

Equally helpful and courteous have been the members of staff who have assisted me at the Bishopsgate Institute, the British Library (St Pancras and Colindale), Cambridge University Library, the Centre for Kentish Studies at Maidstone, Companies House, Fort Pitt Girls' Grammar School, Greater Manchester County Records Office, Guildhall Library, the Imperial War Museum, the Internationaal Instituut voor Sociale Geschiedenis, Amsterdam, Kettering Library, the London Metropolitan Archives, Loughton Library Local Studies Dept., Oxfordshire Library, the Public Record Office, Sittingbourne Library Local Studies Dept., the United Services Club Ltd., Bromley, Waltham Forest Archives and Local Studies Centre, and the Wellcome Medical Library

And finally, I must thank Betty Harrison, who has spent so much time in helping me with the layout of this book, and without whom its publication would not have been possible.

Sources of Information

The websites of the International Vegetarian Union and the Mahatma Gandhi Research and Media Service have both proved fruitful sources of information, and I am also indebted to the Family Welfare Association for permission to access their records.

Reference books, journals and newspapers consulted include

Abramovski, O.L.M. - *Fruitarian Diet and Physical Rejuvenation*

Ashby, Roy - *History of Margaret Manor*

Ashby, Roy - *Never a Dull Moment*

Axon, William E.A. - *Fifty Years of the Vegetarian Society*

Barkas, Janet - *The Vegetable Passion*

Beard, Sidney - *Our Real Relationship with God* and *Testimony of Science in Favour of Natural and Humane Diets*

Bird, James - *Early Volunteer Movements in Walthamstow and Leyton*

Bromley Local History Pamphlet No.1 - *The Lady Margaret Hospital.*

Bullock, Alan - *History of the University of Oxford Vol.VII*

Davies, Margaret - *History of St Catherine's College, Oxford*

Gandhi, Mohandas - *My Experiments with Truth*

Gregory, James - *Biographical Index of Nineteenth Century British Vegetarians and Food Reformers* (Thesis)

Hook, John - *Dawn was Theirs: Air Raids on former London Metropolitan Boroughs*

Jones, Peter - *Memoirs*

Norrington, Miss - *Memories*

Oldfield, William - *Missionary Failures*

Payne, Reginald - *The Watershed*

Pettman, John - *Kettering and District General Hospital 1897-1997*

Russell, Brian - *History of St John's Hospital for Diseases of the Skin*

Searle, Muriel - *Lost Bromley Hospitals* (*Bygone Kent* **8** No.3)

Selby, Elizabeth - *Teynham Manor and Hundred*

Staff of Fort Pitt Central Military Hospital, Chatham - *Comforts for the Wounded in our Hospital*

Twigg, Julia - *History of Vegetarianism* (Thesis)

Waller, William Chapman - *Loughton 100 Years Ago*

Whitehead, Ian - *Doctors in the Great War*

Bromley Chronicle, Bromley District Times, Bromley Record, Bush's Budget and Directory of Bromley, Crockford's Clerical Directory, Dictionary of National Biography, East Kent Gazette, Encyclopedia Britannica, Epping Advertiser, Herald of the Golden Age, Hibbert Journal, History of Fort Pitt GS, The Hospital, Kelly's Directories, Kentish Times (Bromley), Law List, Leyton Advertiser, Loughton and District Advertiser, Loughton Review, Medical Directory, North Berks Herald, Parrett's Sittingbourne and Milton Directory, Post Office Directories, RAMC Journal, St Bartholomew's Hospital Journal, The Times, Truth, The Vegetarian, Vegetarian Messenger, Vegetarian News, Wakefield and West Riding Examiner, Wakefield Free Press and West Riding Advertiser, Wakefield Herald, Who Was Who, Who's Who.

Census Records, London Vegetarian Association Minutes, London Vegetarian Society Minutes, Mess Minutes of the Oxford Bar Circuit, Minutes of St John's Hospital for Diseases of the Skin, National Farm Survey, Record of 3rd East Anglian Field Ambulance 1914-19, Records of Battersea General Hospital, Annual Reports and Minutes of Board of Management of St John's Hospital for Diseases of the Skin, Templewood Papers (Camb. Univ. Library), Vegetarian Society Minutes.

Index

A Groaning Creation, 30, 33
Abbatoirs and slaughter-houses, 18, 30-31, 300
Abolition of Capital Punishment, 52, 115-119, 271-274
Abortion, 301, 303
Abramovski, Dr O.L.M., 147, 167, 246
Adoption, 263, 303
Advertising, 41-42, 55, 201, 208-209, 220, 224
Agar, Morley Frederick, 74
Algeria, 241
Ali (Ally), H.O., 137-138
Allen, Gordon, architect, 151
Allinson, T.R., 14, 19-20, 77
Allotments, 79, 220
Althorne, 79-81, 83
American Vegetarian Party, 219
Amos, Henry, 209, 236
Animal souls, 92
Animal welfare and rights, 30-37, 51-52
Anti-Vaccination, 77, 94
Anti-Vivisection, 36-37, 51, 65, 93-94, 104, 106-107
Aphorisms, 212, 280, 281, 288
Apples, 82, 83, 169, 172-174
Aristophagy, 14-15
Army camps (Territorials), 175-179
Arnold, Sir Edwin, 20, 69
Ashby, Roy, 264-265, 267-268
Aston, Wilson, 67, 74
'At Home' Company, 46-47
Axon, William, 13, 50, 246

Babbington, Jim, 264
Banana boats, 244
Bannatyne, Naomi, 112
Bateman, Dr, 149-150
Bathing and baths, 164, 233, 254, 270
Batten, Mrs M.K., 153
Bayswater, 12, 20

Bazaars, 63, 146, 152, 209
BBC, 218, 257, 295
Beard, Percy, 92
Beard, Sidney Hartnoll, 32-33, 73, 88-92, 143,150, 239, 245, 288, 289, 295, 298-299, 304
Beauty Aspect of Health and Living, 215, 297
Bedford, Daisy, 195
Begging letters, 100, 198, 218, 254-256
Bell, Ernest, 38, 40, 41, 54, 107
Bell, Dr Robert, 296
Besant, Annie, 21
Best Way to Begin Vegetarianism, 30
Bible, 9, 229
Bible Christians, 14, 276
Bicycles and Cycling, 109-110, 150, 211, 238
Bird, James, 84
Birth Control, 19
Bloomsbury, 216
Booth, General and Mrs, 74-75, 87
Borgstrom, Henick, 139
Bournville, 208
Boys, Agnes, 100
Brahmol Soap, 109
Bread and Food Reform, 49, 54
Brightlingsea, 139
British Medical Journal, 40, 68
British Union for Abolition of Vivisection, 37
Broadcasts, 218
Broadstairs, 161, 194-196
Brochures, 147-148, 163, 197, 283
Bromley & Beckenham Joint Hospital Board, 144
Bromley Ex-Servicemen's Club, 155-156
Bromley Park School, 130
Browne, Sir James Crichton, 213
Bromley Women's League, 146
Burleigh Castle, 181, 184
Butler-Harris, Capt.A., 84

Camberwell, 102, 105, 107
Cambridge, Duke of, 100
Campbell, Hon. Dudley, 60
Cancer, 65, 71, 101, 295-297
Capital Punishment, Abolition of,
52, 115-119, 271-274
Carn Brae, 129-131, 144
Carthew, Charles, 94-95, 101, 105,
134-135
Castralle Oil, 109
Census return 1901, 131, 139
Central Hall, Westminster, 217
Chapels
    Bromley, 156-157
    Doddington, 205-207, 221, 226,
234, 267-269, 294, 305-306
Charity Organisations Society,
101, 136
Charity Record, 42
Cheese recipe, 124
Chesterfield, Earl of, 40, 43
Chipping Campden Grammar
School, 5, 141
Christian Brothers, 18, 274
Christian Missions in India, 120-
121, 125-126
Churton, Stanley, 148, 156
Claims of Common Life, 34
Clare, Evelyn, 217, 229, 291
Clifford, William, 160, 289
Clubs, 246
Cocking, Harry (Henry), 74, 170
Cockling, Mary Ann Yates (May
Yates), 46, 49-50, 61
Condiments, 110-111
Condover, 1
Congregational (Farringdon)
Memorial Hall, 16, 50-51, 54, 130
Conscientious Objectors, 182-183
Coomaraswamy, Ananda, 127
Coomaraswamy, Lady, 70, 127
Cooper, Sir William Earnshaw,
128, 145
Cooper, Lady Earnshaw, 259

Cosmetics, 36, 281
Cosmic children, 36, 279
Cost of Living, 19
County Terrace Street, 97, 109-110
Cousins, Miss C.A., 151
Crown of Grapes, 9, 33, 184
Crowther, Miss Clark, 67, 74
Cruelties of the Flesh Traffic, 33
Cyder, 172-173

Daily Express, 210
Daniel, C.W., 215-217
Daniel, Mrs Maude, 191
Darlene, 110
Davies, Miss E.M., 74
Dawson, Geoffrey, 220
DCL Degree, 8, 81, 116, 236, 271,
273, 300-301
Dental matters, 72, 125, 136-138,
244, 307
Dervishes, 242
Desai, Trimbakrai, 112-113, 120,
123, 127, 150
Dickens, Charles, 194-195
Dietetic Reformer, 10, 13
Dietetic Reform Society, 14, 16
Diet, 12-13, 25, 27-28, 48, 60, 69,
71, 82, 87, 123, 146, 164, 165,
167, 169, 182-184, 185, 189, 210,
243, 270, 285, 296
Dockerell, Dr Morgan, 38, 40
Doddington, 155, 159-166, 197-
198, 226-233, 237-238, 253-259,
262-266, 267-270, 282-284, 290,
294, 305-308
    Church, 228, 290
Doremus, F.Pierce, 52
Dow, Dr Boothby, 38
Dreams, 245
Drinking, 60,170-171, 284-285

1st Eastern General Hospital, 186-
187, 189

316

3rd East Anglian Field Ambulance, 181-183
Eat and Be Happy, 164, 211, 216, 302
Eat and Keep Young, 111, 188, 286
Educational Food Fund, 49-50, 52
Ellen's Oast (Ellen's Court), 160, 163, 203, 264-5, 266, 268, 282, 298, 306, 307
Encyclopaedia Britannica, 21, 212, 276
English-Speaking Union, 246
Entertainment, 63, 284
Epilepsy, 202-203, 223, 266, 278
Epping Forest, 67, 71, 85, 159
Esdras, Book of, 127, 288
Essex Volunteer Brigade, 86
Eugenics, 299
Euthanasia, 302
Evening Hymn, 157-158
Evils of Butchery, 30, 32, 208

Fabians, 14
Farringdon Street, 12, 14
Farming at Greet, 160, 262-263
Fasting, 126-127, 204, 211
Fasting for Health and Life, 126, 204, 217, 245
Fees, 43, 67, 70, 102, 105, 132, 134, 136, 148, 159, 192, 222, 284
Fickling, Hugh, 105-106, 108, 149-150, 164, 198
Field Ambulance, 175-183, 188, 284
Financial queries, 43, 50, 53, 95, 105, 135, 200, 221-223, 258
Fire at Doddington, 231-232
Flower show, 229
Footwear for vegetarians, 110
Fort Pitt Hospital, Chatham, 188-190
Forward, Charles W., 16, 34
Foster, Rev.Joseph, 5, 141
France, 240, 243
Freeman, R.Austin, 149

FRESH Network, 169
Fruitarians and their philosophy, 9, 10, 81-83, 130, 167-171, 185, 208, 220, 229
Fruitarian Guesthouse, 228
Fruitarian Hospital, Doddington
  See Lady Margaret Hospital
Fruitarian Society, 89, 106, 167-171
Fruitarian village, 143, 159-166
Fruit trees, 51, 82, 83, 224, 289

Galton, Francis, 299
Gandhi, Mohandas, 12, 19-21, 59, 120, 127, 136-138, 196, 226-227, 269, 289
Garrett, Miss, 216, 229, 253, 291
Gaymers Cyder, 172-173
Get Well and Keep Well   , 125, 188, 216, 265, 266
Gill, Eric, 234
Gleeson, Dr Olaf, 251
Gnosis, 276-277
God the Mother, 304
Gould, Symon, 219
Grapes, 82
Greet (Gritt), 159-160, 207, 233, 289
Greetynge Lodge (Cottage), 265, 267, 283

Hall, Richard, 110
Hanging for Murder, 118
Hanson, Miss, 160-163
Hanwell Asylum, 266
Harley Street, 28, 112, 120, 201, 274
Harrison, William, 69-70
Hauser, Benjamin Gayelord, 214, 280-281
Harvest Festival, 72-73, 229-230, 269
Healing and the Conquest of Pain, 90, 243, 276, 300
Health Farms, 200

Hemlock Sunday, 229-230, 235
Herald of the Golden Age, 74, 89-90, 130, 139, 142, 178, 185, 208, 240, 288, 299, 301
Hermitage, The, 307
Hibbert Journal, 123, 128, 277-278
Hick, Gertrude (Oldfield), 67, 96, 112-114, 129-131, 133, 139-140, 144, 150, 151, 290, 297
Hick, Matthew and Henry (brothers), 113
Hick, Matthew(father), 112-113
Higgins, Wendy, 37
Hills, Arnold Frank, 15-17, 34, 50, 52-53, 62-64, 65, 70, 76, 101, 289, 295
Hindus, 33, 123-128
Hitler, 250-251, 301
Hoare, Sir Samuel (Lord Templewood), 220, 271-274
Holding, R.E., 30
Holmby House, 130
Honey, 13, 110, 201, 212, 285, 289
Honey for Health, 12, 230, 285
Hospitals
1st Eastern General, 186-187, 189
Anti-Vivisection (later Battersea), 106, 250
Bromley and Beckenham Joint Board, 144
Fort Pitt, Chatham, 189-190
Kettering, 112, 144
King's College, 102, 105
Lady Margaret, Bromley, 106, 110, 129-138, 144-158, 160, 193, 200, 221-222
Lady Margaret, Doddington, 160-166, 197-207, 222-223, 249, 253-260
Margaret Hall Soldiers' Hospital, 197
Oriolet, Loughton, 65-76, 96, 101, 295
Phillips Homeopathic, 145

St.Bartholomew's, 22-28, 36, 199
St Francis, New Kent Road, 65, 70, 74, 93-107, 131, 133
St Francis, Red Lion Square, 248-249
St John's for Diseases of the Skin, 38-45, 80, 208
Hospital Sunday, 96
Hospital, The, Report 1902, 102-104
Hotel Cecil, 138
Howard, Len, 156
Humanitarian ideals, 119, 146, 161, 166
Humanitarian League, 30, 33, 119
Human spirituality, 90, 126-127

Ideal Publishing Union, 17, 34
Idiots and imbeciles, 300, 302
India, 117, 120-128, 137, 139, 187, 241
Influenza, 18, 24, 172
Inner Temple, 12, 55,101,150
International Vegetarian Union Congress, 64

Jacob Street Mystery, 149-150
Jamaica, 57, 188, 243-246, 254, 267, 271
Jelf, Q.C., 55, 57, 58, 59
John Bull, 224
Jones, Peter, 266

Kellogg, Dr.J.H., 87
Kingsford, Anna, 127

Lady Margaret Hall, Oxford, 141
Lady Margaret Home, 135
Lady Margaret Hospital, Bromley 106, 110, 129-138, 144-158, 160, 193, 200, 221-222
Lady Margaret Hospital, Doddington, 160-166, 197-207, 222-223, 249, 253-260

Lancet, The, 40
Langford-James, Francis, 246
Langford-James, Rev.Richard, 150, 157
Lavender-growing, 160, 229
Lawn House, 191, 194
Lawrence, D.H., 300
Lawrence, T.E., 219
Laxmidas, Labshankar, 148
Leach, William, 252
Leicester Square, 38, 39, 41, 45
Lincoln's Inn, 12, 58, 59
Literary Lunch, 280
Little Greetynge, 231-233
Llangattock, Lord, 135, 145, 148
London children, 48-49, 63-64, 162, 197
London Vegetarian Association, 61-64, 108
London Vegetarian Society, 15-21, 30, 46-54, 61, 75, 78, 112
Longevity, 174, 254-256, 267, 281, 289
London workmen, 162, 203, 255-256
Loughton, 65, 71
  Debating Society, 77
  Historical Society, 76
  School Board, 76
Loughton newspapers, 65, 68, 72, 76
Lowestoft, 186-187
Lyveden, Lady Julia, 132-134

Mackenzie, Compton, 84
McCowan, Mrs., 134, 191
Maidstone Choral Union, 284
Maitland, Edward, 50, 127
Manchester Vegetarians, 14, 16, 50, 61, 64
Manley, Norman, 243-244
Margaret Chambers, 117
Margaret Dispensary, 105-106, 136
Margaret Hall, Upper Tulse Hill, 191-193

Margaret Lectureship, 148, 155
Margaret Lodge, 160-162
Margaret Manor, 105, 197-199, 219, 230, 246, 252, 253-254, 261-268, 283
Margaret Nursing Home Ltd., 134, 153
Margaret Samaritan Guild, 151
Margaret window, 156-157
Marriage, 112-114, 129, 297-298, 299, 304
Marshall, Dorothy, 249-250
Maternity Society, 74, 94, 129
Mayor, Prof.J.E.B., 14, 16, 68-69, 73, 113
Mearns, Mr, 101
Medical Defence Union, 149
Medical Establishment, 68, 149
Mentally disturbed patients, 193, 265-266, 269, 306
Midwifery, 23-24, 74, 201-202, 259, 263
Mildmay Mission, 95
Millennium Ltd., 106, 107-109
Millionaires, 150, 210, 247
Milton, John Laws, 38, 41-42
Miscegenation, 299-300
Missionary Failures, 121, 126
Mitre Court, 55, 60, 119
Monks Hut, 233, 265, 307-308
Morell, Lady Ottoline, 238
Morphine, 106, 302
Myrrh and Amaranth, 142, 204, 304
Mystery of Birth, 72, 140, 141, 150, 187, 276, 279
Mystery of Death, 71, 263, 276, 277, 280, 283, 292, 302
Mystery of Marriage, 139, 141, 241, 276, 297, 298, 303
Mysticism, 127

National Farm Survey, 82, 262-263
National Food Supply Association, 49-50

319

Nettles, 4, 10-11, 171
New Kent Road, 97-107, 109, 117, 131, 148
New York Times, 217
Newlyn, 228
Newman, F.W., 14
Newport Grammar School, 4-5
Nicholson, Florence, 63-64
Norrington, Lucy, 228-230, 235
Northern Heights district, 63
NSPCC, 194
Nurses, 42, 136, 153, 162, 165, 204, 237, 253
  Uniform, 68, 153
Nursing Homes
  Broadstairs, 161, 194-196
  Bromley, 134, 153
Nye, Charles, 130
Nye, Miss, 135

O'Callaghan, Mr, 50, 63
Oldfield, David, 1-4
Oldfield, Frederick, 1, 68, 134
Oldfield, Gertrude
  See Hick, Gertrude
Oldfield, Irene Dorrien, 129, 133, 140, 290
Oldfield, Josiah
  As Schoolmaster, 5, 230
  At Oxford, 6-9, 83, 87, 265
  Barrister, 55-60, 284
  Becomes Vegetarian, 8-9
  Boyhood, 1-5
  Builds hut at Althorne, 80-81
  Company Director, 107-109
  Contentious views, 295-304
  Death, 289
  Disturbing reports, 95-96, 149, 194, 197, 200
  Dresser at Barts, 25
  Eccentricity, 188, 230, 235, 238, 270
  Gravestone, 291, 293
  Illness, 2, 187-188, 289, 295
  Law student, 12, 21
  Lectures, 211-212
  Legal misdemeanours, 55-58
  Marriage, 112-114
  Medical training, 22-28
  Military career, 175-190
  Prose style, 38, 87, 93, 122, 156-157, 211, 276, 279
  Renounces cruel sports, 8-9
  Theology, 276-279, 288-289, 292
  Travels, 120-128, 240-247
  Views on women, 140-142, 169, 204-2-5, 238-239, 297-298
  Visits India, 120-128
  Will, 291
  Writes DCL Thesis, 81, 197
Oldfield, Josie Magdalen, 186, 197, 199, 205, 226, 238, 260, 269, 287, 289, 290-291, 298, 299, 305
Oldfield, Josie Margaret, 129, 133, 140,
Oldfield, Julia, 1, 140
Oldfield, Margaret, 1
Oldfield, Mary Ellen, 1, 134, 141, 226, 228-229
Oldfield, Sarah, 1, 140
Oldfield, William, 1, 8,16, 44, 113, 120-121, 126, 245, 292, 302
Olive oil, 108-110, 171, 218, 242-243
Oliver, Miss, 270
Operations, 72, 74, 133, 136, 144, 147, 187, 188, 307
Orange Flour Company, 106
Order of the Golden Age, 33, 87-92, 93, 127, 150, 170, 212, 296
Oriolet Hospital, 65-76, 96, 101, 295
Oroea, 67
Otterden, 195
Overseas Club, 246
Oxford Circuit, 55-59
Oxford University, 6-8, 74, 83, 87, 141, 235, 236
Oxford Vegetarians, 8-9, 16

Ozanne, James, 234, 246

Pannus Corium, 110
Parfitt, Ken, 270-271, 281-282, 289, 294, 298
Pasteurisation, 277
Patrons and donors, 42, 70, 93, 95-97, 104-105, 131-132, 134-135, 222-225, 259, 295
Patterson, Mrs.J., 92
Payne, Reginald, 14, 106, 180
Penal reform, 52, 115, 273
Penalty of Death, 2, 116, 240, 271, 273
Pengelly, J.I., 92
Pepys, Samuel, 218
Perkins, Evelyn, 88, 150
Philips Homoeopathic Hospital, 145
Plague, 121
Pomona, 67
Port Sunlight, 208
Povey, Charles, 94
Prahnamin, 125
Prince of Wales Fund, 93

Railway travel, 83
Raisin Cure, The, 82, 215, 217
RAMC (Royal Army Medical Corps), 153, 175-176, 188, 261
Raw food, 82, 167, 169
Red Lion Square, 216, 248-252
Regimental Medical Officer's duties, 176
Registrar of Friendly Societies, 95
Reincarnation, 279, 292-294
Ringworm, 82
Roman Catholics, 91, 96, 125, 276, 291, 294
Romilly society, 115-119, 209
Rumours, 149, 185, 193, 197, 237-238, 303
Rundell, T.W., 151
Russell Hotel, 260
Ryton, 2

Sacrifice, 83, 277
Salt, Henry , 14, 16, 50, 53, 209
Salvation Army, 74-75, 276
Sayers, Dorothy L., 221
School Meals, 48-49, 51, 52-53, 63-64
Scott, F., 203-204
Scrumping, 228, 268-269
Semple, Dugald, 167
Sermons, 204, 206, 211, 235, 277
Services, 44, 70, 166, 228-229, 234
Shaftesbury Convalescent Home, 40
Sharpe, Louisa, 134, 151, 152, 191
Shaw, George Bernard, 14, 21, 50, 219, 254-255, 257-258, 269
Sister Ellen, 199
Sister Francesca, 164, 197-199
Slaughterhouses, 30-31
Sleep, 245
Smithfield, 23-24
Smoking, 239, 281, 285-287
Society for the Abolition of Capital Punishment, 106, 117-119
Socrates, 230, 235, 301
Southampton Street, Strand, 93, 97
Soup Barrows, 49
Soup Recipe, 48
Stansfield Association, 231, 264-265, 307
Stansfield boys, 264, 267
St.Bartholomew's Hospital, 22-28, 36, 199
St Edmund's, Broadstairs, 161, 195-196
St Ethelburga's Home, 75
Sterilisation, 301
St John's Hospital for Diseases of the Skin, 38-45, 80, 208
St Margaret of Antioch, 206
Stopes, Marie, 303
Stretcher bearers, 180
Sullivan, Mrs, 163, 166, 197

'Swami case', 76, 136, 149

Tagore, Rabindranath, 269
Tea-drinking, 239, 281, 284-285
Tegetmeier, Edith, 94
Templewood, Lord (Sir Samuel Hoare), 220, 271-274
Territorials, 166, 175-182, 307
Theobald, William, 63, 94, 108
Theology degree, 6-7
Theosophy, 21, 127
Thomas, Miss, 191
Times, The, 61, 82, 217, 220, 223, 270
Tomatoes, 177
Toshers, 6
Tovey, Philip, 96, 100
Tree-climbing, 238, 267
Tree-planting, 18, 79, 81, 224-225, 289
Truth, 42-43, 199-200, 209, 220, 221-225
Tuberculosis, 31, 68, 72, 83, 162, 163, 164, 165
Tunisia, 241-242
Turner, Commander, 95-96

United States, 246
Unmarried mothers, 201, 237, 303
Universal Food Cookery Exhibition, 154

Vaccination, 77, 85, 130, 263
Valley of the Pilgrims, 282, 289
Vaughan Morgan, Alderman, 100
Vegetable Oil Co.Ltd., 106, 107
Vegetarian Federal Union, 20, 39, 50-52, 62, 64, 94, 212
Vegetarianism, 78, 87, 194, 208-209, 212, 257-258, 276, 285
Vegetarian Messenger, 11, 13, 50-51, 52, 67, 112-113, 129, 209
Vegetarian Review, 34
Vegetarian shoes, 18, 110
Vegetarian Society, 13, 50, 69

Vegetarian, The, 17, 20, 34, 42, 49, 56, 83, 240, 274, 277
Virgin Mary, 304
Vitamins, 4, 171, 172, 213, 285
Vitol (Vytalle) Oil Company, 108, 110
Vivisection, 33-37, 51, 93, 146, 151
Voice of Nature, 33, 35
Volunteers, 83-86, 124, 175

Wakefield, 112-114, 139, 140
Walker Lectureship in Dietetics, 148, 155
Waller, William Chapman, 75-76
Walthamstow, 84-85, 181
War damage, 251-252
Weekly Illustrated, 255-256
Welsh, Inspector, 101
Wheatenade, 172
Whiston, Daisy, 130
Wilkes, Dr Samuel, 34
Wilkins, Daisy, 151
Williams, Howard, 16
Wodehouse, P.G., 213
Women's Christian Temperance Union, 217
Women's Role - Josiah's view, 140-142, 169, 204-205, 238-239, 297-298
Women's University Settlement, 162
Workmen from London, 62, 203, 255-256

Yarnitz, Philip, 206, 234, 257
Yates, May (Mary A.Y.Cockling), 46, 49-50, 61
Youth Hostel, 270, 282-283

Rainmore Books was set up in 2006 with its main aim the publication of books connected in some way with North Kent. Titles already published are:

Yesterday's Medway,
from Rochester Bridge to Chatham Intra

The Medway Shore as it was,
from Burham to Borstal

Riverside Remembered:
the Medway from Chatham Intra to Lower Rainham

all written and illustrated by John Austin

Maidstone Choral Union 1902-2002:
a Centenary Souvenir

About the Author

After graduating from St Hilda's College, Oxford, Rosemary Dellar had a brief career as a Research Chemist before becoming a full-time wife and mother with two sons, one born in Essex and the other in Gloucestershire. When her husband's career next took the family to Preston, Lancashire, she worked for the BBC carrying out Audience Research, an ideal way in which to meet people from all walks of life. Then came a final move to Rainham, Kent, where she spent thirteen years teaching at Chatham Grammar School for Girls before changing hats once again to become Manageress at the Rainham Bookshop. It was at this period she developed an interest in Local History, and published numerous articles in *Bygone Kent* and elsewhere.

She first found a reference to Josiah Oldfield, in a query addressed to the Editor, while compiling the Index to that magazine, and followed it up with a view to writing a short piece about him. Research over several years turned what had been originally planned as a 1500-word article into a 300-page book...